The Hardest Part

The Hardest Part

A Centenary Critical Edition

G. A. Studdert Kennedy

Edited by
Thomas O'Loughlin
and
Stuart Bell

scm press

© Thomas O'Loughlin and Stuart Bell 2018

Published in 2018 by SCM Press
Editorial office
3rd Floor, Invicta House,
108–114 Golden Lane,
London EC1Y 0TG, UK
www.scmpress.co.uk

SCM Press is an imprint of Hymns Ancient & Modern Ltd
(a registered charity)

Hymns Ancient & Modern® is a registered trademark of
Hymns Ancient & Modern Ltd
13A Hellesdon Park Road, Norwich,
Norfolk NR6 5DR, UK

British Library Cataloguing in Publication data

A catalogue record for this book is available
from the British Library

978 0 334 05656 0

Typeset by Regent Typesetting
Printed and bound by
CPI Group (UK) Ltd

Contents

Illustrations

Acknowledgements

With the exceptions noted below, the images are drawn from the private collections of the editors.

The portrait of Geoffrey Studdert Kennedy on page 4 is reproduced by kind permission of Andrew Studdert-Kennedy, the photograph having been digitally enhanced by James Atkinson for reproduction in the book *Life after Tragedy*. The photograph of the 'Calvary' on the First World War memorial outside St Paul's Church, Worcester (page 163) is © James Atkinson. The painting *Hope*, by G. F. Watts (page 145), is reproduced by permission of The Tate Gallery; © Tate, London, 2017. Crown Copyright has expired on the several images containing that notice, and also on that of the 15-inch howitzer from the Imperial War Museum (page 22).

The transcription of the draft chapter and the image of the first page of the manuscript (page 164) are published by the kind permission of the Trustees of the Museum of Army Chaplaincy. We are grateful to Tim Watkinson for the digital enhancement of the image of the manuscript and to Patrik Indevuyst of Ieper, Belgium, for the provision of the pictures on pages 43, 55, 56, 90 and 118.

The text of *The Hardest Part* is taken from the first printing of the book by Hodder & Stoughton in 1918, with the exception of the 'Author's Preface to New Edition', taken from the undated new edition, which internal evidence indicates was published in 1925.

We are grateful to Frances Knight for introducing the co-editors of this volume to each other.

Introduction

Geoffrey Anketell Studdert Kennedy was undoubtedly one of the most famous chaplains of the Great War. His books – especially the collections of poems, often written in a Cockney dialect – sold in huge quantities, and his most popular anthology was republished as recently as 1983 (SK, 1927b). His early death, at the age of 45, served only to reinforce the public perception of a saintly man who, in the words of his own hymn, 'Awake, awake to love and work', had throughout his adult life exemplified the call to 'give and give and give again . . . to spend thyself, nor count the cost'. Whether serving as a parish priest in the slums of Worcester, as a chaplain on the Western Front or as a missioner for the Industrial Christian Fellowship (ICF), Studdert Kennedy gave sacrificially of every resource at his disposal, including himself.

Yet even in his own lifetime he attracted controversy. His use of colourful language, which may well have been effective in communicating the gospel to ordinary soldiers in the theatres of war, had the opposite effect when used in post-war Britain, especially when his fame provided an entrée into upper-class society. Most famously, his work for the ICF, seeking to mediate between the competing claims of 'capital' and 'labour' in a time of rapidly increasing industrial unrest, led to his being labelled as a socialist by the Dean of Westminster, who refused to countenance that Studdert Kennedy's funeral should be held in the Abbey – he had died on 8 March 1929. As the immediate post-war hope of the reconstruction of a better and fairer society in a 'land fit for heroes' was eclipsed by the national turmoil of the later 1920s, so attitudes to the war changed and reputations were challenged. In particular, Robert Graves published *Goodbye to All That* in 1929. Perhaps best described as a 'heavily fictionalised autobiography' (Snape, 2011, p. 329), not only did it include a second-hand account of atrocities committed against German prisoners of war but it also characterized Anglican chaplains as lazy and ineffective cowards. Although Graves later admitted that his primary intention had been to boost sales with his controversial text, much of the 'mud' stuck for many decades.

As increasing numbers of scholars, within the context of broader examinations of the impact of the war on faith and the Churches, have in recent years begun to re-examine the role played by chaplains in the conflict, it has become clear that Graves' critique does not stand up to close analysis (Madigan, 2011; Snape, 2011; Snape and Madigan, 2013). However, responses to Studdert Kennedy's sometimes eccentric wartime activities have not always been entirely positive. Michael Snape drew attention to Studdert Kennedy's practice, when attached to a group charged with touring British army units in France to encourage zeal and enhance competence with the bayonet, of sparring in the boxing ring to entertain the troops before delivering his sermon (Snape, 2005, p. 108). It has been noted also that he spent only three brief periods on the front line, although he was awarded the Military Cross for his bravery during one of those spells. Andrew Totten has argued that in praising the sacrifice of the British Tommy, he was fusing him with the crucified Christ (Totten, 2015, p. 216). Certainly, Studdert Kennedy's *Rough Talks* (SK, 1918a; Bell, 2012), given to soldiers in Rouen in 1916, expressing a type of belligerent and sanctified patriotism that he would later totally repudiate, do nothing to enhance his reputation (Bell, 2017a).

While much has been written about Studdert Kennedy's life (Mozley, 1927; Purcell, 1962; Grundy, 1997; Holman, 2013), there has been only a limited attempt to address his theology, either when it was published or in the one hundred years since. Several writers have acknowledged that Studdert Kennedy was one of the first – and of those by far the most prominent – to challenge conventional understandings of the nature of divine power and to advocate belief in a suffering God (Bell, 2013; Brierley and Byrne, 2017). That advocacy appeared in his first published work (SK, 1917), and then in several of his poems (as reproduced in Appendix 3). Certainly, in *The Hardest Part* we have an extended critique of conventional belief in an impassible God – one who remains unaffected in any way by the suffering of his children. However, this volume is far more than an extended essay on divine suffering, for its author also engages with many of the great contemporary challenges to faith, such as the role of God in history, the nature and purpose of prayer, and belief in life eternal. Looking at *The Hardest Part* from a modern perspective, it is evident that Studdert Kennedy was writing a work of theology – though it might not seem to fit well with the rather academic vision of what many people mean by 'theology'. The pattern of each chapter in which a recollection of a particular location or experience on the battlefield is succeeded by a theological and pastoral reflection makes Studdert Kennedy's use of his experiences as the 'raw material' of his theology quite explicit. This style of theologizing – starting from a moment of experience – is now common among theologians (including academic theologians); in 1918 it was revolutionary. This fact alone makes a new edition desirable.

At first sight, those theological reflections could be mistaken for a series of quick jottings hurriedly recorded in the hours after a particular incident or conversation. However, careful examination shows not only that Studdert Kennedy drew on an immensely wide range of theological sources, often necessarily recalled from memory, but also that what we have in the published work is the result of careful editing and reworking of the material, perhaps weeks or months after the actual event. The significant differences between the apparently original manuscript of chapter 3 (shown in Appendix 1) and the published version demonstrate that.

Furthermore, it is now clear how original and, by the standards of his day, how unorthodox Studdert Kennedy's theology was. At a time when many of his fellow Anglicans were engaged in sterile debates about limits to what priests may believe (or disbelieve), and while biblical scholars were processing the insights of 'higher criticism' that had come from Germany in the pre-war years, Studdert Kennedy was trying to make some of the great Christian themes of the incarnation, suffering, Christology, resurrection, eschatology and moral theology accessible to the general reader and meaningful in the new world of hard questions generated by the experience of war. He knew that true orthodoxy was not repetition from the past but dynamic translation of the experience of faith in the world of the present; incarnation is a constant and ongoing process. His question, 'Where is God in all this?', was directed not only at the carnage of the Western Front but at the whole historical span and geographical breadth of human experience.

Inevitably, he was a child of his age, constrained, as we all are, by our context. However, as we shall see, it was not only in his advocacy of a suffering God that Studdert Kennedy could be said to be theologically innovative. Largely ignored by those who have focused on his more immediately accessible poems, *The Hardest Part* still merits reading a century after its publication, and we trust that this volume will help readers to engage with Geoffrey Studdert Kennedy's responses to some of the eternal questions of Christian belief.

Thomas O'Loughlin
Stuart Bell

The Man, the Padre and the Theologian

Thomas O'Loughlin

Praying for the strength of Sandow

I don't believe I could carry another one to save my life. Lord, how my shoulders ache. I wish I were Sandow.

These are the opening lines of the second chapter of *The Hardest Part* – where a note introduces Sandow. Hardly, you might argue, the most distinctive statement in this very distinctive book! But what sort of a book is this that while challenging some of the most widely held assumptions about the reality we call 'God', begins a chapter in this way: with a statement that is a personal sigh, indeed a prayer, for personal strength in a particular situation? The author is not focused on the premises of his argument, nor on the common discourse with the reader on which they are about to enter, nor even on the state of the academic debate. Rather the man, Geoffrey, is engaged with something far more urgent: another human being suffering and in need. His awareness – and so too ours – is devoted to the fact that around him are men, wounded and dying, who need to be carried to what will help them right now: the nearest point of medical aid. That place will not be safety – both carrier and carried were still on a battlefield being searched by artillery fire – nor is there any certainty there will be a 'happy ending' of survival or recovery from wounds; but getting a wounded man to a medical post is a first, best step. And it is this step that Geoffrey is trying to take. Alas, he cannot carry another wounded man due to the physical exhaustion. But you, the reader, are engaged in another activity: reading a theological argument. And you too have to start just there: right in the middle of things, right in the darkness of limited possibilities, where only a tiny next step may make sense. In such a scene, the author is reminding you, you too have to forsake comfortable global clarity and abstract certainties, and engage step by step, starting with 'the facts' while 'not blinking those facts' (a phrase he used repeatedly) around you.

The Hardest Part is like no other work of theology before it. This is because it draws you into a specific scene in real life and then asks you to begin *doing* theology rather than just studying theology as an intellectual exercise and then debating points that arise in the calm of the library or common room. In some respects – as a statement of declaring faith in God revealed in his Word, Jesus – it is reminiscent of Augustine of Hippo's *Confessiones*, and it shares a theology of the incarnation as theologically central that is very Augustinian. In its probing of the author's inner reactions it is reminiscent of Pascal's *Pensées* and shares that staccato movement from thought to prayer and back again. With John Henry Newman's *Apologia pro vita sua*, it looks to details of biography to make sense of theology and why certain questions are pressing. But *The Hardest Part* is also very much its own work and one that belongs unmistakably to the modern world: faith is not a datum simply assumed, an uncontroversial given, but rather a way, a movement of the individual that is arrived at in the pain and confusion of life; and so it is probably the first work of theology that can be said to represent the theology of the twentieth century. And in the century of most rapid technological development and greatest mechanized slaughter, it seeks to probe what Christians can and should say about God. The theology of the post-1945 period would seek to address the same situation when it said that theology was now called 'to do theology in the aftermath of

Auschwitz', but already in 1918 Studdert Kennedy was adopting a broadly similar approach.

But having said this we are faced with another puzzle. *The Hardest Part* addresses the greatest questions in theology but does so completely without fanfare and with explicit notes of self-deprecation. Its author doubts he could write a theological treatise – he says so in his apologia to his first critics towards the end of the book – yet the reader is invited to jettison approaches that had gone unquestioned for centuries. The book encapsulates the paradox that the enormity of the task can only be approached by the whisper of a small voice. Moreover, many ideas that would have been blandly labelled as 'heresies' are brought again to the fore and the reader is asked to appraise them for what they say, rather than label them as intellectual deformities catalogued for a priori rejection. Little of the accepted edifice of beliefs is left untouched by the end of the book's ninth chapter.

In keeping with Studdert Kennedy's approach of working from the small and accessible to the larger picture, the work is tied down to moments and places – we can locate some of them with chronological and cartographic precision – yet its sweep is universal. It challenges each of us as individuals, because Studdert Kennedy does not set out a party manifesto, to revise what we say about God, the nature of the creation, prayer and our vision of human purpose within the universe. The book is short, conversationally written, willing to use dialect without apology, but at the same time offers a critique of church structures, the accepted 'norms' about the Bible, engages with scientific questions and even presents a new way of looking at worship: no stone is left unturned! The book looks small, adopted a style of smallness, yet it is a work of enormous range and gigantic ambition. Unless one has the knowing certainty of a doctrinal or biblical fundamentalist who only reads with red pen in hand to identify errors/departures from 'established' teaching, one does not read this book and remain unchanged.

The book's fascination imperceptibly becomes a fascination

with the man who wrote it. What sort of man would utter the sort of prayer that seeks the strength of a Sandow? Indeed, what sort of a prayer is it that asks for the strength of a performing 'strong man' of the popular theatre rather than that of a saint (and the author would have known the iconography of 'St Christopher') or a classical hero (Hercules is the proverbial strongman for those polished people with a degree in classics, which he had)? Moreover, what sort of prayer is it when the one praying is a minister in the established Church who should have known the traditional formulae? To pray to be 'a Sandow' is, I suspect, to remind us that Christianity – 'following Christ' as he will say at the conclusion to chapter 8 – is not engaging in a mental exercise of thinking through religious questions, but rather a way of living 'out there' where we may not want to be. Consequently, what we think and say in reflection on that experience has to be true to that harsh and fragmented reality. It is such honesty to the situation that alone gives our thoughts the character of being genuine and true.

Lastly, this sentence is – be it a sigh, a reflection, a prayer or an exclamation – enough to show us that the Reverend Geoffrey Anketell Studdert Kennedy, priest, poet, sometime army chaplain, Master of Arts, Military Cross (awarded for tending the very wounded on Messines Ridge in early June 1917, when he prayed for the strength of Sandow), is a far more complex man than he seems at first sight or, indeed, than he gives us to suspect in the odd comment he makes about himself in his writings.

The man

The details of Studdert Kennedy's brief life – he died when he was 46 – are straightforward (Rowell, 2004). Of Irish background (and he considered himself an Irishman), he was a child of the rectory, born in Leeds in 1883, where his father's ministry in the slums gave him a very particular view of the place of religion in society.

Studdert Kennedy arrived at ordination to a curacy in Rugby in 1908 and his own formal ministry began. However, some of the structures of his later work were already laid down. He had taken a degree in 1904 in classics and divinity from Trinity College Dublin, followed by two years' teaching in a school in Liverpool and a year of ordination training in a theological college. In *The Hardest Part* we are presented with what looks like a rough and ready book (and are reminded of the word 'rough' in other works by him), but on closer inspection we find something far more polished and an argument set out with the clarity of someone who has worked – and worked well – in the classroom. His classical learning just peeps through in his use on two occasions of Lucretius' *De rerum natura*, and we notice that far from just 'citing a classic', we see him entering into a close reading of the text, adopting a critical approach to it and offering his own translations. Likewise, amid stories and snippets of his own dialect poetry, we see that he had very orderly habits of reading. We rarely get more than a name – and even these are sparse – but there is enough description of others' ideas to identify not only specific works but to show that these had been closely read and digested. This is not the reading of someone who just read out of interest and general engagement with topics that touch on Christian faith, but of someone who has been carefully pursuing research, topic by topic, over many years. Then when he comes to write, what is on one level a stream of consciousness is also a teacher's story that leads the reader from a problem, over a set of explorations, to a conclusion. This is the method of teacher leading the less than knowledge-hungry class rather than that of the systematician seeking an argument that is internally cohesive and consistent.

From the start of his ministry Studdert Kennedy had viewed service to the poor and those marginalized by society to be an essential part of the Church's work. He combined this concern with a High Church view of worship, with a 'high' theology of incarnation and a very critical reading of the history of Christianity, whether that was those writings that became part of the biblical canon or later productions. From the perspective of the twenty-first century this combination of liturgically 'traditional' with the theologically 'radical' might seem strange – but it was far from uncommon in the period. The High Church insistence on the value of the tradition within the Church allowed them to be far more critical of the past and the present (for perfection was solely a future reality), in contrast to those who sought an ideal in a past age of the saints or in a perfect book. Again, when we see these approaches in *The Hardest Part* it is easy to assume that Studdert Kennedy came to his ideas in a flash of inspiration – perhaps the image should be of a star-shell or a Verey light exploding over no man's land – but the evidence is wholly against this. He had come to many of his positions in careful study and reflection after serving in the darkness and grime of city slums, and the shock of the mud and trenches was but the occasion that brought these studies and reflections to a conclusion.

So after four years in Rugby, in 1912 he moved to be a curate in Leeds and then again less than two years later to become vicar of St Paul's, Worcester. And in the same year he married Emily Catlow, with whom he would eventually have three sons. We meet Emily on several occasions in *The Hardest Part*, in that the work is dedicated to her and, more poignantly, because he knew that at any moment his own life could end – we shall read of men close to him, speaking with him and then hear of their deaths a moment later – and she would be a widow with their son Patrick (whom we shall also meet in the book), and they shall have to grieve, explain, pray and continue bravely in discipleship.

The work of Studdert Kennedy the padre would begin from Worcester, and after he was demobbed in 1919 he would return there and stay a further three years, until 1922. During that time he would produce several other writings, but one in particular needs to be noticed: *Food for the Fed-Up*. This was written during 1920, and in the form of a series of lectures on the Apostles' Creed he takes the arguments of *The Hardest Part* and lays them out against a well-known system of Christian teaching. Seeing the same themes examined using a familiar teaching/liturgical formula and without the urgency of the man at the front shows us that Studdert Kennedy had developed an embracing theological vision deeply rooted in personal study, prayer and careful reflection. And it is the form of that theology as found in these two works, but in style more closely resembling *Food for the Fed-Up* than *The Hardest Part*, that will animate his writings for the remainder of his ministry and life.

1922 saw Studdert Kennedy leave Worcester for a post in the City of London that did not involve parochial duties. Instead, he could devote all his energy to being a travelling preacher as part of an organization called the Industrial Christian Fellowship (ICF). It was a movement that sought to realize social transformation through a social teaching based in the Christian vision of human fellowship and the Gospels' concern for the poor. Seeing both capitalism and Marxism as inadequate to the full range of human needs, it conducted missions across Britain, and Studdert Kennedy, never in the strongest of health, was, with his great wartime reputation, its star speaker. He did not spare himself and the work took its toll on him. At the same time he developed other aspects of his theology – themes that are but implicit in *The Hardest Part* – on the dignity of the human endeavour to bring the creation to its divine finality. The eschaton he preached was not a Utopia but the completion of all that was the New Jerusalem, which was in the presence of God. He first outlined this part of his vision in his 1923 book *The Wicket Gate*, and gave it a fuller expression in a book published just a year before his death: *The Warrior, the Woman, and the Christ*. Through all these works one theological image, met with explicitly in *The Hardest Part*, remained central: what we know about God is what we see in Jesus – and, most particularly, Jesus suffering on the cross. That reality was not to be replaced by abstract speculations nor pious thoughts, but facing the crucifix each human being had 'to take up his' own 'cross and follow' (Matt. 16.24), building the world of justice, peace and love. Studdert Kennedy's own following came to an end when he was preaching at an ICF 'crusade' in Liverpool on 8 March 1929 – and this has become his feast day in the current liturgical calendar of the Church of England (Chapman, 1999).

The padre

If there is one item of common knowledge about Studdert Kennedy it is that he was an enormously popular chaplain during the First World War who had even earned an affectionate nickname: 'Woodbine Willie'. This name – derived from the then popular brand of cigarettes and his habit of having them to offer to the troops who, especially while 'in the line', were invariably short of 'fags' (cigarettes), and an activity we see him engaged in in the closing scene of chapter 6 of *The Hardest Part* – encapsulated his view of chaplaincy as having 'a box of fags in your haversack, and a great deal of love in your heart' (Mozley, 1927, p. 141).

Studdert Kennedy's involvement with the army began while he was still in Worcester, when he was called on to preach to recruits in training camps located on the city's outskirts. In these sermons he developed his conversational tone of earthy rapport with his audience. The style was more than a dumbing-down communications stunt; it was based within his conviction that God was to be sought by each human being in his/her own experience and location. The preacher's task was to get to that location and help the hearer there to find God *because God was already there*. His preaching style was a function of his belief in the incarnation as a continual event, a mystery, within the universe. If the Word had become flesh (John 1.14), then the words about God could take form in the language of the everyday. The language of the Tommy is a point of departure, not a destination. From being a preacher in Worcester he moved to being a chaplain in France in 1915, and over the following months he developed his unique style of ministry that took him right up to the front line – and then into the thick of battle.

The Man, the Padre and the Theologian

The Studdert Kennedy we read – the man of many poems and half a dozen books – cannot be seen as simply the product of the war. This is because the underlying ideas found in poem after poem – or as he would have said, in his style of self-deprecation, 'rough rhymes' – and in chapter after chapter were the result of deep studious reading and long reflection. The problems of human suffering, the image of God as enthroned potentate and the need for courage to follow the Christ were as real for him in an inner city slum or industrial wasteland as on the battlefield. The difference was that in the mud of Flanders the issues were more starkly drawn in terms of the speed of life and death; and it is this starkness, this horrid unblinkable vision into the depths of human destructiveness, that brought his thought to an issue. The war did not produce his thought but it did bring it into the open and give it rigorous focus. Whether his desire to start publishing – and *The Hardest Part* is his first book of prose – was an awareness that if he did not publish he might not survive, or that the issues were now so urgent that he could no longer postpone writing, we shall never know. What we can see in *The Hardest Part* is someone who has been gathering and organizing his thoughts over probably a decade, and then marshals them into a chain of reflections set in Flanders – the current province of West Flanders in Belgium around Ieper, then known as Ypres – during the series of battles beginning in June 1917 that are conventionally referred to as 'Passchendaele'. If the cues given in the book are to be trusted, this period of reflection and writing began with the Battle of Messines Ridge on 7 June and continued until the opening battles in August just east of Ypres. In all it was a period of perhaps two, at most three months. The work of the years was distilled into a series of individual reflections 'in real time', which took place in the very middle of his work as a chaplain.

Because of the way Studdert Kennedy engaged in his theological reflection, as responses to the actual situations in which he finds himself as a human being, a believing Christian, and a chaplain, *The Hardest Part* is itself the best guide to his work as a padre, how he set about the work and what it meant to him. But should we also ask: What was Studdert Kennedy like as a theologian?

The theologian

Studdert Kennedy would almost certainly have rejected 'theologian' as a designation: he always denigrates his work as if it is little more than rough ideas sketched out! But we should be very reluctant to accept this as more than an expression of intellectual humility before the task that faces every Christian thinker. By contrast, we should be aware that he puts forth a new and distinctive theological vision and as such needs to be reckoned alongside the major innovators of twentieth-century theology – as should become clear from reading Stuart Bell's essay in this book.

However, many who like the appealing figure of Woodbine Willie may baulk at the idea of that man as a theologian. This may say more about the popular image of what a theologian is than about the life and work of Studdert Kennedy. The still-popular idea – and it was probably shared by Studdert Kennedy, from the hurt we see in his epilogue about reactions he received from those who read proofs of his book – is that a theologian is a professional academic and that their theology is always produced in the stolid forms of academic monographs replete with an arcane jargon and copious footnotes. It is the image portrayed on so many canvases hanging in universities: a cleric with wrinkled brow from long study, gown as uniform, book in one hand and pen in the other, and learned tomes on the desk and as backdrop. This is a caricature. Many of the most influential theologians created new ways of thinking about God and discipleship using other means. John Milton and John Bunyan both created works of literature that gave expression to their theology, while John and Charles Wesley created a theology of a merciful God of gentleness in their sermons and hymns. Theology takes many shapes, and theologians can be found far from the classroom. Indeed, academic theologians have begun to take this phenomenon far more seriously in recent decades, recognizing that theology can be found in literature, drama, art and in every other medium in which humans reflect on their situation, the traditions of faith and the mystery greater than all that is. From this perspective it is necessary to consider Studdert Kennedy the theologian.

At the core of his theology stands a particular way of understanding what Christians refer to as the mystery of the incarnation. For him, the incarnation is not just one aspect of understanding of the significance of Jesus, the man acclaimed as the Christ and addressed as Lord, it is an insight into the whole relationship of God with the creation. God has entered the creation in the man, Jesus, and thus established in his life and all it involved the paradigm for the human relationship to God. We see this in the number of times Studdert Kennedy appeals to John 1.14 as a basic insight – indeed the foundation – in his arguments. But the incarnation is not a puzzle of metaphysics for students trying to grasp the terminology and arguments of christological conflicts of the fourth and fifth centuries, it is confronting the reality of God sharing the human lot in Jesus of Nazareth. This is facing the fact of the crucifix: the Word made flesh became the flesh suffering on the cross. Just as 'incarnation' is not a one-off event that happened long ago at the conception of Jesus but an ongoing mystery of God's dealing with the universe, so the crucifixion of Jesus is not simply a one-off event but an insight into the mystery of the universe. And that universe is developing, struggling, growing, evolving, 'travailing' – a word Studdert Kennedy often uses – and suffering.

This focus on the Word incarnate crucified is set out in a story, told twice in *The Hardest Part*, of the need to look on the crucifix for an image of God: the story of suffering is looked on as the story of God in relation to the creation. Later, in *Food for the Fed-Up*, Studdert Kennedy presented it in a more systematic way as a basic aspect of Christian believing, and it is the key to much of his thought (1921a, p. x). To start elsewhere than with the crucified, dejected anointed one is to create one's own illusion about 'God' based not on infinite love but the experience of human power exaggerated to a notional infinity. So for Studdert Kennedy the starting point is with recognizing that God is willing to share our human condition and so must share in our suffering and pain. Studdert Kennedy thus arrives at his distinctive willingness to speak of divine suffering – 'the divine passibility' – not as a result of an abstract deduction from cosmology but as a consequence of his theology of the incarnation.

This God who shares our condition, and so our suffering, is also calling us towards the fulfilment of ourselves and the universe. God is not relating to the universe as a master over a game who rewards those who play and punishes those who refuse to, but as one who, taking a share with us in the Christ, invites us to live in a particular way. So Christianity is a 'way' rather than a body of religious ideas. This invitation calls forth a response in love that requires that we bravely collaborate and set out on a distinctive path of discipleship. In this vision of faith as movement, Studdert Kennedy combines themes from Christology, eschatology and moral theology within a new arrangement. The question is not simply who is Jesus in terms of his relationship with God; nor a question of who is 'saved' in terms of keeping the rules or having the right set of beliefs; nor a question of heaven as the place of perfection post-mortem: it is within this world that the building of the kingdom takes place, even if the fullness of the kingdom is a reality as transformed/different from this world as the resurrected body is transformed/different from this one. Indeed, in chapter 9 of *The Hardest Part*, 'on eternal life', Studdert Kennedy is at pains to draw attention to the distinction between the Christian belief in the resurrection – foreshadowed in the mythic images of the resurrection of Jesus after the crucifixion – and notions of the survival of the soul/individual post-mortem, which would reduce the resurrection to being just 'life after death'. This is also the key to why his use of the biblical image of 'the New Jerusalem' is not simply a utopianism.

The integrated approach to the traditional doctrines can be seen very well in chapter 9, which is the lynchpin of his theology. Here Studdert Kennedy takes life after death, the 'immortality of the soul', as simply a fact within the universe: it is a matter that might even be approached using the methods of empirical science. He shows that he has been reading works on this by leading psychics/spiritualists, such as the philosopher Henri Bergson or the scientist Sir Oliver Lodge, who just then was attracting great attention among a people grieving the loss of their loved ones in the war. It is certain that Studdert Kennedy had been reading Lodge – he says so explicitly – but it is not clear whether he had read *Raymond*, which appeared in 1916, in which Lodge published séances that had taken place with his son, who had been killed on the Western Front. But such immortality was not to be confused with the resurrection. This created universe, what an older theology would call 'nature', is to be investigated empirically in all its wonder, but it is not to be confused with the new life, the transformation, that realm of 'grace' captured in the mythic term 'resurrection'. Just so, the utopia for which so many good people dream and work is not to be confused with the destiny of the world and each person – as God's creations – that is the fullness of life, the eschaton, the 'omega-point' or what is conveyed in Studdert Kennedy's favourite myth: the 'New Jerusalem'. This strict awareness of the chasm between the divine and the created, nature and grace, the world of the empirical – which for him is much more than the material – and the world that demands the courage of faith, animates *The Hardest Part* and is expressed again as a basic insight in *Food for the Fed-Up* (1921a, p. xiv). And these two realms are only linked in one moment: that of the mystery of the cross, which again is not the event of an afternoon on a 'hill far away' but the ongoing state in which we live, believe and follow.

It is only when we appreciate these theological foundations that we can understand why Studdert Kennedy believed that it was necessary to challenge the widely accepted view of God as 'the passionless potentate'. So for him, 'god' is not primarily 'omnipotence' writ infinitely large – an abstraction rooted in our human perceptions of power – but the creator who brings all into being and who loves the creation as its finality. And at the centre of the process is located the suffering Word made flesh. God shares in the travail of the creation and endows us with the courage to collaborate in the work of the creation as it moves towards that finality. The universe Studdert Kennedy imagines is not a fixed universe that is there to be used as a test bed for humans – and those who pass the test are the saved. For him, the universe is God's great progressing work. The creation has its own integrity as it evolves – and Studdert Kennedy rejects 'the god of the gaps', even as a propaganda device. Within this great process, human beings exist: conscious, and with a share of freedom and responsibility. And within it also is the involvement of God, who both gives courage to us – and so this is the pattern of our prayer in difficulties – and shares our sufferings. It is this aspect of his theology that is most original and – as becomes clear in Stuart Bell's essay – has received the most attention among professional theologians.

Once one has challenged the notion of the extraterrestrial passionless potentate, one needs to adopt a different stance both as an individual believer and as a member of the Christian Church – and Studdert Kennedy does both. As an individual it means that it is never sufficient to imagine that one is doing theology – as distinct from narrating an account of the theological speculations of others – by repeating formulae handed down within Christianity, whether these come from the Bible, the liturgy, some saint or a catechism. You can only declare authentically that which is your own response to what you have experienced. This issue had been broached in the nineteenth century in terms of 'notional assent' to doctrines (i.e. ticking a box saying 'I accept') versus 'real assent' (i.e. 'this is something I really believe'), but Studdert Kennedy goes much further: my faith is that which is my response to what I know, given my situation and experience, fits the facts. Thus he works through the arguments in *The Hardest Part*, basing each statement he makes on his own real perceptions – and he lets us know that it would be inauthentic of him to adopt the 'perceptions' of others because he can only stand over, in his conscience, what he has perceived. Then if he preaches this, even if he were later proved wrong (and he is explicit that no one is infallible), he can still uprightly say he has been honest and borne witness to the truth to the best of his ability. In the face of the painful facts, authenticity and being true to one's self is the basic commodity of religious discourse. The preacher must be as honourable as the message and so must never be the salesman of religious commonplaces.

If this is the case, theology is not a set of doctrines joined together by some logic, nor a bundle of ideas to be taken on board as so many 'true' propositions; rather it is a reflection on the situation with which one is confronted, and to be a disciple is to be called to engage in this reflection. Theology and discipleship are thus closely related activities, and one must continually draw on what one experiences as central to that process. This seeing has a direct honestly that cannot be set aside for doctrine, a book (e.g. the Bible) or an opinion, however venerable (e.g. the formulae of the liturgy); but it then issues not in some vague feeling but in a creed-that-is-owned and a commitment to taking part in the journey of the creation towards its finality (1921a, p. 10). This starting point of personal authenticity, combined with reflection, followed by an act of commitment, will be found in many of those twentieth-century theologians who have been seen to be influenced by 'existentialism', itself an ill-defined but very useful notion; and so we can say that Studdert Kennedy is one of the earliest representatives of this approach.

Perhaps the most significant expression of this existentialism is to be found in the way Studdert Kennedy places each chapter of *The Hardest Part* on or very near the battlefield, within the sound of the guns. This might seem little more than an author's device to give a theology book some excitement or some local colour: in effect, these are the views of a padre at the front rather than a scholar at his desk. However, I believe his use of specific scenes for each question/chapter is also far more than a matter of literary form or a preacher's device. We today often speak of theology having to take account of the crises that affect people in their lives: does this theology stand up to scrutiny when people are being exploited? Does it stand up in a world in which we are aware of discrimination – for example over gender – or does it silently endorse some form of power domination? Does a particular way of presenting the message of Christianity collude with oppression? Does it still make sense in the heat of the day when confronted with evil, pain and destruction? These are modern questions and add a dimension to the examination of theology undreamt of when the key questions in any evaluation were concerned with consistency with the past – orthodoxy, coherence as a piece of intellectual argument, and competence in its relationship to the body of academic scholarship. Studdert Kennedy bypasses the traditional tests of a theology in favour of existential categories: does this still make sense when men are dying around you, when you are in a trench or bunker, when you have to decide if you should go to help a wounded man just feet away from you, know-ing that if you do it might be the last step you take? The scenes, therefore, of *The Hardest Part* are an implicit statement: theology is too serious a matter to be left in the study, and its coherence needs to be tested in the furnace of living. In Worcester, Studdert Kennedy had already tested his preaching by seeing if it would be worth the while of the soldier to listen to it, and later he would test what he said about society by whether or not it made sense in situations of economic hardship. In *The Hardest Part* he tested a theology of pain and suffering by locating them in the situation in which he was living during the Battle of Passchendaele. The scenery is a statement that the twentieth century had to find a new locale for the practice of theology.

As a member – indeed a minister – in a real community, a Christian Church, Studdert Kennedy was aware that how one located oneself in relation to the facts around one would have a profound effect on how one imagined and represented the community of faith (chapter 8), its memory (chapter 4) and its central celebration of its mystery (chapter 7). In each of these areas – each of which merits extensive studies – he can be seen as the forerunner of what would happen in the twentieth century and in some cases may indeed have been the catalyst of later developments. In terms of the approach to the Scriptures, he found himself engaging in the task of demythologization (not yet a concept in Anglophone biblical studies in 1918), aware that every decoding is another encoding – and he sought in this book and in all his later writings to create a new mythology of God and the location of humanity within that myth. In the case of the Church he questioned the notion of it as a constituent 'institution' of society that facilitates the worship of God in an orderly way, in favour of its being the mystical gathering of the disciples – those who have chosen to follow the Christ – on pilgrimage. The Church is the big pilgrim group moving along the road towards a destiny; and this notion of it as the 'pilgrim people of God' would become a commonplace in theology by the mid-twentieth century, challenging at every level the older models of 'religious institution' and the 'perfect society'. In the matter of the Eucharist, Studdert Kennedy not only cut new ground in moving away from the sterile questions of the scholastic period that dominated Reformation debates, he was also one of the first theologians to think of the Eucharist in terms of Christian activity. In 1917 he was exploring the paradox of how the sacrament of Christian community was actually the great cause of division and strife between churches and within churches between different factions. In a nutshell, 'sacraments' were not objects – somehow 'holy' and 'religious' – but were encounters with God. Indeed, in *Food for the Fed-Up* (pp. 19–20) he presents his view of sacramentality in terms that would later be found in the work of Edward Schillebeeckx. However, the most surprising aspect of *The Hardest Part* is that he works around to a position – then unheard of – of the Eucharist as the centre and summit of the Christian life: the very position that would be adopted officially by the Roman Catholic Church just under half a century later in the documents of its Second Vatican Council (the details can be found in the notes to the texts).

One cannot do justice to the range and depth of the work of Studdert Kennedy in a brief introduction like this. It will require many studies, following themes through all his writings, and it will then need to be set against his background theological culture and what has been happening since he wrote. This book is an attempt to set this process in train by bringing a work of genius, *The Hardest Part*, back into circulation with some notes that make its appreciation easier after the passing of a century. And as for this introduction, it is merely a preliminary sounding to show that there are depths in Studdert Kennedy's work that deserve to be studied. When I set out to write this piece I checked all the usual dictionaries and survey works in theology with this interesting result: while every general guidebook, for instance *The Oxford Dictionary of the Christian Church* (Oxford University Press, 2005), has an entry on the man and the padre, I could not find a single dictionary of theology/theologians that mentioned him! We, the editors of this edition, will have succeeded if this is soon recognized as an oversight.

Gone and Almost Forgotten: The Reception of *The Hardest Part*

Stuart Bell

Introduction

While the life of Geoffrey Studdert Kennedy has been widely recounted in a number of biographies, which are listed in the References and Further Reading section, it would be well to locate *The Hardest Part* in a brief summary of his active service and his other works of poetry and prose. Studdert Kennedy arrived at the Western Front at Christmas 1915. The first four months of his chaplaincy were spent at the huge army base at Rouen. Later in the conflict he served at three infantry training schools and was stationed in the base at Boulogne to play his part in the National Mission of Repentance and Hope, on the orders of Deputy Chaplain General Gwynne and contrary to his personal preferences (Carey, 1929, p. 130). In his account of Studdert Kennedy's time as a chaplain, Chaplain General D. F. Carey detailed three 'comparatively short periods in the front line': in June 1916; in 1917, when Studdert Kennedy was attached to a brigade involved in the attack on Messines Ridge; and in 1918, as part of the Allies' final advance (p. 135). In 1917 Studdert Kennedy was awarded the Military Cross for 'conspicuous gallantry and devotion to duty' during that attack on Messines Ridge, searching out the wounded while under heavy fire and helping them to the dressing station (p. 143).

The Hardest Part

Critically important to understanding his change of attitude to the war, which seems to have been caused by those brief periods at the front, is a personal recollection of Carey, who had met Studdert Kennedy soon after he received the Military Cross: 'He told me he had seen things . . . Then he added: "You know, this business has made me much less cocksure of much of which I was cocksure before."' (p. 154)

In 1917 Studdert Kennedy contributed to *The Church in the Furnace*, a collection of essays by 17 temporary army chaplains, addressing matters of faith they believed to have been raised by the war (SK, 1917). His chapter was entitled 'The Religious Difficulties of the Private Soldier', and in it he addressed for the first time the challenge the horrors of the war posed to the conventional understanding of God as 'almighty' or the reconciliation of divine power with the self-evident presence of evil on such a vast scale. Before *The Hardest Part* was published in 1918, Studdert Kennedy had already produced *Rough Talks by a Padre*, a book of addresses espousing the kind of sanctified patriotism he would later totally repudiate, first given in Rouen in 1916 but subsequently repeated across the Western Front. More popular was his *Rough Rhymes of a Padre*, a collection of his poems, some of which had been published in leaflet form for distribution to soldiers. It was reprinted three times in the first month of its publication. The title of *The Hardest Part* derives from a line in one of his dialect rhymes, 'The Sorrow of God', in which he wrote:

The sorrows o' God must be 'ard to bear
If 'E really 'as Love in 'Is 'eart,
And the 'ardest part i' the world to play
Must surely be God's part. (SK, 1918b, p. 19)

Prophetic and radical

> The Hardest Part has a prophetic and radical force rather like
> that of Barth's Epistle to the Romans, which came out at about
> the same time. In fact it deserved even greater attention than
> Barth's book, for the theology of the suffering God is more
> important than the theology of the God who is 'Wholly Other'.
> What was able to stand the test of the battlefields of Flanders
> and created faith even in the hells there was the discovery of
> the crucified God. (Moltmann, 1981, p. 35)

Thus wrote the German theologian Jürgen Moltmann in 1981. He
quoted Studdert Kennedy at some length: 'It's always the Cross in
the end – God, not Almighty, but God the Father, with a Father's
sorrow and a Father's weakness, which is the strength of love.
God splendid, suffering, crucified – Christ.'

Moltmann was undoubtedly one of the outstanding theologians of the latter part of the twentieth century. Perhaps his
most influential work was The Crucified God, published in 1974.
In it he argued that we must speak of God 'within the earshot
of the dying Jesus', challenging the traditional understanding of
God as impassible – unaffected and unchanged by events in the
created world. Moltmann's thesis was that while it was the Son
who suffered and died, the Father suffered the death of the Son.
Furthermore, he argued, not taking seriously the history of suffering in God's world leads to an idolatrous understanding of God.
It appears that Moltmann had not read The Hardest Part before
writing The Crucified God. However, given that he was expressing
very similar views to those of Studdert Kennedy, albeit in a far more
formal academic style, it is hardly surprising that when he did
discover The Hardest Part, he thought that its theology deserved
more attention than that of Karl Barth. Of particular significance
are the similar personal contexts in which Studdert Kennedy and
Moltmann developed their theology: the former from the horrors
of the Western Front; the latter from the experience, at the age of

17, of a firestorm generated by Allied bombing that caused the death of 40,000 men, women and children in Hamburg. In his autobiography, Moltmann wrote: 'At that time the eclipse of God descended on my world, and the dark night of the soul destroyed my spirit' (2007, p. 190). Echoing the similar questions asked by Studdert Kennedy, he wondered whether God was present in the burning inferno of those days, 'or was he untouched by them, in the heaven of a complacent blessedness?' Coming from a secular family, his first encounter with the Bible had come when, as a prisoner of war in Scotland, he was given a copy by a British army chaplain. His witnessing of trains full of emaciated prisoners being transported to concentration camps significantly influenced what has been described as a Christian theology 'after Auschwitz', although Moltmann prefers the description 'theology . . . after the crucifixion of Christ'. In his autobiography, Moltmann made particular mention of an English hymn that has become quite widely sung in recent years, appearing in numerous hymnbooks:

And when human hearts are breaking
Under sorrow's iron rod,
Then we find that self-same aching
Deep within the heart of God.

The hymn-writer was Timothy Rees, an Anglican clergyman who both served as a chaplain in the First World War and was also Bishop of Llandaff in South Wales in the 1930s. Clearly, either of those experiences could have motivated the writing of a hymn speaking of a God moved by human suffering.

Moltmann stressed the significance for him of Studdert Kennedy's context in a series of interviews that he gave to Patrick Oden in May 2011:

He then asks me a question, 'Do you happen to know this old British chap, Studdert Kennedy, "The Sorrow of God"?' I reply that I didn't. He goes on, while turning and looking for a book on the shelf behind him. 'I was deeply impressed by him, because he was a chaplain in the trenches, not in the gazebos. Part of his poem on the sorrow of God, the hardest part is the heart of God. Therefore he developed an understanding of the suffering of God . . . and he understood how God must feel in World War I.' (Oden, 2011, pp. 43f.)

Given their respective experiences of the two world wars, it is perhaps unsurprising that their theological responses were similar. What is undeniable is that the sheer scale of suffering in the latter conflict, including the Holocaust and the dropping of atomic bombs on Hiroshima and Nagasaki, raised with even greater urgency the fundamental question that had been asked on the Western Front: 'Where is God in all this?' Consequently, Moltmann's theological explorations received far more attention and led to a far greater scale of debate than had *The Hardest Part* a generation earlier. Indeed, it was Moltmann's discovery and re-presentation of Studdert Kennedy that arguably rescued *The Hardest Part* and his poems about a suffering God from theological obscurity. We shall return to what might be termed the 'post-Moltmann' reception of *The Hardest Part* later.

Pre-publication reception

While there is limited evidence of any immediate reaction to the publication of *The Hardest Part*, it is remarkable that Studdert Kennedy felt it necessary to write and include in the first edition a Postscript to respond to the hurt felt by some of those who had read his pre-publication text. That there was such a response is indicative of how radical his theology was felt to be in 1918. While describing the book as 'a very poor attempt to express the inexpressible', and denying that it was 'a theological essay', Studdert Kennedy defended his 'main idea':

We must make clear to ourselves and to the world what we mean when we say 'I believe in God the Father Almighty.' The conditions under which these meditations were made account for the repeated and constant denial of the popular conception. I may have railed at that conception very fiercely, but my raillery is mild and good-natured compared with the outspoken comments of the guns.

There is further internal evidence of the reception of *The Hardest Part* in the 1920s in the author's preface to a new edition published in 1925 (see Appendix 2). In looking back at the seven years since the first edition, Studdert Kennedy observed:

Men said this was a crude and cruel book when it was written, and I said that it was not as crude or as cruel as the war. I would now say that it was mildness itself compared with the cruelty and brutality of a godless peace.

He reaffirmed his belief that the 'doctrine of the Kaiser-God' was 'as dead as cold mutton' and restated his revolt against 'the doctrine of the glorified policeman'. For Studdert Kennedy, the seven years of a peace, characterized by 'chaos, poverty, disease, and hosts of unemployed', had simply reinforced his case against the conventional view of God almighty.

Reception on publication

One of the few religious or theological publications to respond to the initial publication of *The Hardest Part* was the *Church Times*. In a composite review of November 1919 that also discussed *Rough Talks* and *Rough Rhymes*, together described as 'three books of a sincerity almost terrible in their directness', the editor, E. Hermitage Day, wrote with implicit approval of 'dramatic sketches of scenes and passing thoughts, steeped in blood and horror, coarse and tender, daring and shuddering, running through a whole gamut of emotions'. Significantly, the review opened with a recognition of the 'distressingly mean streets and ironworks' of the parish in Worcester from which Studdert Kennedy had departed for the Western Front. It also quoted affirmative comments from soldiers about his parade services in Worcester cathedral. The reviewer was certainly sympathetic. Accusations of Patripassianism were, wrote Hermitage Day, 'grotesque', since Studdert Kennedy was not teaching formal theology to the British Expeditionary Force. Although the review recognized that when used in a theological treatise such language 'might imply a leaning toward that ancient heresy', yet 'What we know about Him is what we see in the Crucified.' While identifying the 'kinship of thought' with H. G. Wells, Hermitage Day observed that Studdert Kennedy had none of Wells' 'awe and hatred' of the 'inscrutable Unknown', and concluded that 'He holds the Faith.'

After summarizing the fundamental arguments of *The Hardest Part*, the review concluded:

> Not everything spoken or written by the padre is to be approved without reserve. Some things seem to be crudely thought as well as cruelly said. It is possible that he himself could not pass a very stiff examination in dogmatic theology. But he goes straight to the heart of the Catholic Faith ... It is significant. (Hermitage Day, 1919, p. 356)

Three weeks later, however, a letter to the *Church Times* from Lt Col. Pythian-Adams complained about Studdert Kennedy's 'Loose reasoning [and] defective theology' in *The Hardest Part*, which would do 'incalculable harm' to readers who are not well instructed in matters of faith. The phrase 'well instructed' is powerfully indicative of the traditional manner in which theological understanding was assumed to be 'handed down'.

In contrast *The Expository Times*, in its brief discussion of *The Hardest Part*, simply focused on Studdert Kennedy's claim about democracy: 'Everywhere I find among the men of the army that this is the one great thing that touches them and rouses real enthusiasm. They do believe in Democracy' (Hastings, 1918, p. 101). 'Those are Mr. Kennedy's words', added the editor for emphasis. There is a parallel here with *The Expository Times'* earlier treatment of *The Church in the Furnace* collection mentioned above, when its informal review had focused entirely on some chaplains' calls for revision of the Prayer Book, ignoring, along with everything else, Studdert Kennedy's advocacy of a suffering God.

A Hodder & Stoughton advertisement for its recently published books frequently quoted from a review of *The Hardest Part* published in *Challenge*: 'This is undoubtedly the most arresting religious book which owes its origins to experiences with the army in France.' ('W.T.') The actual review was generally highly positive. It noted his 'lashing out' at familiar phrases in the Prayer Book and drew attention to the chapter 'God and Prayer', in which Studdert Kennedy offered this response to his experience of a man 'shivering out pious supplications to God for protection and safety': 'I wish that chap would chuck that praying. It turns me sick. … It isn't religion, it's cowardice' (see page 89). The reviewer recognized that the gospel, for Studdert Kennedy, 'is the Cross interpreted as the complex revelation of God', and observed that he 'is constantly on the verge of Patripassianism'. Without offering an explicit endorsement, the review contained an implicit approval in summarizing Studdert Kennedy's argument: 'The Cross is an inspiration because it lifts our anguish and sorrows to the level of God's perpetual triumph over evil in the power of his self-forgetful love.'

Searches for other reviews or responses at the time of the publication of *The Hardest Part* have proved fruitless. In 1925 the *Anglican Theological Review*, published in Ohio, simply noted that the new edition of *The Hardest Part* was one of many 'books received', quoting Studdert Kennedy's new preface to what it described as 'a book of nine terrible chapters on the one theme, "What is God like?"'

Soon after his death in 1929, *The Times* carried an obituary for Studdert Kennedy. Although it ran to around 1,000 words, his advocacy of a suffering God claimed just three lines (9 March 1929, p. 14). A few days later 'an appreciation' by H. R. L. ('Dick') Sheppard was published, also in *The Times* (15 March 1929, p. 23). It paid fulsome tribute to his oratory, his eloquence, his advocacy of Christianity, his lovable nature, his wisdom and his efforts to address the problems of British society in the 1920s. Of his theology there was nothing; of *The Hardest Part*, no mention.

How do we account for such a muted response to an indubitably theologically controversial book? First, we have to recognize the sheer volume of publications that addressed every conceivable aspect of the war, including religion. Popular newspapers and magazines carried whole-page advertisements while the religious press offered thoughts on the war from well-known religious leaders and preachers of every denomination. *The Hardest Part* had to compete for attention with that avalanche. Studdert Kennedy's fame no doubt helped to give his books some prominence, but it was a crowded market and his books of poetry had a more obvious appeal for the general reader.

However, there was a more fundamental reason for *The Hardest Part* to be ignored by the theological journals of the time, and that is the contemporary understanding of how, and by whom, theology was 'done'. Theological insight and development of thought were seen as the exclusive province of a small and elite group of theologians. Such people, almost invariably men, were typically professors or dons at Oxford, Cambridge or, just occasionally, London or one of the Scottish universities. Examples of such prominent Oxbridge theologians include S. R. Driver, Charles Gore, Arthur Headlam, Henry Scott Holland, William Sanday and B. H. Streeter. To that group were added the so-called 'best brains' of the bishops' bench, and the occasional dean or canon, obvious examples being Hastings Rashdall, Dean of Carlisle, and J. K. Mozley, Canon of St Paul's. They were the theologians. Thus the biographer of Randall Davidson, Archbishop of Canterbury, could offer without any implicit criticism the comment that his subject was 'not himself a theologian' (G. K. A. Bell, 1952, p. 1135). Similarly, the former army chaplain D. F. Carey, writing shortly after Studdert Kennedy's death, insisted: 'Studdert was the last to make any claim to be a theologian in the exact sense of the word' (Carey, 1929, p. 149). In an environment in which discourse on theology was confined to a highly educated elite, no ordinary parish priest, let alone an army chaplain with a colourful reputation, was expected to publish original theological ideas or offer a distinctive answer to the question 'Where is God in all this?' from the Western Front. Consequently, *The Hardest Part* was not, it would appear, thought worthy of review by 'proper' theologians.

In later years, when his theology was commented upon it was often treated in a somewhat dismissive and patronizing manner. J. K. Mozley wrote the classic historical survey of changing attitudes to divine impassibility, publishing his Cambridge DD thesis on this subject in 1926. He also edited what soon became the standard biography of Studdert Kennedy, *G. A. Studdert Kennedy: By His Friends*. In the former work he wrote:

The thoughts of *The Hardest Part* came to its author on the battlefield of the West, and their intensity, both in idea and in expression, reveals clearly enough the pressure and tension of such tremendous experiences. But the same theology reappears, and as something which belongs to the heart of religious truth, in later works. (1926, p. 160)

In Mozley's survey of British theology from 1889 to 1946 he described *The Hardest Part* thus:

The title was meant to express in arresting manner the belief that in the experience of suffering it is God, not man, who had most to endure. The book was written under the stress of personal immersion in the war, and its emotional aspect is largely due to that fact. (1952, p. 52)

In stressing the effect of the 'pressure and tension' under which he worked and in apparently feeling the need to excuse the 'emotional aspect' of *The Hardest Part*, Mozley seems to have been implying that something more 'balanced' might have come from the usual sources of theological insight, such as the senior common rooms of Oxford or Cambridge.

The marginalization of *The Hardest Part* within Studdert Kennedy's corpus and the rationalization of his theology as being a temporary consequence of wartime conditions continued after the Second World War. In 1947 'a friend' edited *The Best of Studdert Kennedy*, bringing together extracts from his poems and prose. Significantly, the vast majority of the poems on God's passibility, most notably 'The Suffering God' and 'The Sorrow of God', were omitted from the anthology. Furthermore, in a book of 240 pages, just eight were given to one chapter from *The Hardest Part*, 'God and Prayer', in which the suffering of God is hardly mentioned. In contrast, however, it should be noted that William Temple, in his contribution to *G. A. Studdert Kennedy: By His Friends*, showed that he recognized the significance of *The Hardest Part* among Studdert Kennedy's prolific output by quoting a whole chapter of the book – 'God and Prayer'.

In his overview of Anglican theology from 1889 to 1939, Michael Ramsey described *The Hardest Part* as being 'written for readers sensitive to the agony of the world'. He viewed the 'tendency' to believe that traditional understandings of divine impassibility must be modified, and that God suffers, as particularly characteristic of the 1920s (1960, p. 58). However, in not drawing any links between *The Hardest Part* and the ideas of divine suffering that developed after the Second World War, he was far from alone.

Reception after Moltmann

Searching a hundred years of issues of *The Expository Times* reveals a far greater theological interest in Studdert Kennedy in the 1980s and 1990s than at any time during his life or immediately after his death. Gordon Wakefield observed in 1995 that the '"rough rhymes" express a theological revolution in his attack on the notion of divine impassibility' (1995, p. 138). Since then a number of writers have engaged with Studdert Kennedy's advocacy of a suffering God, often relating it to contemporary experiences.

In 1999 Desmond Tutu, in his memoir of his chairing of South Africa's Truth and Reconciliation Commission, reflected not specifically on *The Hardest Part* but on selected verses from Studdert Kennedy's poem, 'The Suffering God', concluding with:

Then must it mean, not only that Thy sorrow
  Smote Thee that once upon the lonely tree,
But that to-day, to-night, and on the morrow,
  Still it will come, O Gallant God, to Thee. (SK, 1918b, p. 61)

Tutu wrote:

I thought of God's sorrow many times as we listened to harrowing tales of the kind of things we are capable of doing to one another. Awful things that seemed to beggar description and called into question our right to be considered fit to be regarded as human at all. (1999, p. 93)

Then followed numerous witness statements and confessions of torture and murder on an immense scale, descriptions that more than justified Tutu's pondering about actions that call into question the designation 'human'.

Writing in 2005, Robert Ellis argued that Studdert Kennedy's writing revealed him to be 'what we now think of as a "pastoral theologian"' (p. 168). This is key to understanding his theology.

In coming to this conclusion, Ellis saw Studdert Kennedy first as 'someone whose poetic voice has a decidedly personal perspective' but also as one who has a wider perspective than the purely pastoral: 'I mean to speak of the way in which pastoral experience and theologizing about it – rather than being the application of theology acquired elsewhere – actually becomes the raw material of that theology' (p. 170). The depth and breadth of Studdert Kennedy's theological expression, made explicit in the annotated text of this volume, show that while his methodology may indeed have been that of a pastoral theologian, his thought fully merits the unqualified designation of 'theologian'.

Ten years later, in a chapter in *A Handbook of Chaplaincy Studies*, Andrew Totten linked reflections on the Second World War experiences of John McManners – later editor of *The Oxford Illustrated History of Christianity* – with Studdert Kennedy and *The Hardest Part*. His criticism was that 'Studdert Kennedy ended up fusing the suffering Christ with his deified Tommy' (2015, p. 216). He quoted from the chapter 'God in the Bible', unhelpfully omitting the first phrase and others that might be seen to undermine his critique. The full paragraph reads:

[All men are learning to worship patient, suffering love, and] the muddy bloody hero of the trenches is showing us Who is the real King. [The darkness is being cleared away, and men at last are growing proud of the Cross.] Beside the wounded tattered soldier who totters down to this dressing-station with one arm hanging loose, an earthly king in all his glory looks paltry and absurd. [I know nothing in my real religion of the Almighty God of power.] I only see God in Christ, and these men have shown me – *Him*.

When the whole paragraph is considered, it is clear, I think, that Studdert Kennedy was not 'fusing' Christ and the Tommy. His phrase, 'I only see God in Christ' was not meant as an interpretation of his observation of the 'wounded tattered soldier' but rather to be set against the 'religion of the Almighty God of power' (a phrase omitted by Totten), which Studdert Kennedy consistently rejected.

What he was doing was affirming the suffering God of the cross, rather than the omnipotent almighty, as the 'real King'. Neither was there here a deification of the Tommy. That Studdert Kennedy saw a revelation of a suffering God in suffering men does not mean that he was equating them. Indeed, while many of his contemporaries did virtually deify the Tommy, Studdert Kennedy famously ridiculed Horatio Bottomley's description of all the British soldiers as 'saints' (Carey, 1929, p. 131).

In his 2011 book *Religion at Ground Zero: Theological Responses to Times of Crisis*, Christopher Brittain set the theological responses to the First World War, in particular those of Paul Tillich and Studdert Kennedy, within a wider context, not least of the Holocaust and 9/11. While his chapter on the First World War could be criticized for its mis-stating of Studdert Kennedy's home parish (p. 53), misquoting Winnington Ingram's Advent sermon (p. 50) and taking somewhat at face value later critiques of Anglican chaplains, Brittain not only engaged constructively with the theology of *The Hardest Part* but also set it in a wider context, drawing links with later 'times of crisis' and comparing theological responses. He noted that Studdert Kennedy understood how religion had been used by the military as an ideological tool and how ideas of sacrifice and duty had been used for propaganda purposes.

Most significantly, Brittain drew a parallel between *The Hardest Part* and the writing of Paul Tillich, serving in the German army as a chaplain at the time of its publication, and who would later become one of the leading theologians of the twentieth century. In a 1918 sermon, Tillich declared: 'God suffers with us in all our affliction. He does not come to us as an enraged God to increase our suffering, but comes to us to carry us as Friend, as Father, as our God' (Brittain, 2011, p. 57). Unsurprisingly, just as did Studdert Kennedy, Tillich engaged in conversations about the power of prayer in the context of the Western Front. In Tillich's case, a disagreement with a senior officer who could not accept his argument that prayer could not protect a soldier from enemy fire led to Tillich being transferred to another unit (Pauck, 1977, p. 50). From the very start of the First World War it was recognized that it was a conflict between two Christian – or nominally Christian – countries, both sides claiming divine endorsement of their cause. Christopher Brittain's helpful setting alongside each other of the writings of Studdert Kennedy and Tillich in 1918 shows that two opposing chaplains were coming to similar conclusions about the nature of God.

Conclusion

While *The Hardest Part* was largely ignored by the theologians of the time, it is surely significant that its advocacy of a suffering God was both being offered at the very same time by Paul Tillich, serving on the Western Front as a chaplain just a short distance away from Studdert Kennedy, and then would be echoed by Jürgen Moltmann, pondering on the sight of a blazing Hamburg, just 25 years later.

Once peace had come, and the guns that had most obviously raised the questions about God's relationship with the carnage were standing silent, Studdert Kennedy's answer to those questions in *The Hardest Part* suddenly appeared redundant. God had given Britain and her allies the long prayed-for victory, and questions about the divine nature were no longer being asked. It took another war for those questions to be asked again, with even greater urgency, given the unprecedented scale of suffering and death.

While very few people appear to have pulled a copy of *The Hardest Part* off their shelves, perhaps until Moltmann did so in the late 1970s, so much of the 'theology after Auschwitz' – certainly the Christian theology – can be seen to be offering similar solutions to the problems raised by traditional understandings of divine omnipotence. While, as a book, *The Hardest Part* may indeed have become almost forgotten, its theology of a suffering God would be echoed far and wide in the second half of the twentieth century.

The Hardest Part

BY THE REV.

G. A. STUDDERT KENNEDY, M.C., C.F.

("WOODBINE WILLIE")

Author of "Rough Rhymes of a Padre"

The sorrows of God mun be 'ard to bear
If 'e really 'as Love in 'is 'eart
And the 'ardest part i' the world to play
Mun surely be God's Part

TO

MY WIFE

Geoffrey Anketell Studdert Kennedy, 1883–1929.

Preface

THIS collection of essays needs no preface, but as Studdert Kennedy has asked me to write one, I can perhaps best comply with his request by telling those who read this book something about the man who wrote it.

Of Irish extraction he was brought up in Leeds, where his father was vicar of a parish in a poor district. Kennedy was educated at Leeds Grammar School and Trinity College, Dublin. In 1908 he was ordained by the Bishop of Worcester and went to work at Rugby under the present Dean of Windsor.

He eventually returned to assist his father in his slum parish in Leeds, and in 1914 he was appointed Vicar of St Paul's, Worcester, a very poor parish of some 3,000 souls.

As a parish priest Studdert Kennedy proved himself a diligent visitor, who by his sympathy and unselfish devotion won the hearts of many.

He is a speaker of extraordinary power, and I know none so effective with men. His powers of vivid description, his absolute naturalness and manifest sincerity attract and interest.

In the early days of the war, when a large number of men were in training at Worcester, some 2,000 attended the Cathedral on Sunday mornings. When Kennedy preached, as he sometimes did, Church Parade lost all its stiffness and boredom, every man was all attention, and the addresses with their racy remarks and telling illustrations were the chief topic of conversation during the ensuing week.

At the end of 1915 Kennedy, having been able to make arrangements for the duties of his parish, went out as a chaplain. His geniality and good fellowship endeared him to the men, and his bravery and sincerity won their respect. He went through a good deal of fighting, and the brutal realities of war brought him face to face with the problem of reconciling belief in the love of God with the omnipotence of the Deity.[1]

These essays[2] are an attempt by a thoroughly religious man to solve this and other problems, and bring religion into relation to the stern realities of life, and free it from deadening conventionalities in thought and practice.

These pages express the thoughts which came to the writer amid the hardships of the trenches and the brutalities of war. It is literally theology hammered out on the field of battle.

Some may disapprove of what he has written and dissent from his conclusions, but they will profit by reading the book and learning how an earnest man endeavours to do for the British soldier what the writer of the book of Job and the prophet Isaiah endeavoured to do for the men of their times.

Kennedy expresses in a striking and graphic manner what multitudes who have not his power of expression are dumbly thinking.

Expert theologians before condemning should read the author's postscript. Its revelation of the spirit of the man and his object in writing will do much to disarm criticism.

W. Moore Ede.
Deanery, Worcester.
May 1918

---

1 Moore Ede played down the extent to which SK threw down a challenge to traditional textbook theology. As set out here, *The Hardest Part* is another exercise in reconciling two aspects of God as studied in theology: on the one hand the interested and loving figure, on the other the all-powerful deity. There is no hint that SK would use the problems of suffering and evil in the world as a basis to challenge that central notion of philosophical theology: the divine impassibility. Likewise, there is no hint of the challenge to traditional Christology and church preaching.

2 Moore Ede presented them as a series of essays – trial pieces of a thesis – rather than a worked-out single, unified work (albeit one presented as a string of meditations).

Author's Introduction

WHEN I had been in France as a chaplain about two months,[1] before I had heard a gun fired or seen a trench, I went to see an officer in a base hospital who was slowly recovering from very serious wounds. The conversation turned on religion, and he seemed anxious to get at the truth. He asked me a tremendous question. "What I want to know, Padre," he said, "is, what is God like? I never thought much about it before this war. I took the world for granted. I was not religious, though I was confirmed and went to Communion some times with my wife. But now it all seems different. I realise that I am a member of the human race, and have a duty towards it, and that makes me want to know what God is like. When I am transferred into a new battalion I want to know what the Colonel is like. He bosses the show, and it makes a lot of difference to me what sort he is. Now I realise that I am in the battalion of humanity, and I want to know what the Colonel of the world is like. That is your real business, Padre; you ought to know."

I think that this question sums up in a wonderful way the form which the spiritual revival is taking among men at the front. First there comes a wider vision of humanity. This arises partly from the new sense of comradeship and brotherhood which exists in our new citizen armies, and unites them with the citizen armies

---

1 SK arrived at the massive Army base outside Rouen just before Christmas 1915. This was located well behind the lines, so it is unsurprising that he neither heard a gun nor saw a trench while based there.

of the allied nations, and partly from the worldwide scale of this tremendous conflict. The cutting of the world in two by the sword has helped men to see it whole. Men's minds are of necessity less parochial, less insular, and more cosmopolitan, in the best sense, than they were. As a consequence of this there is a quickened interest in ultimate questions, a desire to know the meaning of it all. This grows in some cases to a positive hunger for the knowledge of God and a conscious seeking after Him; in others it remains a kind of dim dumb longing for some ultimate truth. Finally, there is a certain, partly wistful, partly disappointed, turning to the Churches in the rather forlorn hope of obtaining information and light. Sometimes the question is put to the Church anxiously and sadly, sometimes with bitterness and contempt.

In the vast majority of cases, of course, it is not put in words, because those who would ask it have no words in which to express it. It appears rather in the attitude of mind, and is hinted at in the conversation of these splendidly dumb soldiers who act and cannot speak. But the question is there in the heart of the army and of the nation, "What is God like?"

When a chaplain joins a battalion no one says a word to him about God, but every one asks him, in a thousand different ways, "What is God like?" His success or failure as a chaplain really depends upon the answer He gives by word and by deed. The answer by deed is the more important, but an answer by words is inevitable, and must be given somehow.

When the question was put to me in hospital I pointed to a crucifix[2] which hung over the officer's bed, and said, "Yes, I think I can tell you. God is like that." I wondered if it would satisfy

---

2 A cross with a figure of the dead Jesus on it. In 1914 such crucifixes would have been rare in Britain outside the Roman Catholic Church and High Church circles within the Church of England. However, in France the crucifix would have been the most common form of cross – and would have been very common in hospital contexts.

him. It did not. He was silent for a while, looking at the crucifix, and then he turned to me, and his face was full of doubt and disappointment. "What do you mean?" he said; "God cannot be like that. God is Almighty, Maker of heaven and earth,[3] Monarch of the world, the King of kings, the Lord of lords,[4] Whose will sways all the world. That is a battered, wounded, bleeding figure, nailed to a cross and helpless, defeated by the world and broken in all but spirit. That is not God; it is part of God's plan: God's mysterious, repulsive, and apparently perfectly futile plan for saving the world from sin. I cannot understand the plan, and it appears to be a thoroughly bad one, because it has not saved the world from sin. It has been an accomplished fact now for nearly two thousand years, and we have sung hymns about God's victory, and yet the world is full of sin, and now there is this filthy war. I'm sick of this cant. You have not been up there, Padre, and you know nothing about it. I tell you that cross does not help me a bit; it makes things worse. I admire

---

3 A quotation from the Apostles' Creed, much used in the Church of England's liturgy, and a text that, as we shall see throughout this book, was very dear to SK and on which he wrote another book in 1921: *Food for the Fed-Up*.

4 Cf. Rev. 17.14. SK almost always cited Scripture from memory and consequently there are often slight variations between what is found here and the version he had in mind (the Authorized Version of 1611). Sometimes he placed these quotations in inverted commas, sometimes not. In these notes, such quotations are given in the form 'Mark 12.30', and only if a variation is significant is it noted. On many other occasions he used scriptural phrases almost without noticing he was doing so, or made an oblique reference to a biblical incident, and in these cases the reference is preceded by 'cf.'. When a Gospel quotation could be assigned to more than one Gospel, that closest to SK's usage is cited; otherwise the Matthaean reference is given. When the editors quote Scripture in the notes, they use the New Revised Standard Version (Anglicized edition) when they wish to make clear they are not quoting something from SK. However, in several places the version quoted in notes is the Authorized Version, since it is its wording that SK is echoing in *The Hardest Part*. In these cases the initials 'AV' follow the quotation.

Jesus of Nazareth; I think He was splendid, as my friends at the front are splendid – splendid in their courage, patience, and unbroken spirit. But I asked you not what Jesus was like, but what God is like, God Who willed His death in agony upon the Cross, and Who apparently wills the wholesale slaughter in this war. Jesus Christ I know and admire, but what is God Almighty like? To me He is still the unknown God."[5]

How would you answer him? How would you answer the thousands like him, who feel all that but cannot put their feelings into words? That is what I have tried to do in this small book. For two years I have been serving with the army, always learning more than I could teach. Part of the time I have been with the men in the line, part of it I served at the base, and part I spent touring about from base to front and from front to base, preaching to great crowds of men, and trying to answer their questions. I have learned a great deal about the mind of the ordinary man, and I have learned to love and respect him, and to be ashamed of myself.

All my experience has grouped itself round and hinged itself upon the answer to this question, asked me at the beginning, "What is God like?" because it appears to me to be the only question that ultimately and really matters and must be answered. The form of meditations in battle which the answer takes is the result of an experience which much surprised me. During active operations I was very busy and intensely preoccupied, and unconscious of any connected thinking, and yet when a lull came I found in my memory whole trains of thought that had been working themselves out all the time. Each train of thought I have tried to write down as memory gave it to me, without elaboration, and they fall into a kind of reasonable sequence.

I only hope that what I have written may help those who are dumbly asking this great question, and those who are try-

5 Cf. Acts 17.23.

ing to answer it for them. It is all of necessity very sketchy and incomplete, but I hope and pray it may serve to help those in difficulty, as the vision of God I have tried to express has helped me.

G. A. STUDDERT KENNEDY, C.F.,[6]

Army Infantry School, B.E.F.[7]

---

6 CF = Chaplain to the Forces.

7 BEF = British Expeditionary Force. This was the collective name of the British Army – including troops from Canada, Australia, India, New Zealand, South Africa and elsewhere in the Empire – fighting in France and Belgium. SK may well be referring to the 4th Army Infantry School at Flixecourt, to which he was attached in autumn 1917. See Snape, Michael, 2005, *God and the British Soldier*, Abingdon: Routledge, pp. 107–8.

Map of the Battle of Messines Ridge.

*The bold line on the left of this map shows the front line at the moment,
0310 on 7 June 1917, Studdert Kennedy chose as the location for the
beginning of his book. He was located to the west of the series of hills
marked '80' [metres above sea level], '63' and '65' on this map – these
hills and the high ground between them formed 'the ridge'. The series of
19 enormous mines that exploded – and to which he refers – were along
that front line, leaving craters that can still be seen today.*

The Michelin Guide to Ypres and the Battles of Ypres *(Clermont-
Ferrand, 1919, p. 21)*

I

What is God like?

June 7th, 1917.

*I*N *the assembly trenches on the morning of the attack on the Whyschaete-Messines Ridge. The ——— division attacked first, and our men went through their lines to the last objective.*[1]

* * * * *[2]

---

1 The assault on Messines Ridge began at dawn on 7 June 1917 with the detonation of a string of 19 mines – the work of nearly two years of tunnelling – at exactly 0310 hrs, along the top of this little hill just south of Ieper (then called Ypres). This was the greatest man-made explosion up to that time, and could be heard in London. One has to have an image of that explosion to envisage the scene SK wants us to imagine. The troops he was with were not part of the first assault wave but were to push the assault eastwards towards a succession of objectives laid out for that day. Consequently SK was not in the front line but in a trench further back (an 'assembly trench'), which had been specially dug so as to hold extra men needed after the initial wave had gone 'over the top'. This was a very dangerous location – even if as he looked around it seemed safe for the moment – in that if the Germans suspected an attack, these packed trenches would have been the most inviting target for their artillery. For a succinct narrative of this event, see S. Usborne, 'A blast that obliterated 10,000 Germans' at www.independent.co.uk/news/world/world-history/history-of-the-first-world-war-in-100-moments/a-history-of-the-first-world-war-in-100-moments-a-blast-that-obliterated-10000-germans-9517223.html; retrieved 31 May 2017.

2 SK used this device to indicate that there was a break in his process of reflection. We might think of it as a short pause that allowed him to move in time and location before resuming his thoughts.

13

It is God alone that matters.[3] I am quite sure about that. I'm not sure that it is not the only thing I am sure about.[4] It is not any Church of God, or priest of God; it is not even any act of God in the past like the Birth of Christ or His death upon the Cross. These may be revelations of what God is or means by which He works; but it is God Himself, acting here and now upon the souls of men;[5] it is He alone that can save the world.

There is only one commandment really: Thou shalt love the Lord thy God with all thy heart, with all thy mind, with all thy strength[6] – with the whole bag of tricks in fact. It's got to be a whole hog, go-ahead and damn the consequences kind of love – a complete and enthusiastic surrender of the whole man to the leadership of God.[7] It is funny the body isn't mentioned; it

---

3 Each chapter is a single self-contained reflection presented by SK as taking place at a specific place and moment (the reflection took place in the midst of life, work, war), and that starting point was all important to him for his theology that 'faces facts' squarely. Consequently each chapter has to be read at one sitting as a single train of reflective thought. SK was not *writing* theology but '*doing* theology' and sharing his activity with his readers.

4 Note SK's starting point: he was out in the field, not in a study, when he began his theological reflection. This starting point was explicitly recognized by Jürgen Moltmann in his advocacy of SK's theology – see page xxxv. Likewise, SK did not start with an abstraction or an authoritative statement but with his own experience. His starting point was trying to make sense of what he was encountering in life and so it must be true to that experience. This approach, now common, was then revolutionary, and we shall refer to it as his 'existentialism'.

5 This interest in God's 'acting here and now' was fundamental to SK's existentialism: it was a real activity that SK felt, rather than a record of an action (e.g. of the birth of Christ recorded in the Bible), that is his starting point. He emphasized this starting point repeatedly in the book and drew out its implications in the later chapters, especially chapter 4.

6 Mark 12.30; note he omitted the phrase – common to all three Gospels – 'and with all thy soul' (Matt. 22.37; Luke 10.27).

7 For SK, the whole of life and faith was a process, a movement, a journey located within a larger cosmic movement from an act of creation, an 'Alpha', towards a consummation, an 'Omega', which takes place under God's

comes in here a bit, the giving of the body.[8] It's about all some of these dear chaps know how to give, and they give like kings: better than many kings, God bless 'em. There is the whole of vital religion, and therefore the whole of life, in a nutshell – Love God all out, and then live with all your might. The other commandment is only a bit off the big one. You couldn't help loving your neighbour if you once loved God.[9] You may love churches and services and hymns and things, and not love your neighbour; lots of people do, but that is not loving God. These things become ends in themselves, and then they are worse than useless. That's always been the bother with religion.

It's a difficult business. I suppose loving God means knowing God. You can't love a person unless you know him. How can a man know God? "By their fruits ye shall know them."[10] I suppose that rule applies. By God's fruits ye shall know Him. That is the queerest yet. It fairly beats the band – God's fruits. Where do they begin, and where do they end?

*　　*　　*　　*　　*

leadership. We shall see repeatedly in the book that he was not only reformulating a view of the relationship of humanity and God but presenting it within a theology of discipleship. The believers are following God's leadership now rather than following the dictates of a religion or using 'following' as simply a synonym for accepting or believing in a credal statement.

8 The 'here' was the battlefield on which he stood. As he looked around (c.0300 hrs) he knew that soon some of the bodies of the men beside him would be mangled in death or with wounds: they would then have given their bodies. SK saw these deaths or wounds as acts of love fulfilling the 'one commandment'.

9 Mark 12.31: 'The second is this: "You shall love your neighbour as yourself."'

10 Matt. 7.20. The use of this criterion is significant in that it relied on the living perception of the individual rather than the establishment of an a priori certainty: SK's existentialism was thoroughgoing.

I suppose it must be getting on time now.[11] Five minutes past three, I make it, and ten minutes past is zero. It will be the devil of a shindy when it starts. What a glorious morning! So still.[12] Now the birds are just awaking in English Wood.[13] How soft the silver dawn light is, and this grey mist that hangs so low makes all the open meadow land just like a dim-lit sea, with clumps of trees for islands. In the east there is a flush of red – blood red. Blood . . . Beauty . . . God's Fruits. I wonder what—

* * * * *

God Almighty! what's that? It's the Hill gone up. Lord, what a noise! and all the earth is shaking.[14] It must be like that Korah, Dathan, and Abiram business in the Book of Numbers up there.[15] All the lot went down, women and children and all. I

---

11 SK moved from the mode of reflection to dealing with the actual moment: it was now 0305 hrs. We shall see this movement between the moment of reflection and the historical moment again and again throughout the book.

12 Every reader of this book in 1918 knew one thing about Messines Ridge: that it began with the great explosion of the mines. As a chaplain, SK would not have known at the time that the battle would open with this detonation: it was one of the greatest secrets of the day. So here he both recreated his scene and prepared us for his surprise.

13 By June 1917 this was the remains of a copse that had been given this name by the army as part of their identification of the topography around them. English Wood was located near the village of Vijverhoek, around 2 miles south-west of Ypres.

14 0310 hrs – the moment of the detonation. On the previous afternoon, Major General Charles Harrington, Chief of Staff of the British Second Army, had quipped to his staff: 'We may not change history tomorrow, but we will certainly change geography!'

15 Num. 16.1–35. Little read today, this story of the earth swallowing these three men for speaking against Moses, and with them 250 other men along with their wives and children, was described in 1900 thus: 'Most readers of the English Bible are familiar with the story of Korah's rebellion, and the terrible fate that overtook him and his followers.' See Selbie, J. A.,

always thought it was hard luck on the children.[16] It's like war though. War is just a mighty earthquake that swallows all before it. Now for it. Here come the guns. Listen to that big 12-inch.[17] It sounds like the man with a loud voice and no brains in an argument. I thought I'd get the wind up, and here I am laughing. We are all laughing. We're enjoying it. That's the stuff to give 'em. It is a glorious sight, one silver sheet of leaping flame against the blackness of the trees. But it's damnable, it's a disgrace to civilisation. It's murder – wholesale murder.

We can't see the other end – ugh – damn all war! They have wives and kiddies like my Patrick, and they are being torn to bits and tortured.[18] It's damnable. What's that, lad?[19] Shout a bit

---

1900, 'Korah, Dathan, Abiram', in Hastings, James (ed.), *Dictionary of the Bible*, Edinburgh: T. & T. Clark, vol. 3, p. 11.

16 SK was thinking here of the biblical story rather than Messines Ridge. The biblical narrative is remarkably like that of the mines he witnessed: the earth opened up and swallowed them and all they had (Num. 16.30) and 'wives' and 'little children' (16.27). A fire came of out the pit consuming men and then closed over them (16.33 and 35). SK would reflect on such incidents of divine wrath in the Bible in chapter 4.

17 Most probably SK meant the 12-inch howitzer which, due to its size, was built on to a railway carriage: 138 of these monsters were built and they had a maximum range of 14,500 yards. A howitzer, as distinct from a 'gun', fired its shell (750 lb/340 kg in weight) high into the air. It then plunged to its target under gravity. There were also four 12-inch guns built in 1917, from which the 850 lb shell was sent directly to its target, range 33,000 yards, by the force of its propellant. Once the mines were detonated, the artillery opened fire, and since SK could hear the gun's loud report, it was probably not far behind him – suggesting that it was a howitzer.

18 Here and elsewhere in the book, SK did not speak of an abstraction such as 'humanity' but related it to his own family – his wife and son Patrick. This allowed him to appreciate that the Germans who had been swallowed up in the mine had wives and children too. This is a detail of his existentialism; it is his connectedness with the world he experiences that is his way to understanding.

19 His reflection is interrupted by a little snippet of conversation with one of the soldiers near him. We shall meet this return from reflection to the moment and those around him repeatedly in the book.

louder. It is, you're right, it is the stuff to give 'em. They can't stand much of that; they'll have to quit.

* * * * *

How wonderful that sky is, golden red, and all the grass is diamond-spangled like the gorgeous robe that clothes a king. Solomon in all his glory.[20] Look at that lark. Up he goes. He doesn't care a tuppeny dump for the guns. His song is drowned, but not his joy.

God's in His heaven;
All's right with the ——[21]

* * * * *

What awful nonsense! All's right with the world, and this ghastly, hideous —— But, by George, it's a glorious barrage, and English girls made 'em.[22] We're all in it – sweethearts, mothers, and wives. The hand that rocks the cradle wrecks the world. There are no non-combatants. We're all in it, and God, God Almighty, the loving Father Who takes count of every sparrow's fall,[23] what is He doing? It is hard to fathom. God's fruits, singing birds and splendid beauty, flowers and fair summer skies, golden mists and bloody slaughter! What is a man to make of it?[24]

---

20 Matt. 18.29.

21 This well-known couplet is from Robert Browning's 1841 verse drama *Pippa Passes*. For SK it was a stock phrase emblematic of a whole attitude to God and the world that denied the facts of suffering, pain and evil.

22 By 1917 most of the labour in the munitions factories was being provided by women. Women involved in occupations traditionally seen as 'men's work' were still a cause of wonder.

23 Matt. 10.29: 'Are not two sparrows sold for a penny? Yet not one of them will fall to the ground unperceived by your Father.'

24 It is in the face of this contradiction of facts within experience that he began his core reflection on God and suffering. What is different from a traditional theodicy is that it is forced on him by experience rather than by an exercise in the calm detachment of the study, and he had already ruled out

What is God like?

* * * * *

"Almighty and everlasting God, we are taught by Thy holy word that the hearts of kings and governors are in Thy rule and governance, and that Thou dost dispose and turn them as it seemeth best to Thy godly wisdom."[25] . . . I think that's right. It's in the Communion Service, anyhow. I suppose it includes the Kaiser. Anyhow, it is nonsense.[26] What unspeakable blackguards some kings and governors have been, and what utter ruin they have caused! Why should we start a prayer with such a futile falsehood? Their hearts can't be in God's rule and governance when they are evil and base. There it is in the Communion Service.[27] If it is true, what is God like?

* * * * *

What is God like? I remember that's what that officer in hospital asked me.[28] "You ought to know; that is your business, Padre," he said. I suppose it is, and I ought to know. But do I? Do I know and love God? Jesus Christ I know and love. He is splendid. I love His superb courage, His majestic patience, and His perfect

---

as simplistic declarations that it was not a real problem as 'awful nonsense'. SK had to confront the bloody reality around him openly. It would either lead him to a new faith (as it did in his case) or to an abandonment of faith altogether (as it did in the case of some of those soldiers he was serving alongside).

25 This is the opening sentence of one of the two alternative forms of 'The Collect for the King' from the Communion Service of the Book of Common Prayer (BCP). SK wondered if he had quoted it correctly from memory: he had.

26 SK made this declaration at the outset: much of what is inherited was useless when confronted with experience, and he did not even try to justify it.

27 It is significant that SK took as the starting point of his reflection something experienced in liturgy – because that is where many people hear the phrases they put together to express their theology. The liturgy is an experiential rather than an abstract starting point.

28 In his introduction to the book, SK had already referred to this incident – a crucial moment in the development of his own thinking – that occurred soon after he arrived in France (see p. 7).

love. I love His terrible wrath against all wrong and His tender kindness to the weak. Tender as a woman and terrible as a thunderstorm, Jesus Christ, I know and love; but Almighty and Everlasting God, High and Mighty, King of kings and Lord of lords, the only Ruler of princes,[29] to Whom all things in heaven and earth and under the earth do bow and obey,[30] do I know anything at all about Him? Do I believe in Him?[31] How can I find Him in this welter of sin and cruelty. I have said such words a thousand times. What did I mean? What did the men who wrote them mean? It all seems like silly sentimental nonsense in the face of this.

They are supposed to be expressions of reverence. Just now they sound like expressions of blasphemy, accusations against God. Are they superficial compliments necessary in the court of the Most High? How God must hate them if they aren't true! and how can they be true? I wish they would not put such things in the Prayer Book. It makes one sick in the light of scenes like this. This war is the very devil; it seems to scupper all one's ancient understandings.

* * * * *

We're off now, over the top.[32] I think I'm frightened. But that's bosh. I can't die. That's another thing I'm sure about. "Thanks

---

29 This was a partly remembered quotation from 'A Prayer for the King's Majesty' from Evening Prayer in the BCP. In the light of what he would say later it is significant that he began this with the stock liturgical address 'Almighty and Everlasting God' (*Omnipotens aeterne Deus*), whereas the collect he was using began: 'O Lord, our heavenly Father, high and mighty, King of kings. Lord of lords, the only Ruler of princes . . .'.

30 A phrase from the BCP order for the Visitation of the Sick. Cf. Phil. 2.10.

31 Note the existentialism – he had to be responsible to himself; he did not ask 'Can one believe?' or 'Is belief possible/justified?'

32 SK was on the move; consequently, in this section the text moved between the action, conversation with those around him, observations of what is before his eyes, and theological reflection. It is a demonstration to the reader that one does theology in the activity of life.

be to God Who giveth us the victory through Our Lord Jesus Christ."[33] Anyhow, I'm a skunk to think about that now.

What does it matter if I do die? . . . except to her . . . and it is better for her and the boy for me to go out decent and respectable than to have me live on a beastly funk; so come on, you silly old fool, come on. Lord, that boy looks bad. Buck up, lad, it will be all right. We've got 'em stiff. Look at that chap's boots, all bust at the back, and his feet are blistered too, I bet, and that pack, and ammunition, like a travelling cheap jack.[34] What torture! I say, damn all war, and those that make it! The kings and governors whose hearts God is supposed to turn and govern.[35] Come on, you chaps. That barrage is perfect.[36] A cat couldn't live in it. Now we're well away. Lord, what a howling wilderness the guns have made![37]

It's about my time to strike off to the left – on my own. There's the wood in which I've got to find a place for an Aid Post.[38] It's being shelled pretty heavily. I believe I'm getting windy again.[39]

---

33 1 Cor. 15.57.

34 An infantryman carried about 60 lb (27 kg) of kit with him into battle, and may have had to carry a shovel or pick in addition, as tools would be needed to put a captured position into a defensible state. Problems with both poor-quality boots and also 'trench foot', caused by standing in water and mud for many hours, were widely reported by soldiers.

35 An echo of the already quoted Prayer for the King from the BCP's Communion Service.

36 We may use 'barrage' and 'bombardment' interchangeably, but SK used it here in its technical sense: the barrage moved just ahead of the advancing infantry and was to act as a barrier to stop the enemy coming out to repulse them – a 'perfect' barrage such as the one SK mentioned would have prevented the Germans firing on them as they advanced.

37 The phrase 'the guns' is a standard way of referring to the artillery.

38 A major element of chaplains' work when at or near the front was assisting with the operation of first aid posts, for example by acting as stretcher bearers. By going off towards a wood on his left to set up a first aid post, SK was heading towards the northern part of the ridge. In a wood near there at this time was serving a German corporal named Adolf Hitler.

39 'Windy' was army slang for paralysing fear.

A British 15-inch howitzer about to fire on 27 Sept 1917 near Ypres.
Though larger than the 12-inch weapon mentioned by Studdert Kennedy, this
picture conveys the sense of size and power of the weapons used during the
Battle of Passchendaele. This Coventry-made 94-ton monster, one of only 12
built, was used to bombard the remains of the village of Langemarch (NE of
Ieper). For Studdert Kennedy the noise made by these giant weapons sounded
'like the man with a loud voice and no brains in an argument'.

Damn all nerves! Dear Christ, Who suffered on the Cross and
wouldn't take that sleeping stuff,[40] give me strength to be a
decent chap. Come on. How I hate being alone. It's rotten. One
pal makes all the difference. But He was alone. It's funny how
it is always Christ upon the Cross that comforts; never God
upon a throne. One needs a Father, and a Father must suffer
in His children's suffering. I could not worship the passionless
potentate.

---

40 Cf. Matt. 27.34 and Mark 15.23. Note that SK thought of the crucifixion in terms of the synoptic Gospels rather than the scene in John 19.25–30.

He who did most has borne most, the strongest has stood the
   most weak;
'Tis that weakness in strength that I cry for, my flesh that I
   seek.
In the Godhead – I seek it and find it.[41]

I don't know or love the Almighty potentate – my only real God
is the suffering Father revealed in the sorrow of Christ.[42] That
was a near one. These Boche shells can't have as much in them
as they used to have or I would be – "Today thou shalt be with
Me in Paradise."[43] Yes, that's it.

*   *   *   *   *

Good Lord, what's that? A dead Boche. I kicked him hard, poor
little devil. He lies like a tired child that has cried itself to sleep.
He looks puzzled, as if he were asking, Why me? My God, my
God, *why me?*[44] What had he to do with it, anyhow? Not much
great blond beast about him, He couldn't hurt a decent well-
developed baby. That little chap is the very fly-blown incarnation
of the filth of war. You can see all Europe asking questions in
his weak blue eyes.[45] War serves them all alike; good and bad,
guilty and innocent, they all go down together in this muddy,
bloody welter of mad misery. How can a man believe in an
absolute Almighty God? What is He doing? "Peradventure He

---

41 This is a quotation from memory of part of stanza XVIII of Robert
Browning's poem 'Saul'.

42 In most chapters of the book SK came to a place at which he expressed
his central point in just one or two sentences: this is that kernel of his thought
in this chapter.

43 Luke 21.43.

44 Cf. Matt. 27.46.

45 Within his existentialism, SK's theology originated in suffering questions
rather than certainties.

sleepeth."[46] The God that answers by fire let Him be God.[47] It is an odd thing God doesn't seem to work that way now. It would be a simple way of solving things, but Heaven makes no sign.[48]

*   *   *   *   *

Here's the very place I'm looking for. It will make a splendid Aid Post. I wish it was not shelled so heavily. The Red Cross makes no odds. Nothing makes much odds. God Himself seems non-existent – the Almighty Ruler Whom all things obey. He seems to have gone to sleep[49] and allowed all things to run amuck. I don't believe there is an absolute Almighty Ruler. I don't see how any one can believe it. If it were a choice between that God and no God, I would be an atheist. But how near the God Whom Christ revealed comes at a time like this: nearer than breathing, nearer than hands and feet, the Father of sorrow and love Who spoke through the crucified Son.

O Christ my God, my only God, so near, so suffering, and so strong, come down into my soul, and into the souls of all my comrades, and make us strong to suffer for honour and for right. Christ the Lord of courage, kill my fear and make me now and always indifferent to death that I may live and die like Thee.

*   *   *   *   *

That is the lot now, Doc. The sergeant died, so we did not bring him down. I'll bury him up there to-morrow. It's quiet now.[50]

---

46 1 Kings 18.27; to appreciate the appropriateness of this quotation, we need to recall that SK assumed his reader knew the whole story of Elijah and the prophets of Baal (1 Kings 18.17–40).

47 1 Kings 18.24: 'and the God that answereth by fire, let him be God' (AV).

48 Cf. Matt. 12.38–9 and 16.1–4. SK assumed knowledge of the story of the Pharisees asking a sign from heaven as a proof of divine involvement, but according to the Gospel no such sign was to be given.

49 Cf. 1 Kings 18.27.

50 This series of insights and reflections had occurred over a 20-hour

They're all going well over.[51] What a lovely night! A million stars, like an army with torches marching through the darkness to the dawn. Points of light they seem, and they are shining worlds. All our astronomy does not bring us much nearer to the truth. I suppose all astronomy started with

Twinkle, twinkle, little star,
How I wonder what you are.[52]

And it leaves us wondering still – only more so. Almighty God! When you look at them, "Almighty" seems the right word still. It kind of says the mystery right, the mystery of life that science only makes more deep. God's fruits, the silent silver beauty of the stars, but – ugh! how that poor chap groans. All my togs[53] are covered with his blood. Doc, I'm going to sleep. Call me in an hour. "Father, into Thy hands."[54] It's always the Cross in the end – God, not Almighty, but God the Father, with a Father's sorrow and a Father's weakness, which is the strength of love; God splendid, suffering, crucified – Christ. . . . There's the Dawn.[55]

---

period from 0305 hrs until after dark, probably around midnight. SK must have been awake for over 24 hours at this point.

51 The shells – from either side – were going further east or west of his position: it was a relative 'quiet' of which he wrote.

52 This is, of course, a quotation from the children's nursery rhyme, first published in *Rhymes for the Nursery* in 1806.

53 Togs – a colloquialism for clothes.

54 Luke 23.46: the final words of Jesus before he died on the cross according to Luke's Gospel; the verse is also a standard element in the traditional final prayers before going to sleep. Both contexts seem to have been in SK's mind.

55 SK ended his reflection ambiguously: just as he was going off to sleep for an hour he noticed the first streaks of dawn in the eastern sky; implicitly drawing a parallel with the fact that the crucifixion and death of Jesus were followed by mentions of the dawn (cf. Matt. 28.1 and Luke 24.1).

II

God in Nature

June 15th, 1917.
In a shell hole near the pill-box which was B.H.Q. The dawn of day
after a battle. All night the evacuation of the wounded had gone on
without a stop. There were many casualties.[1]

* * * * *

I don't believe I could carry another one to save my life. Lord,
how my shoulders ache. I wish I were Sandow.[2] It's a good thing
there are no more to carry. I wonder – will that last chap live?
His thigh seemed all mash when we pulled him in. It was a

---

1 This entire reflection was located in one place, out in the open air, early
in the morning before breakfast. He could rest in a shell-hole and was near
the Battalion Headquarters, which had set itself up in the safest place on
the battlefield: a reinforced-concrete bunker captured from the Germans.
These bunkers, which barely protruded above ground, were similar in shape
(cylindrical or hexagonal) to the boxes in which medical pills were once sold
– hence the name given them by the British infantry. The battle of 14 June
marked the final assault of the engagement officially known as the Battle
of Messines Ridge. Its aim was to push the British line eastwards from the
ruins of the town of Messines, but there was no element of surprise and the
casualties were consequently heavy. SK's situation was a real place on a real
battlefield, and his theologizing should be situated there.

2 Eugen Sandow (1867–1925) was 'the father of modern body building'.
Born in Germany, he made his home in Britain and became famous not only
for live performances of feats of strength (e.g. in the Albert Hall in 1901) but
on Edison films. Widely admired as a model of strength, he was reputed to be
a friend of King George V.

German bunker on Messines Ridge.
After a century the robust reinforced construction of this German bunker is still visible – and it was in such a bunker as this that Studdert Kennedy located the reflection that constitutes this chapter. Today this bunker is part of the New Zealand Memorial Park on the crest of the ridge. In the background can be seen the rising ground over which the British Army advanced. It was for his work with the wounded in this landscape that Studdert Kennedy was awarded the Military Cross.

beastly job. He cried for mercy and we had to drag on just the same. He is strong though, a splendid body all broken up. It's quiet now, only for those 5.9's over on the right.[3] They never stop. I'm glad to sit and think. How I do love quiet.[4] What a perfect morning it is. All the sky burns red with the after-blush of dawn, and here I seem surrounded by a soft grey sea of mist. What unutterable beauty there is in Nature. No wonder artists despair. God's fruits. I suppose the first of all God's fruits by

3 The German 5.9-inch howitzer (referred to in speech as 'a five nine') was a medium-weight weapon, one of the main purposes of which was to break up an attack.

4 As with the quiet of the early hours of 8 June referred to in the previous chapter, this is a relatively quiet time.

which we may know Him is the world of Nature.[5] Nature drives a man to belief in something, or rather some one, behind it all.[6]

The basis of religion is Nature worship. H. G. Wells wants me to give up wondering who made the world, because it has nothing to do with religion, being a purely scientific question.[7] What a comic person he is in many ways. He is the most utterly civilised man I know. He is as civilised as Piccadilly. He could never write poetry or really understand religion; they are both too primitive.[8] Like most apostles of the superman he is not

---

5 Matt. 7.20; he has already mentioned this as a criterion for thinking about God in chapter 1.

6 Traditionally, discourses on the human knowledge of God – 'proofs for God's existence' – began with 'the cosmological argument' and the notion of perceptible order pointing to an 'orderer'. SK started elsewhere, with his own relationship to nature as a human being; and then he turned the 'cosmological argument' on its head. Moreover, SK did not provide the reader with an argument but rather lets us share in the movement of this single moment of reflection.

7 H. G. Wells (1866–1946). While now largely remembered for his science fiction stories such as *The Time Machine* and *The War of the Worlds*, two of his wartime works attracted huge interest at the time, not least from clerics, including SK. Wells' novel *Mr. Britling Sees It Through* (London: Cassell, 1916) told the story of a respected writer – with much in common with Wells himself – whose family experienced numerous crises as a consequence of the conflict, in contrast to their rather idyllic pre-war existence. In his chapter in *The Church in the Furnace*, SK quoted Wells: 'After all, the real God of the Christians is Christ not God Almighty; a poor, mocked, and wounded Christ nailed on a cross of matter . . .', describing him as 'not yet a fully conscious Christian' (p. 381). However, Wells' 'God' was, unlike that of SK, a defeated God for whom there was no ultimate victory. SK and several other chaplains took issue with Wells' bleak view of the divine, including F. W. Worsley, who wrote a booklet from 'somewhere in France': *Letters to Mr. Britling* (Oxford: Oxford University Press, 1917). In 1917, Wells published *God, the Invisible King* (London: Cassell), which made more explicit his religious beliefs, including a denunciation of the doctrine of the Trinity. His call was for a modern form of religion without the supernatural, and without belief in God as creator – hence SK's comment here. Rather, Wells advocated a finite God as a human construct. Later he would renounce all religious belief.

8 Later in the chapter SK will make it more explicit that he considered

really advanced so much as defective. He wants to build a future which has no real relation to the past. I wish he could have come out here; it would have given him the knowledge of naked Nature that he lacks. He might have understood religion because he has a soul, only it is a soul that has always lived in streets.

You cannot leave Nature out of religion when you love it, and all natural men do. The natural man's first argument for God is always flowers or trees or brussels sprouts or something. You have to worship Nature or the Maker of it. It calls you. You are part of it. You draw your very life, your power to worship and adore, from the vitals of this poor battered earth. Nature means well, and the beauty of its million colours and the music of its million sounds just pull your heart-strings and you have to worship. It will take more than Wells to still the pipes of Pan,[9] and they play the oldest religious music in the world. "Behold the lilies of the field; they toil not, neither do they spin; yet I say unto you that Solomon in all his glory was not arrayed like one of these."[10] So the pipes of Pan found echo in the soul of Jesus Christ. You can't leave Nature out. It's like telling a man to leave out his heart and lop along with his liver. Nature is one of God's fruits by which we have to know Him. I know it is hard to see in Nature what God is; its many voices seem to contradict one another. Its tenderness and cruelty, its order and its chaos, its beauty and its ugliness, make discords in its song and mar the

poetry rather than prose as closer to the attitude necessary if he was to think of God. This awareness of the analogical/poetic nature of religious awareness set him apart from the doctrinal positivism – the notion that one could make statements about God in much the same way one could describe the material world – of much theology in his day.

9 This reference to the pastoral music-playing god Pan, from Greek mythology, amounted in SK's reflection to the celebration of the inner beauty of nature and a reminder for him that this beauty had always been associated with the divine in human culture: this was an appeal to what he considered a basic human experience.

10 Matt. 6.28.

music of its message to the soul of man. There is much truth in the charge that Nature is red in tooth and claw.[11] It is hard to see God in a cobra or a shark.

Nevertheless, the heart of the ordinary man will always turn away from these things and come back to the glory of a summer dawn and worship the Maker of it. "The Veiled Being," Wells calls Him,[12] and He may be that; but still I stretch my hands out toward the veil and worship Him in gratitude, although I cannot see His face.[13] I've *got* to worship Him. It isn't my intellect that wants Him, it's my "me," my innermost essential me. I want to paint or draw or put into words some expression of my love and praise. It calls and grips. For me the world will always be a vast and star-lit temple[14] where every bush and flower flames with God, and I believe in that I am just an extension of the average man.

Still, there is truth in the statement that Nature's God must always be an unknown God,[15] because the revelation of God in Nature is a contradiction of itself. It looks like that on the surface. Flowers and summer skies tell of a God of beauty and love, but snakes and earthquakes, volcanoes, plagues, and floods cry

---

11 This familiar phrase came from Alfred Lord Tennyson's 1850 poem *In Memoriam A.A.H.* (Canto 56). The whole verse is so linked to SK's thought that it is very likely that he is thinking of the charge made against the cosmological argument in the poem, rather than just using a stock phrase:

Who trusted God was love indeed,

And love creation's final law,

Tho' Nature, red in tooth and claw

With ravine, shriek'd against his creed.

12 A key theme in Wells' *God, the Invisible King.*

13 SK may be thinking of 1 Cor. 13.12 or more generally of scriptural passages that refer to 'the face of God', such as Ps. 42.2, which express such a desire in terms of worship.

14 This Temple imagery was more than a pious metaphor: SK thought the world a place where God's presence and glory could be encountered, just as in the Old Testament this divine glory could be encountered in the Temple in Jerusalem.

15 Acts 17.23.

out against that message. The lamb and the lion do not lie down together,[16] but are at war. I can remember how Haeckel's *Riddle of the Universe* shook my faith in God. "The cruel and pitiless struggle for existence which rages through all living nature, and which must for ever rage . . . is an undeniable fact."[17] I remember that sentence, and it seems so true. It is all war, and it does look heartless and cruel.

But is not the difficulty really in the attempt to see in Nature an Almighty God – a Being Who can do everything which we imagine to be possible, a God Who could have made a perfect, painless, sinless world at a stroke, but Who, for some inexplicable reason, chose to adopt this slow, tortuous, and painful method of evolutionary creation. We are invited to find a meaning and a use for everything in Nature – even sharks and poisonous snakes. We are asked to regard floods, famines, pestilence, and disease as visitations of the Almighty, exhibitions of His supreme power. We are told that Nature is a perfect system of balances in which there is a place for everything and everything has its place. There is supposed to be no failure and no possibility of failure in Nature, inasmuch as every detail of it is the work of absolute

---

16 Isa. 11.6 (and cf. Isa. 65.25).

17 Ernst Heinrich Haeckel (1834–1919) was one of the best-known rationalist thinkers at the end of the nineteenth century. He argued that notions such as 'God' were illusory facile answers that could not stand before the questions posed by the advances in human knowledge in areas such as evolutionary biology. A professor in Jena, he published *Die Welträthsel* ('World-riddles') in 1899, translated by Joseph McCabe and published in 1901 as *The Riddle of the Universe* (London: Watts & Co.). However, in that translation, the only one made at the time, the phrase quoted by SK cannot be found. SK's immediate source was Karl Pearson's *The Grammar of Science* (London: A. & C. Black, 1900), p. 364, which contained a long quotation from Haeckel that Pearson translated directly from the German text. SK had remembered this sentence from *The Grammar of Science* word for word. This familiarity not only with Haeckel but with other works on the topic (e.g. Pearson), and the fact that such a sentence was retained accurately in his memory, shows that SK was concerned with these questions long before he reflected on them when 'facing the facts' of the cruel bloodiness of the battlefield.

omnipotence. The result of this attempt to adapt Nature to an imaginary conception of God based upon abstractions is utter bewilderment. The materialism of Haeckel and the pseudo-Darwinites seems honest and illuminating beside it.[18] Men still prefer materialism to this blind piety, because, sad and hopeless as its teaching is, it does at least seem to be honest and to face the fact of Nature's horror chambers unafraid.

Yet materialism is hopeless even from a purely intellectual point of view. Mechanical evolution is as incredible as the six days creation.[19] Darwin seemed sufficient for the eyes of a cod-fish,[20] but he won't do for Coleridge's poems[21] or the eyes of Jesus Christ.[22]

And they are all part of one big show. You cannot separate the cod-fish from Coleridge, or snakes from Shakespeare. The attempt to believe that "Macbeth" or "The Hound of Heaven"[23] is the result of a mechanical process gives me intellectual dys-

---

18 One of the themes of this chapter, and of the book more generally, was the need to 'face the facts' – a phrase SK uses repeatedly – of what is happening in the world around us in our experience, and to avoid taking refuge in simplistic 'solutions'. Part of this gritty realism is taking very seriously the attacks of those who oppose belief.

19 Cf. Gen. 1.1—2.4a.

20 While the philosopher William Paley had, in 1802, declared the eye to be a miracle of design, Charles Darwin, in *On the Origin of Species*, having admitted that the evolution of the eye seemed absurd, argued that that process, 'though insuperable by our imagination, should not be considered as subversive of the theory [of evolution by natural selection]'.

21 As noted above, SK saw poetry as a particularly human activity. He was a poet himself, and one whose mode was particularly suited for discourse about God.

22 This reference to Jesus was not an appeal to him as the salvific figure at the heart of Christianity, but to Jesus as a human individual. It was the individuality of each real person, Jesus or the drunken, spitting engine-driver he once knew, rather than the abstract notion of a 'human' that interested SK here.

23 'The Hound of Heaven' is a long poem by Francis Thompson (1859–1907), published in 1893, the theme of which is the soul being pursued by God in all the vicissitudes of life.

pepsia. It is easier to believe the Virgin Birth,[24] and that's hard enough. Science has not really answered a single ultimate question. It leaves us where we were before. It is incurably abstract, and can only work by abstraction; which means taking out what you don't want and leaving in what you do. Real Nature refuses to be bound down to a rigid system of laws. They suffice for rough results in practice, but they don't come near the truth. Queer things happen in the universe, and science is against what's queer. That is why, from the human stand point, it is often such an insufferable bore. It wears gold spectacles, doesn't believe in fairies, and tries not to look startled when something in Nature jumps,[25] or a man displays superb self-sacrifice and disregards the natural laws which made him. This system of mechanical creation gave Europe an awful fright in the nineteenth century. We thought we would have to worship an engine – an engine! – not even an engine-driver. Personally, I might have managed an engine-driver. Engine-drivers are alive, and do strange things. I knew one who used to get drunk and spit in unexpected places. I did not worship him, but I did like him. He was at any rate a person. But worshipping an engine, a

---

24 This is the Christian belief, based on a particular reading of a mosaic of biblical texts focused on Luke 1.34–35, that Jesus was born of a virgin and so did not have a human father. Long ridiculed by those who rejected the possibility of miracles, it became more problematic for many Christians in the later nineteenth century due to the growth of new ways to read biblical texts that did not see them as primarily a factual record. Additionally, the biological discovery that conception involved both an ovum and sperm – whereas in earlier thinking the woman was merely a 'seedbed' – undermined the traditional theological arguments for the appropriateness of a virgin birth. It was a particularly sensitive issue at the time SK wrote.

25 The principle *natura non facit saltus* ('nature does not jump'), which can be traced back to Leibniz, is an expression of the steady movement of natural processes, for example in evolution, and was used by materialists to reject any notion of divine intervention. SK contrasted the universe of surprises and irregularity he experienced with the completely known world of those who considered it such a fundamental principle of cosmology that it also applied in the sphere of religion.

mechanical system, makes me feel like a cog – a little cog in a big wheel. That is what it does make men feel. It is soul-destroying, because it denies liberty. It is German; that's what it is; in fact, it's the devil. It is as intellectually impressive and as vitally futile as Pan-Germanism,[26] because it has no psychology, and does not believe in freedom or in souls.

The truth is, that the piety which bade us find in Nature absolutely omnipotent benevolence is maddening, because it will not face the facts of Nature's failures and refuses to look into its horror chambers; while materialism is even more maddening, because it will not face the facts of Nature's most astounding successes nor look into its treasure stores of wonder and beauty with open eyes.[27]

We must look at both. I am sure that Lamarck[28] was nearer than Darwin, and that what is behind the Universe is a will or a wish. It is not an accident or a series of accidents, it is a design. But there is no use pretending that it is a perfectly expressed design. I agree with old Lucretius there; I cannot believe the world is perfect – *tantis stat prædita culpis* – it has too many faults.[29] Behind all the vast history of effort, ceaseless effort, that Science has disclosed, I can see a will, but not an abso-

---

26 What SK meant by 'Pan-Germanism' becomes clearer in the next chapter: it is the nationalist belief that God had destined Germany to be the dominant race and that it would achieve this position, and the land it needed, through warfare that removed threatening inferior races.

27 This paragraph encapsulates the core idea of this chapter.

28 Jean-Baptiste Lamarck (1744–1829) was the first biologist to put forward a complete theory of evolution. He was a deist who held that evolution occurred following laws written in nature by 'the sublime author of nature'. His thought became widely accessible through A. S. Packard's 1901 book, *Lamarck, the Founder of Evolution: His Life and Word* (London: Longman, Green & Co.). SK's passing reference to Lamarck was another indication that he was reflecting on the arguments against traditional theism for a long time before the shock of the war.

29 Lucretius, *De rerum natura*, V.199. SK quoted from memory; the exact text is *natura tanta stat praedita culpa* ('there are so many faults in nature'). Lucretius, first century BC, was famous among Christians as the most thorough-

lutely omnipotent will that knows no failure and no strain. I cannot see the calm, serene, untroubled potentate whose word at once creates perfection. The paths of natural development are strewn with species that have failed, like the dead horses on the road from Hell-fire Corner to the line.[30] The story of this strange world's growth, as I have read it, is the story of a ceaseless war, with perfection of personality as its end in view. It is the story of many failures, out of which has come success; it is a tale of mysterious obstacles marvellously overcome, and of victory wrung by stupendous effort from the very heart of defeat. Nature is a triumph, a victory over enemies and obstacles the nature of which we cannot comprehend. The Spirit that labours behind Nature seems always to be up against difficulties, the utter necessity of which we cannot grasp because they arise from the nature of matter which is the final mystery – the thing we do not understand at all. I believe H. G. Wells is right when he sees in the crucified Christ the revelation of the true God, bearing titanic pain and nailed upon a cross of matter,[31] – if only we remember that behind the Cross there is the Empty Tomb, and that Christ, Who suffered pain and death, rose again un-conquered, to go on suffering and conquering down the ages.[32]

That is the picture of God which Nature gives when you look square in her face and refuse to blind yourself either to her failure

---

going atheist of Latin antiquity. It was in the fifth book, cited here, that he took issue with the notion that the universe's order pointed towards a god.

30 This was a crossroads a little east of Yprcs and just in behind the front line on the road to Menin – 'the Menin Road' – which, because it was a place of high-density traffic, was kept under more or less constant artillery fire by the Germans. Today it is a roundabout where the N8 to Menin is crossed by the N37. It was located at the intersection of two roads and a railway line to the east of Ypres on the map on page 12.

31 H. G. Wells, 1916, *Mr. Britling Sees It Through*, London: Cassell, p. 406.

32 SK's theology of Easter was that this was an ongoing event within the creation and life rather than a single miracle that took place at one moment in the past. This has become a commonplace among modern theologians, using the phrase 'the paschal mystery'.

or her success. God was forced to limit Himself when He undertook the task of material creation.[33] He had to bind Himself with chains and pierce Himself with nails, and take upon Himself the travail pangs of creation.[34] The universe was made as it is because it is the only way it could be made, and this way lays upon God the burden of many failures and of eternal strain – the sorrow of God the Father which Christ revealed. That is why one's heart goes out in love to the Spirit that labours behind Nature. If one believed Him to be the absolute omnipotent monarch seated on a throne, high and lifted up in power, and capable of accomplishing absolute perfection at a stroke, then one would curse Him for Nature's manifest imperfections and many cruelties – floods, famines, volcanic eruptions, disease, plague, pestilence, and the like. All these horrors which He could prevent, and will not, one would curse Him for, and rightly so.

> But Thou, with strong prayer and very much entreating,
> Willest be asked, and Thou wilt answer then;
> Show the hid heart behind creation beating,
> Smile with kind eyes and be a Man with men.

> Were it not thus, O King of my salvation,
> Many would curse to Thee; and I, for one,
> Would spit on Thy bliss and snatch at Thy damnation,
> Scorn and abhor the shining of the sun.[35]

When in Nature one sees God suffering and striving as a creative

---

33 This notion of God's self-limitation in creation is often invoked in modern Jewish theology; see David Birnbaum, 1989, *God and Evil: A Jewish Perspective* (Hoboken, NJ: Ktav Publishing House).

34 Cf. Rom. 8.22–23.

35 SK was quoting – from memory and therefore imperfectly – two verses from the poem 'St Paul', written by F. W. H. Myers in 1867. The 146 verses include four that were later sung as a hymn, 'Hark what a sound, and too divine for hearing', which has appeared in numerous hymn books since around 1925. It seems quite possible that SK had learned the whole poem.

Father Spirit,[36] and when one sees how much that His sorrow has produced is quite perfect, like this red dawn and that white bird upon the wing, the rose that blooms at the cottage door, and the glory of sweet spring days, and the eyes of my dog, and the neck of my horse,[37] and a million other perfect things and when one sees all this as the fruit not only of God's power, but also of God's pain, then the love of Nature's God begins to grow up in one's soul. One remembers the great words, "He that hath seen Me hath seen the Father,"[38] and there a burst of light, and one sees Nature in Christ, and Christ in Nature. One sees in Christ the Revelation of suffering, striving, tortured, but triumphant Love which Nature itself would lead us to expect. I can see the face of Jesus Christ staring up at me out of the pages of a scientific text-book which tells me the story of the patient, painful progress of a great plan.

I have no fear of Nature's horror chambers; they are just God's Cross, and I know that the Cross is followed by an Empty Tomb and victory. God is limited now, and has been ever since creation began,[39] by the necessities inherent in His task; but those necessities are not eternal, they are only temporary and contingent, and God will overcome them in the end. That is our faith. He that hath seen Christ has seen the Father,[40] and Christ not only died, but conquered death and rose again. God the Father is suffering, striving, crucified, but unconquerable. We see His triumph now in Nature's glory, and we hear Him calling to us to join Him in the task of conquering the evils which arise

---

36 SK did not use the traditional terminology regarding the Spirit but referred separately to the Father Spirit and the Spirit of Christ – at times he seemed to use 'Spirit' for the presence of God dwelling within creation.

37 This was not only an expression of his existentialism – he wanted to reflect on individual real objects in his experience – but also a reminder that chaplains had the use of a horse to get around on their duties, although horses would be left behind when serving at the front.

38 John 14.9.

39 Rom. 1.20.

40 Cf. John 14.9.

from the necessities of creation.[41] He calls us to combat floods and famines and pestilence and disease. He hates them, and wills with us to overcome them, and they shall be overcome. The Doctor, the Pioneer, the Scientist, are workers with God like the Priest. All good work is God's work, and all good workers do God's will. They are labouring to make a world. That seems to me to be the truth of God in Nature, the truth of Christ crucified and risen again to reveal the suffering but triumphant Father. In the light of the Cross and the Resurrection Nature's many voices make no discords, they all tone into one, and that is the voice of Christ.

*   *   *   *   *

What's that, Colonel? Breakfast? I'm coming. I'm hungry, too. Good old earth, what would I do without you? Poor old patient mother earth, with all your beauty battered into barrenness by man's insanity.

He who made you is not dead, though crucified afresh.[42] Some day He will rise again for you, and all this wilderness that man has made will blossom like the rose, and this valley will laugh[43] with laughter of summer woods and golden grain, and cottage homes in whose bright gardens children play at peace and unafraid. Yes, I'm coming, Colonel. What is it? Bacon and eggs? Good old pigs and hens.[44]

---

41 For SK, human beings were called to become part of the creative process. This, and the idea of faith as moving along a road, became central planks of his theology of discipleship.

42 Another expression of the paschal mystery: the Christ is being crucified now and continues to be until the end of time; SK was distancing himself from the notion of it being a one-off event – as in the nineteenth-century hymn, 'There is a green hill far away' – that is simply recalled to mind.

43 SK was not in a valley but on very level ground. This was an allusion to the time when the creation will come to its completion, imagined in terms of Luke 3.5 (and Isa. 40.4) and Luke 6.21, which present those weeping now as laughing when the universe comes to its blessed perfection.

44 It seems that, for SK, the goodness of these simple creatures within creation was emblematic of the goodness towards which creation is groaning.

III

God in History[1]

IN a German concrete shelter. Time, 2.30 a.m. All night we had been making unsuccessful attempts to bring down some wounded men from the line. We could not get them through the shelling. One was blown to pieces as he lay on his stretcher.[2]

I wonder how much this beastly shanty would stand. I guess it would come in on us with a direct hit, and it looks like getting one soon. Lord, that was near it.[3] Here, somebody light that candle again. I wish we could have got those chaps down. It was murder to attempt it though. That poor lad, all blown to bits – I wonder who he was. God, it's awful. The glory of war, what utter blather it all is. That chap in the "Soldiers Three" was about right:[4]

---

1 For an early manuscript version of this chapter, see Appendix 1.

2 SK did not give more details, but assuming that this reflection took place in the course of heavy fighting after mid-June 1917 and before the end of that year, then it is possible it should be located to the east of Ieper during the Third Battle of Ypres, commonly known as the Battle of Passchendaele, which was fought between 31 July and 10 November. Historians have contested every attempt to estimate the number of casualties, but a total of half a million is unlikely to be an overestimate.

3 There was actual shelling going on – and it was in reaction to hearing the shells explode around him that he wondered if the shelter could withstand a direct hit. Because this was recently captured territory, the German artillery had precise coordinates for every structure on it and one of their bunkers would be a good target as a likely place to be used as a British command post.

4 Rudyard Kipling first published this collection of short stories in India in 1888 as *Soldiers Three: A Collection of Stories setting forth certain Passages*

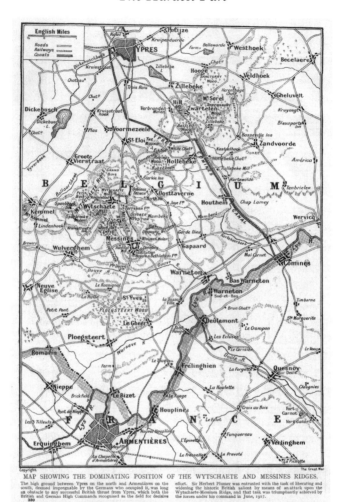

MAP SHOWING THE DOMINATING POSITION OF THE WYTSCHAETE AND MESSINES RIDGES.

The high ground between Ypres on the north and Armentières on the south, deemed impregnable by the Germans who occupied it, was long an obstacle to any successful British thrust from Ypres, which both the British and German High Commands recognised as the field for decisive effort. Sir Herbert Plumer was entrusted with the task of liberating and widening the historic British salient by means of an attack upon the Wytschaete-Messines Ridge, and that task was triumphantly achieved by the forces under his command in June, 1917.

An overview of the southern portion of the Ypres Salient in 1917.

This is the landscape – the names of places linked with war and death rather than the refinement of the academic library or rectory study – in which Studdert Kennedy wishes us to imagine his work grappling with the fundamental questions of Christian faith. This map was produced in Britain in June 1917 and widely reproduced in publications that gave a running commentary on the conflict.
The War Illustrated, *23 June 1917.*

God in History

Says Mooney, I declare,
The death is everywhere;
But the glory never seems to be about.

War is only glorious when you buy it in the *Daily Mail* and enjoy it at the breakfast-table.[5] It goes splendidly with bacon and eggs. Real war is the final limit of damnable brutality, and that's all there is in it. It's about the silliest, filthiest, most inhumanly fatuous thing that ever happened. It makes the whole universe seem like a mad muddle. One feels that all talk of order and meaning in life is insane sentimentality.

It's not as if this were the only war. It's not as if war were extraordinary or abnormal. It's as ordinary and as normal as man. In the days of peace before this war we had come to think of it as abnormal and extraordinary. We had read *The Great Illusion*,[6] and were all agreed that war was an anachronism in a

---

in the Lives and Adventures of Privates Terence Mulvaney, Stanley Ortheris and John Learoyd. It was republished in Britain in 1899, and by 1917 Kipling was at the height of his fame as the balladeer of the army and the Empire. His poem 'Recessional', with its repetition of 'Lest we forget', written for Queen Victoria's Diamond Jubilee in 1897, became a key component of memorial and remembrance ceremonies. The loss of his son, John, in the Battle of Loos in September 1915 was, unsurprisingly, a devastating experience for Kipling.

5 This was a favourite theme of those 'at the front', on both sides; that for many people at home the war was little more than a game, a great international competition that would finally reveal which was the 'top nation'. It can be seen all too vividly in Erich Maria Remarque's 1929 novel, *Im Westen nichts Neues* (published in English, also in 1929, as *All Quiet on the Western Front*).

6 Norman Angell, *The Great Illusion: A Study of the Relation of Military Power in Nations to their Economic and Social Advantage* (London: William Heinemann, 1910). This argued that the economic interdependence of the countries of Europe had made war obsolete and, therefore, the arms race, then reaching its height, was 'an illusion'. Angell (1872–1967), who won the Nobel Peace Prize in 1933, had propagated this view before the book's appearance and had drawn considerable attention to his thesis before 1914. There is an useful assessment of the position by Cornelia Navari, 'The Great

OFFICIAL PHOTOGRAPH, CROWN COPYRIGHT RESERVED.

R.A.M.C. PICKING UP WOUNDED IN A CAPTURED VILLAGE. Nº 10

Caring for the wounded.

This is one of a series of official postcards produced during the war; and this postcard was intended to show the efficiency of the Royal Army Medical Corps in caring for the wounded. While today we often hear of the numbers who died (e.g. 60,000 men on the first day of the Somme), a far greater number were wounded and their suffering continued for years afterwards. We can take it for granted that if one needed an ambulance – as did so many in this photograph – one was seriously wounded. It is this sheer volume of suffering that spurred Studdert Kennedy to re-open the question of the relationship of God to human suffering and to write The Hardest Part.

civilised world. We had got past it. It was primitive, and would not, could not, come again on a large scale.

It is "The Great Illusion" right enough, and it is an anachronism in a civilised world. We ought to have got past it; but we haven't. It has come again on a gigantic scale.

I say, keep that door shut; the light can be seen. I believe they are right on to this place. There was a German sausage up all day just opposite,[7] and they must have spotted movement here-

---

Illusion Revisited: The International Theory of Norman Angell', *Review of International Studies* 15:4 (1989), pp. 341–58.

7 An observation balloon, tethered to the ground, used to spot the fall of shot for the artillery. It was called a 'sausage' because the bag of the balloon was shaped like a sausage or a kidney.

A sausage balloon.
The observation balloons – referred to as 'sausage balloons' by the troops – were very important platforms for artillery observation and were used by both sides. While they lacked the mobility of an aircraft and were vulnerable to attack, they had two advantages: they could give a very accurate fix on a map for artillery and could communicate instantly with the guns by telephone – neither of which could be done so quickly by planes. To be spotted by a 'sausage' meant that shells would soon follow. Studdert Kennedy wanted us, his readers, to read with the consciousness that we could be shelled at any moment: these are serious thoughts because they are being thought through with the existential urgency that they could be our last.

abouts this morning. There it goes again. Snakes, that's my foot you're standing on. Anybody hurt? Right-o, light the candle. It's no fun smoking in the dark.

Yes, war has come again all right. It's the rule with man, not the exception.[8] The history of man is the history of war as far back as we can trace it. Christ made no difference to that. There never has been peace on earth.[9] Christ could not conquer war. He gave us chivalry,[10] and produced the sporting soldier; but even that seems dead. Chivalry and poison gas don't go well together. Christ Himself was turned into a warrior and led men out to war. Few wars have been so fierce and so prolonged as the so-called religious wars. Of course a deeper study of history reveals the fact that they were not really religious wars. Religion was not the real, but only the apparent cause of them. They were just political and commercial struggles waged under the cloak of religion. I don't believe that religion had anything to do with the Inquisition, it was a political business throughout. Still these struggles, with all their sordid brutalities, proved Christ helpless against the God of War. He is helpless still. God is helpless to prevent war, or else He wills it and approves of it. There is the alternative. You pay your money and you take your choice.

---

8 In this SK was in agreement with many of those who were the opponents of belief and who argued that life was to be explained solely as an evolutionary struggle 'red in tooth and claw' (see the previous chapter). However, while this dismal vision of the human condition had been taken by many Christian theories before SK, they had usually justified it by an appeal to some form of a doctrine of original sin. SK did not even hint at such an idea but rather argued that the universe was incomplete and was a process moving towards completion. In adopting this perspective, SK anticipated the stance of many modern theologians.

9 This was SK's explicit rejection of the notion of an earlier ideal moment – a pre-lapsarian bliss in the Garden of Eden – that was destroyed by original sin.

10 The language and imagery of chivalry remained highly prominent and hugely influential throughout the conflict. This was expressed in personal discourse, hymnody, public speeches and memorialization, often referencing the Arthurian tradition.

Christians in the past have taken the second alternative, and have stoutly declared that God wills war. They have quoted Christ as saying that He came not to bring peace upon the earth, but a sword.[11]

Bernhardi did that quite lately.[12] Luther did it too,[13] I believe. If you cling to God's absolute omnipotence, you must do it. If God is absolutely omnipotent, He must will war, since war is and always has been the commonplace of history. Men are driven to the conclusion that war is the will of the Almighty God.

If it is true, I go morally mad. Good and evil cease to have any meaning. If anything is evil, war is. It is supposed to be a blessing to the nations by those who advocate or apologise for it. It is supposed to make them virile and strong. It is a strange method of doing it, to take all your finest physical and spiritual specimens and set them to kill one another by thousands, and leave weaklings alive to breed the race of the future. It is the best and most direct way of securing the survival of the unfittest. Specially under modern conditions, when by mechanical

---

11 Matt. 10.34.

12 Friederich von Bernhardi (1849–1930) was a Prussian general, a historian who frequently quoted Treitschke (see note 17 below) and a militarist who, citing Goethe, declared '"war" is our rallying cry, onwards to victory!' His most influential book was *Deutschland und der Nächste Krieg* (1911), published in English as *Germany and the Next War* (London: Edward Arnold, 1912). He cited Matt. 10.34 on p. 29 of the translation as part of his opening argument that 'Christianity cannot disapprove of war'. That SK knew this book, the work of Angell and also that of Treitschke demonstrated that, just as with his awareness of scientific theories and religion, discussed in the previous chapter, SK had been making a detailed study of these questions for quite some time. While *The Hardest Part* may have been written in the heat of battle, it was the result of long-term reflection on these problems.

13 In his 1520 letter to Georg Salatin, Luther wrote: 'The Word of God can never be advanced without whirlwind, tumult, and danger . . . One must either despair of peace and tranquillity or else deny the Word. War is of the Lord who did not come to send peace.' See P. Smith (ed.), *The Life and Letters of Martin Luther* (London: Murray, 1911) p. 72.

contrivances weaklings can slaughter splendid men by scores with shells hurled at them from miles away. War is evil. It is a cruel and insane waste of energy and life. If God wills war, then I am morally mad and life has no meaning. I hate war, and if God wills it I hate God, and I am a better man for hating Him; that is the pass it brings me to.[14] In that case the first and great commandment is, "Thou shalt hate the Lord thy God with all thy heart, and Him only shalt Thou detest and despise."[15]

Then I give it up. I can't see God, and I can't love Him. I turn back to Christ. I can see Him and love Him. He could not will war. He brought strife upon earth,[16] because He roused the powers of evil by challenging them; but He did not will strife: He suffered agony and death because of it, and pleaded with men to conquer evil and learn to live at peace.

This is the only attitude I can accept without degradation, and if that is not God's attitude, if God does not suffer agony because of war, and if He does not will that men should live at peace, then I cannot and will not worship Him. I hate Him. This is not merely an intellectual alternative, it is a moral one. It lives and burns. It is a matter of life and death which side you take. If it were merely intellectual it would not matter.

Intellectually the Almighty God Who wills war has a lot to say for Himself. Heinrich von Treitschke is His prophet,[17] and the

---

14 That SK must be true to his own perception of good and evil, even if this led to it being morally right to hate God, was another aspect of his existentialism.

15 Cf. Matt. 22.37.

16 Cf. Luke 12.49.

17 Heinrich von Treitschke (1834–96) was one of those influential popular historians of whom few today have heard. He influenced the development of German nationalism, stressing its links to race, blood and soil, and saw war, using Christian language, as part of the divine will by which the super-race should reach its 'destiny'. He saw Germany as having natural enemies baulking its divinely willed progress: the Jews, the Catholics and the British Empire. His books became standard texts in German schools until 1918 and he had a revival under Hitler. SK may not have known his works directly, though

Prussians are His chosen people.[18] They have a splendid case. The militarist interpretation of history is an inevitable result of the doctrine of the absolute omnipotence of God.

Progress has everywhere and at all times been accompanied by strife and warfare. It is the eternal law of nature. The struggle for existence and the survival of the fittest are Almighty God's appointed methods of progress. The strong man must survive and the weaker go to the wall. That is the law of nature, and therefore the will of God. How can you argue against that? You can't. You can only oppose sentiment to reason, and that fight is won before it is fought for any reasonable man. This world is not a Sunday School; it is a slaughter-house, and always has been. Peace or war, what does it matter? There is no such thing as peace, and never can be. Competition is just peaceful war with far more cruel weapons than either shot or shell. War is competition stripped of all disguise – without the velvet glove. Who is going to deny that competition is the law of business and the law of life? A few parsons perhaps, and some socialists who want what they have not got. Every sensible man of the world knows that cut-throat competition is the law of life, the cause of progress, and the only real motive of efficiency and work.

You cannot kill knowledge with rhetoric or alter facts by furious abuse. You may rail at the Prussian, but at least he is no hypocrite. He is the honest man of Europe, or at least he was until he was beaten and began to whine. There was no Sunday-School sentiment about him. He did not pretend to apply the teachings of a visionary Christ to practical politics. He took his stand on the rocks of natural fact, and claimed the support of

---

he clearly discerned some of the key ideas and may have encountered him through J. McCabe, *Treitschke and the Great War* (London: T. Fisher Unwin, 1914), which outlined his ideas and showed their prevalence in German cultural ideology.

18 The notion of 'a chosen people' has deep biblical roots (e.g. Lev. 26.12), but it also has a sorry history – implicit here – of the consequential belief that God takes sides in human conflicts between 'his' people and the 'others'.

the Almighty God according to Whose will the everlasting strife of history has been the lot of man. It is absurd to charge the Kaiser with hypocrisy when he claims that God is with him.[19] If God be absolutely Almighty, then He is with him, and was when he declared war, it being the will of God that the strong should seek to conquer the weak. The Kaiser is right when you look at the thing honestly in the cold light of reason, and refuse to use sentiment and religious soft soap.

The Prussian is the really consistent worshipper of the Almighty God Whom Nature plainly reveals as the Author of life.[20] He believes in power, patiently makes himself powerful, and then puts power to the test. If he loses then, it is because he is not powerful enough, and he must set to work again. In the end power must prevail, for that is God's will in the world. Might is right.

And what about the British? We are the hypocrites. God is Love,[21] we say. Right is might. But do we trust in right, or in Love? Not much.

Let us have done with this nonsense. Let us have a bit of Prussian honesty. They are the sincere and consistent worshippers of the Almighty God of strife Whose will has always swayed the world, and led it on and upwards to its appointed end.

It is a great argument, it makes one feel angry and helpless. One feels that it is all wrong; but if God is Almighty, how can it be wrong? It is utterly logical and consistent; but one can't accept it because one's soul rebels. The truth is, that history drives one to the knowledge that God cannot be absolutely Almighty. It is the Almighty God we are fighting; He is the soul of Prussianism. I want to kill Him. That is what I'm here for. I

---

19 From the British perspective, the First World War was for many a 'Holy War' between Godly Britain and a Germany that had rejected God. The Kaiser's claim that God was on his side was widely recognized in Britain, and universally mocked.

20 Cf. Acts 3.15.

21 1 John 4.8, 16.

want to kill the Almighty God and tear Him from His throne. It is Him we are really fighting against. I would gladly die to kill the idea of the Almighty God Who drives men either to cruelty or atheism. This war is no mere national struggle, it is a war between two utterly incompatible visions of God. That is what I'm out for. I want to ensure that men do not worship a false God. I want to win the world to the worship of the patient, suffering Father God revealed in Jesus Christ.[22] But can I find any traces of that God in history? Yes, I find Him everywhere.

> History's pages but record
> One death-grapple in the darkness
> 'Twixt old systems and the Word.
> Right for ever on the scaffold,
> Wrong for ever on the throne,
> Yet that scaffold sways the future,
> And, behind the dim unknown,
> Standeth God within the shadow,
> Keeping watch above His own.[23]

God, the Father God of Love, is everywhere in history, but nowhere is He Almighty. Ever and always we see Him suffering, striving, crucified, but conquering. God is Love.[24] He is the Author of peace and lover of concord,[25] and all true progress is caused by God and moves toward God, the God of Love. Only as we progress toward unity, concord, and co-operation do we really progress at all. The workings of God in history are quite evident and clear. I see the birth of human unity and concord foreshadowed far back in Nature in the union of the mother and the child. I see it spread out into the family, from the family to

---

22 This long paragraph is the kernel of this chapter's argument.

23 This is an extract from 'The Present Crisis' by James Russell Lowell (1819–1891) – apparently further verses remembered accurately by SK.

24 1 John 4.8, 16.

25 A phrase from the second Collect for Peace from the BCP.

the clan, and from the clan to the nation, and from the nation to the empire of free nations, and I look forward, and have a perfect rational right to look forward, to the final victory and a united world. This progress is there, and it is the work of God, but it bears no trace of being the work of an Almighty God. It has been a broken, slow, and painful progress marked by many failures, a Via Dolorosa[26] wet with blood and tears. So far as human unity exists to-day, it is, like all other good things in the world, the result not only of the power but of the pain of God. We see the God of Love in all the splendid dreams of and efforts after brotherhood and unity which have marked the course of human history. All of them splendid failures.

Above all, I see it in the splendid failure of a dream which found birth within the brain of Christ, and has won the enthusiasm and life-long devotion of so many noble souls, the Catholic Church. The Church has always been a failure, like Christ; but out of its failure it has won the high success. In it we see the God Father Whom Christ revealed – struggling, suffering, crucified, but conquering still. Men leave Him for dead, and behold He is alive again. They despise His weakness, and then find His weakness strong. They mock at the folly of the Father Who leads but will not drive,[27] and then come to see the wisdom of that folly in the end. For the foolishness of God is wiser than man, and His weakness is stronger than our strength.[28] If the Christian religion means anything, it means that God is Suffering Love,

---

26 Literally 'the sad way'; the *Via Dolorosa* is a recollection of the route Jesus took through Jerusalem from his arrest until the crucifixion. This route in Jerusalem inspired the devotion known as the Stations of the Cross that can be found in churches of many traditions today. With his High Church background, SK would have been familiar with this devotional exercise, and this was a very significant term for him. Again, this image is a key to his understanding of discipleship.

27 An image from the world of horses: one can drive a horse or lead a horse.

28 1 Cor. 1.25 – the quotation is slightly changed in his memory.

and that all real progress is caused by the working of Suffering Love in the world.

If it means anything, it means that progress is made in spite of, and not because of, strife and war. Human strife is not God's method, but His problem – a problem that arises from absolute but temporary necessities inherent in the task of creation. Strife and warfare arise from the limitation which the God of Love had to submit to in order to create spiritual personalities worthy to be called His sons. War is the crucifixion of God, not the working of His will. The Cross is not past, but present.[29] Ever and always I can see set up above this world of ours a huge and towering Cross, with great arms stretched out east and west from the rising to the setting sun,[30] and on that Cross my God still hangs and calls on all brave men to come out and fight with evil, and by their sufferings endured with Him help to lift the world from darkness into light.

Always that cry from the Cross is answered; but because of sin, and because we are but children yet, it is only very feebly answered. All nations crucify Him, yet all nations desire Him. All men love Him, and yet, manlike, kill the thing they love because He calls for sacrifice. Longing for Him in our hearts, we deny Him in our lives. We are all hypocrites, and our hypocrisy is our salvation. Honesty would damn our souls to hell, because it could only be Prussian honesty of the lower standard. If we were perfectly honest now, it would mean that we had lost the vision of the Highest which makes hypocrites of all.

We cannot be Christian, but we must be as Christian as we can. We cannot even be human, but we must be as human as we can. We can't be saints, but we must be sportsmen. It is beyond us to turn the other cheek,[31] but at least we must not

---

29 SK was returning to one of his key themes: the paschal mystery.

30 This image is based on Mal. 1.11 (and other passages), and was part of SK's theology of sacrifice.

31 Cf. Matt. 5.39.

hit below the belt.[32] That is the form our hypocrisy must take, and it is the only foundation for future honesty. The laws of war, the Geneva Convention[33] and its provisions may be intellectual nonsense, but they are spiritual supersense. They have in them the splendid human inconsistency which is the hall-mark of a man, the super-animal who is always a failure, because his destiny is infinitely high. If one aims at the moon one will not score a bull, but neither will one hit a gooseberry bush.

This is the creed of those who worship the God of Suffering Love, and it is the direct contradiction of the creed of those who worship the supreme untroubled God of power. In this creed, which to men looks like weakness, there lies the source of all true strength.[34] This, I believe, is the real creed of the British Army, if only it could cut itself free from all the complications that have arisen from false teaching in the past.

If we were not fighting this war in order to end all war,[35] and with hatred of war in our hearts, it would be for us, as well as our enemies, another utter disgrace. But that is what the heart of the Allies does mean: it means to end war. The heart of the allied nations means it, for the heart of the nations is in their

---

32 A reference to a low blow in boxing that was not only illegal but considered ungentlemanly.

33 The first Geneva Convention (1864) was inspired by Henri Dunant (1828–1910), who also founded the Red Cross, and it was supplemented by that of 1906. SK seems to have been thinking of the entire edifice of treaties related to conduct in war, such as the Hague Conventions of 1899 and 1907. Britain considered this collection of treaties part of its own military law and they were printed in full in the War Office's *Manual of Military Law*, 6th edn (London: HMSO, 1914), pp. 314–58. By 1918 these treaties were widely believed to be no more than pious aspirations: for example, gas was widely used but had been forbidden in 1899.

34 Again SK appealed to the paradox of 1 Cor. 1.25.

35 The phrase 'the war to end war' was coined by H. G. Wells but soon came into common use. SK frequently expressed that idea, not only in *The Hardest Part* but also in one of his *Rough Rhymes of a Padre* (London: Hodder & Stoughton, 1918), 'What's the Good', in which he wrote: 'But I knows now why I'm fightin' // It's to put an end to war.'

common people, and they all mean it. The heart of the common people knows nothing about God Almighty, except as a puzzle for parsons, but they long for and fight for brotherhood and peace, and therefore, consciously or unconsciously,[36] they long for and fight for the suffering Father God of Love revealed in Jesus Christ.

*   *   *   *   *

Hurrah for the army of splendid human hypocrites who blaspheme the God they die for and kill the thing they love. Here's one of them blaspheming Christ and helping in a wounded Boche.

Yes, lad, you can get through now. It's fairly quiet. Follow the white tape and it will bring you through.[37] I wonder, could we carry old Fritz? I bet that foot is giving him what for.[38]

---

36 This notion of an unconscious awareness of the true nature of God became a major theme in twentieth-century Catholic theology, most notably in the work of Karl Rahner.

37 To help the soldiers find their way towards the enemy, before an attack the engineers marked out routes with white tape. Now SK was advising a bewildered soldier to follow those same tapes back to what had earlier been the front line.

38 Giving someone 'what for' was slang for causing pain or distress. In this case it is the enemy's foot causing the pain, but it was also used to describe one person attacking, verbally or physically, another.

IV

God in the Bible

*SITTING at the door of the Regimental Aid Post. Time about 4.30
a.m., after a very rough night in the trenches, during which we had
many casualties.*[1] *Among those who were killed outright was a very
popular sergeant. In his breast pocket I found a Bible.*

*　　*　　*　　*　　*

I wonder did he read it. It was given him by his wife. Was it
for her sake he carried it, or for what he found in it, or both?
"Yes, I'll 'ave one, sir; you never know your luck; it may stop a

---

1 As with chapter 3, SK did not give us details of his location, except that
he wanted us to review this chapter's content from the perspective of how
these questions must be approached amid the horror of war and the seri-
ousness of confronting life and death at every turn. The scene was probably
in 'the Salient' – the area just east of Ieper (Ypres) during the Third Battle of
Ypres or Battle of Passchendaele. The scene was located in one of the forward medical posts with doctors present – just behind the front line but well
forward of the surgical facilities that were to be found in a 'casualty clearing
station' the equivalent of the hospital in the 1970s–80s TV series *M*A*S*H*).

In the heat of battle, chaplains were expected to support the medical teams,
although inevitably some chaplains would demonstrate greater bravery by
working nearer the front line than might others. In 1917 Studdert Kennedy
was awarded the Military Cross for 'conspicuous gallantry and devotion to
duty' in searching out the wounded. For another perspective on this scene,
see the classic account of the work of a medical officer in situations like this:
J. C. Dunn, *The War the Infantry Knew: 1914–1918* (London: P. S. King & Son,
1938, and much reprinted). Also worth reading is A. A. Martin, *A Surgeon in
Khaki: Through France and Flanders in World War I*, with an introduction by G.
Harper (Lincoln, NE: University of Nebraska Press, 2011).

Helping a bogged-down ambulance out of the mud.
This official postcard shows an ad-hoc group of men trying to get a motor ambulance on its journey to pick up the wounded. This working together to help one another in the midst of suffering and the evil of war was, for Studdert Kennedy, a demonstration of motivation within every human person towards the good and towards a destiny that would only be fulfilled when God 'is all and in all'.

bullet." I remember that remark when I was distributing New Testaments to men going up the line from Rouen.[2] "I'll 'ave one, too, so long as you re giving 'em away. I left my old one at 'ome as a souvenir." Superstition and sentiment, I wonder why she gave it him. Was it superstition? Was it sentiment? Or was it because they both found in its pages the beauty and the strength that come of God? It's no use blinking facts.[3] He was a splendid fellow, but I don't think he knew much about religion. I think he rather despised what he did know as being the refuge of the

---

2 While at the Army base in Rouen, Studdert Kennedy would habitually walk the lines of men waiting to be taken towards the front lines by train, giving out both cigarettes – specifically the 'Woodbines' from which derived his nickname – and also copies of the New Testament.

3 SK repeated his theme that a genuine religious response must begin by a true acknowledgement of the problem and all the experience that is counter-indicative to faith.

Getting the wounded back to hospital.
This postcard, entitled 'English Field Hospital', was produced early in the war – the officer is still wearing a sword frog and there are no steel helmets – and reminds us that while chaplains are remembered for providing religious services, much of their work was with the wounded at the various stages of the evacuation and hospital process. Studdert Kennedy was part of this hospital system and he attributed a key insight, mentioned in his introduction to The Hardest Part, *to an encounter in a base hospital.*

weak. He was so strong and self-reliant in his strength, but, dear God, he was lovable.[4]

Of course you never know with English men, they are so splendidly shy about serious things; but on the whole I don't think he did read it. I'm sorry, but I don't.

There are thousands of Bibles carried that are not read. That is certain. If you give them out broadcast, that is bound to be so. The Bible, specially the New Testament, has an enormous circulation in the trenches,[5] yet I very rarely come across a man

---

4 This was another expression of his notion of 'anonymous holiness': being lovable as a human being is more important than obvious religious piety.

5 SK was aware of the complexity of religious phenomena within actual human situations, and so rejected the notion that the externals of religious usage, such as possession of a Bible, could be used as an index to faith or even religious awareness.

who knows very much about it. I am always surprised and very much pleased when I do.

I find quite common among men a kind of inherited respect for the Bible. They seem to think of it very much as a decent man thinks of his grandmother. It is ancient, and therefore demands respect; but it is utterly out of date and cannot be taken seriously, except by parsons, who, of course, are not quite ordinary men; and even the parsons appear to take parts of it nowadays with a grain of salt. There is, in fact, a vague but widespread feeling that the Bible stands discredited and cannot be appealed to for the solution of the doubts and difficulties of modern life.

There are some men who openly ridicule and despise it; and very often, strange to say, these men appear to have read it quite a lot, in a superficial kind of way. Some of these are not decent men, and some have got beyond the conventional sense of decency and arrived at a sense of righteousness and higher social justice. They despise the Bible as part and parcel of a disreputable past, and hate it because it has been used to bolster up the weakness of a rotten social system.[6]

It is a strange business, but I am not really surprised. The Bible is a queer Book, as queer as life itself. How about myself? I'm a parson, and I've studied it, of course. I study it still; but do I love it?[7] Well, parts of it I do – revel in them; parts of it I

---

6 SK seemed to have in mind the sort of criticism of religion famously expressed by Karl Marx:

> The social principles of Christianity justified the slavery of Antiquity, glorified the serfdom of the Middle Ages and equally know, when necessary, how to defend the oppression of the proletariat, although they make pitiful face over it.

'The Communism of the Paper *Rheinischer Beobachter*' [1847], as found in K. Marx and F. Engels, *On Religion* (Moscow: Foreign Languages Publications House, 1957), p. 74.

7 SK began his questioning with the existential subject: where did he, himself, stand? While this might seem commonplace in 2018, in his time this was a profoundly significant step, in that he did not seek to start his search from an indubitable datum such as the authority of the Bible as a divine work.

don't. I get irritated when I have to read out to people in church some of the stories in the Old Testament.[8] I would not mind if they were read out as legends not supposed to be true, though even then some appear to be pointless and not worth reading out.[9] The worst of it is that we have to read them out without comment, as though we thought them true and valuable. I don't believe that Balaam's ass spoke,[10] or that Jonah lived in a whale's belly,[11] or that the walls of Jericho fell flat.[12] I am bothered about the plagues of Egypt[13] and the passage of the Red Sea.[14]

---

8 SK did not consider the problems in the abstract but in the situation in which the Bible is encountered in liturgy. This was, again, a novel feature of his approach in 1918, and he will return to this point in chapter 8, when he imagines what the Church should do: 'She is not going to read your comrades impossible stories out of the Old Testament on Sundays.' When we link these observations with SK's comments on the BCP, we see that he was one of the first Anglicans to be aware of the need for serious liturgical renewal; and unlike others with such concerns, this was not a medievalistic romanticism. In the collection already mentioned to which SK contributed, *The Church in the Furnace*, several chaplains argued the need for liturgical reform.

9 This seemingly obvious point would have shocked contemporaries as it explicitly rejected 2 Tim. 3.16, which was used as a theological principle in many discussions on the place of the Bible. It meant that SK could be smeared with the label of the heresy of Marcionism (after Marcion, a second-century Christian who argued that the Old Testament was redundant and should be ignored).

10 See Num. 22.5—24.25 for the Balaam stories; the exact incident is found at 22.28–30.

11 See Jonah 1.17—2.10; this story was complicated for SK's contemporaries in that Matt. 12.40 could be adduced to support it as a historical incident.

12 See Josh. 6.1–21, esp. vv. 5 and 20; this story was complicated for SK's contemporaries by the reference to it at Heb. 11.30.

13 Exod. 7.14—12.32; SK was 'bothered' because these stories explicitly state that God punished innocents (e.g. at 12.29) as a form of political sanction.

14 Exod. 14.21–31; the image of 'Egyptians dead on the seashore' as a direct result of divine action (14.30) for merely doing their duty clearly bothered SK, for he remarked on a similar story further on.

Then there are the really bad stories. They are bad, because
they give a false idea of God, and so are really blasphemous
when read as real truth. God hardens Pharaoh's heart and
then destroys him because his heart was hard.[15] That is frankly
immoral. There is the man who put out his hand to steady the
Ark and was struck dead by the hand of God.[16] What a God!
I love Elisha, but some of the stories about him and Elijah
are incredible and immoral. I think Elisha's treatment of the
children that called him "bald pate" showed that he had no
sense of humour,[17] and it's a positive disgrace to drag God into
it, as if He hadn't any sense of humour either, when He made it.
The children were rude and they ought to have been smacked,
but to have them eaten up by bears is the limit. I have heard that
taken as a lesson in an Infants School. That is real blasphemy.
God is not a bogey-man. Elijah calls down fire from heaven to
burn up companies of soldiers who were doing their duty.[18] It is
impossible, and immoral as well. Of course I don't believe in the
truth of the six days creation[19] or the Flood and Noah's ark;[20]
but then, I don't think those pretend to be true: they are just
splendid legends containing great truths.[21]

---

15 The story's rhetorical force is that God keeps hardening 'Pharaoh's
heart' (Exod. 7.3, 13, 14, 22; 8.19; 10.20, 27; 11.10; 14.4), so that even
greater calamities befall his people.

16 The story of Uzzah in 2 Sam. 6.6–7. SK was not simply thinking of this
incident but of the many stories of the ark of the covenant – supposedly the
sign of the divine presence – bringing death by God's will in its wake. His
reference to 'the hand of God' was derived from one such ark story in 1 Sam.
5.10–12.

17 2 Kings 2.23–25.

18 2 Kings 1.9–17; the images of fire from heaven simply destroying in
an instant three companies of soldiers, each of 50 men, must have seemed
strangely like some of the scenes SK was witnessing.

19 Gen. 1.1—2.4.

20 Gen. 6.17—9.15.

21 SK seems to have been forging a rough taxonomy of stories: the legends
(e.g. the Flood), the immoral (e.g. Elisha and the bear) and the impossible

The Hardest Part

I don't wonder that the ordinary man gets muddled about the Bible, yet I love it, and I find within its covers the finest things in life.

I love it, because for me it fulfils its purpose, and that is how it must be judged – upon the whole, like any other book.[22]

What is the purpose of the Book? Is it a book at all? Isn't it just a haphazard collection of writings? No; it is a book. That is one of the queerest parts about it. It is a collection of writings by all sorts and conditions of men at all sorts and conditions of times, that, by some strange process of natural or supernatural selection, have got together and made a real Book. There is something odd about the evolution of the canon;[23] something odder, I mean, than there is about the evolution of a cat. Both, of course, are astounding and God-guided; but if the one is called natural, I should call the other supernatural. Yes, the Bible is a book, because a single purpose runs through it and makes it one. What is that purpose? I think it is to teach the love of God. That is the aim and object of it all.

Has it on the whole fulfilled that purpose in the past? Well, speaking broadly, I think the Bible has a wonderful record. Of course, like that of all other human things, it is not a perfect record. The devil has quoted and misquoted the Bible for his own purpose all down the ages.[24] It's a kind of crooked testi-

---

(e.g. Balaam's ass) – with a large overlap of the 'impossible and immoral' (e.g. the Red Sea).

22 This appeal to 'purpose' wasn't unusual in Anglophone theology at the time, in that most of the defences of the Bible were based on an appeal to its factual truth or its status as inspired/revealed, or a claim to its inerrancy.

23 The 'canon' is the list of texts that form the Bible; the issue of how that list came about – and hence whether the books in the various lists were 'inspired' (a topic to which SK will shortly turn) – was a major concern in the early twentieth century. See e.g. A. Souter, *The Text and Canon of the New Testament* (London: Gerard Duckworth, 1913).

24 This, as a commonplace, is usually traced back to Shakespeare's *The Merchant of Venice*, Act 1, scene 3; but SK was more probably thinking of the

mony to its power that he should do so. Scripture has been used to support the ghastliest of crimes. *"Tantum religio potuits uadere malonem"* ("See thou to what damned deeds Religion draweth men")[25] is as true of Christianity as it was of Paganism. The Bible has been the cause of cruelty, intolerance, and tyranny. It has helped in the suppression of learning and the persecution of great pioneers, both scientific and political. It has made men call good evil and evil good,[26] and they have often played the beast with texts of Scripture on their lips. The pages of Holy Writ are stained with many a victim's blood. That is the one side, and, on the other, stands a goodly company of real saints in whose eyes there shines the light that never was on land or sea, caught from these same blood-stained pages of the Book. Such is its record.

Is it then inspired? Well, accurately speaking, an "it" can't be inspired; you can only inspire a "him." A book can't be inspired; only its writers can. The real question is, "Was the Bible written by men inspired by God?" I think it was.

What do you mean by an inspired man?[27] I mean a man whose spirit has come into direct and conscious communion with the great personal Spirit Who is the final reality of the world. Well,

---

basis of the image, which is the story about Jesus and Satan in Matt. 4.1–11 at vv. 5–6.

25 Lucretius, *De rerum natura*, I.101. SK quoted accurately from memory, but there are two misprints in the text. The line should read: *tantum religio potuit suadere malorum* ('only religion is able to persuade [men to do] such evils'). We have already seen, in chapter 2, SK quoting Lucretius, and it is surely significant that, in a period that loved quoting the classics, the only Roman author he cites is 'the great atheist'. The rather poetic translation, 'see thou to what damned deeds religion draweth men', appears to be SK's own. This would indicate a detailed study of Lucretius at some time prior to 1917; he would cite the translation again in *Food for the Fed-Up*, p. 179.

26 Cf. Isa. 5.20.

27 In moving the focus from the book, or its contents, to the human beings in their search for God, SK was making a theological move that many Christians today are still unwilling to make, but locating himself in the mainstream of later theological thought.

if that is what I mean, and the Bible was written by such men, and collected by such men, doesn't that mean that every part of the Bible is of equal value and of equal truth, since all the writers were in communion with God? No, it doesn't mean that. These writers were still men, not machines nor yet mere clerks taking down dictation. They were sinful, sensual, stupid men; men even who were murderers, adulterers, and thieves like David;[28] but men who, in spite of all that, had come into touch with the highest. When I read my Bible I am talking down the ages to men of like passions with myself, and they are trying to tell me about God, and what He meant to them and to the people of their time. There are all sorts of difficulties which they have to meet before they can get their message home to me.

First of all they have to overcome their own stupidity and their own sin, which weakens and maims their powers of communion with God. They were not miraculously sinless or intellectually perfect men.

Then there is the difficulty of speech. Words are awful things, so strong and yet so very weak. The deepest thoughts cannot be said. All great speech, like all great art, is an effort to express the inexpressible. These men were not endowed with miraculously perfect speech.

Finally, they have to meet my stupidity and my sin before I get the message. Even if an absolutely perfect revelation could be written, I would not have the purity of heart or the clearness of mind necessary to understand it.

With all these difficulties to meet and overcome, do you wonder that their message is not perfect or perfectly expressed?

When men criticise the Bible they tend to take all its shining beauty and illuminating truth for granted, and to pounce upon the faults and falsehoods. Their criticism has no basis of genuine

---

28 David was popularly imagined, on the basis of Luke 20.42, to be the author of the book of Psalms. There is nothing to suggest that SK still held this position. It may be that it was such a strong image to make his larger point that he forgot that it was, by 1918, a claim rejected by scholars.

appreciation. Why do men display this tendency? Why do they allow the mystery of evil to obliterate the mystery of good? Because, I believe, they have at the back of their minds this impossible conception of an omnipotence that knows no difficulties and has no obstacles to overcome. They think that if the Bible is inspired by God Almighty it ought to be perfect and accurate in every detail of truth, and all parts of it equally perfect, since God had only to touch men's lips and Truth, with words wherein to express it, would flow like rivers from their mouths.

There is in the Bible no trace of such omnipotence; it is as foreign to the real spirit of the Bible as it is to any real life. One cannot find God Almighty in the Bible any more than we find Him in Nature or in history. We see in the Bible, as we see everywhere else, the patient, persistent suffering spirit of love and beauty at war with awful and incomprehensible necessities, and slowly conquering them.

The Bible is not merely the history of God's self-revelation to man, it is the history of the making of man capable of receiving the revelation; and it is as slow, as chequered, and as painful a process as the progress of man in any other department of life has been. The whole Bible is a Book of Genesis, and is full of the travail pains of the eternal love.[29] It is not only our sin which we, at any rate partly, will, but our ignorance and stupidity which we do not will at all, that makes, and always has made, love suffer in His work.

By stupidity I mean the lack of imagination, sympathy, and intuition which a man cannot help, because it is a defect in his general make-up so to speak. A man can almost always help being a knave, but millions of men are born fools. It is one of the awful necessities inherent in God's task of creation that He has to suffer fools gladly,[30] and it is no small part of the burden which He has to bear. It is this tragedy of human stupidity which

---

29 Cf. Rom. 8.22.
30 Cf. 2 Cor. 11.19.

lies behind the first word from the Cross[31] – "Father, forgive them, they know not what they do."[32]

This necessary stupidity, which is due to the fact of our incompleteness, for we are only beginnings at the best, is the inevitable burden which the Creator had to take upon Himself. It could not be avoided. We make this burden heavier by adding to our natural stupidity our sin; that is, our deliberate and wilful misuse of the powers we possess. Part of God's sorrow is absolutely necessary, and part is only necessary because we will it to be so. It is absolutely necessary that God should create and suffer in creation, we make it necessary that He should also redeem and suffer in redemption. The Bible is the history of God's agony in creation and redemption. It shows how painfully and slowly God managed to overcome the obstacles of man's stupidity and sin, and show him the truth which is eternal life in Christ. The life and death of Christ are the epoch-making events in that great story of Divine patience and pain, and in the light of the Cross all history becomes luminous.[33] In the Cross God gathers up all history into a moment of time,[34] and shows to us the meaning of it. It is the act in time which reveals to us the eternal activity of suffering and redeeming love all down the ages.

Every nation has its Bible, and that Bible is its history. It is only the fact that the Hebrews were possessed of unique religious genius that makes their Bible take precedence of all others in the world, and it was that which made it inevitable that the Incarnation should take place among them. In the light of the Hebrew Bible all other Bibles can be read and understood,

---

31 SK, following liturgical tradition, was thinking in terms of 'the Seven Last Words [Statements] of Christ on the Cross'.

32 Luke 23.34.

33 The notion of the luminous cross is a liturgical theme found in such hymns as *Vexilla Regis*, which was translated by J. M. Neale and the compilers as 'The royal banners forward go' in *Hymns Ancient and Modern*, no. 96, in the 1906 Complete Edition with which SK was most likely familiar.

34 Cf. Luke 4.5.

since it is the same God Who inspires the writers of them all, the only difference being one of degree.[35]

It would be too much to attempt to describe in detail the slow and painful progress of the knowledge of God among the Jews which is revealed to us in the pages of Holy Writ. One would want one's library, and I have only a Boche helmet and a water-bottle,[36] but the main stages are clear.

They started from non-moral polytheism like all other peoples, but were apparently the first people in the world to discover that God was good and demanded goodness from His children. They did not doubt the existence of other gods, but were convinced that their God was good, and that because He was good He was superior to all other gods, and would in the end conquer them, and make His chosen people lords of all the world.

The Jews, however, were not a conquering, but an often conquered people, and their faith in Jehovah's[37] invincibility was sorely tried. Disaster after disaster crowded in upon them, and in this furnace of affliction they learned a higher truth. There was only one God in all the world, and that God good. He was the supreme Almighty Sovereign of the earth and sky,[38] and all things were according to His will.[39]

---

35 Just as God is creator of all and seeks to inspire every human heart, so every set of humanity's religious expressions – every 'bible' – stands somewhere on the continuum leading to final understanding. Here SK's notions of inspiration, ecumenism and the universal nature of salvation came into harmony with his cosmology.

36 SK lamented that he only had a German helmet, which he perhaps picked up as a souvenir, and his water bottle. We have already noted how widely read he was, hence his regret at not having his library to hand when trying to summarize the development of Judaism.

37 The use of this early sixteenth-century blunder for the Divine Name (sometimes now rendered 'Yahweh') is unlike SK who, though he wore his scholarship lightly, was normally very exact. See E. Kautzsch, 'Names: Divine Names', in T. K. Cheyne and J. Sutherland Black, *Encyclopaedia Biblica* (London: A. & C. Black, 1902), pp. 3320–30.

38 Cf. Luke 12.56.

39 Cf. Luke 12.47.

The cause of all their disasters was the hand of God punishing them for their sins. Famine, fire, pestilence, disease, and war were the weapons that God used to drive His people back to Him and His laws.[40]

It was God Who brought the stranger from the north or south to devastate the land.[41] Caught between two mighty empires, the Belgium of the ancient world, they suffered horribly, and brutal conquerors destroyed their homes and killed their children before their eyes. Their noblest teachers interpreted their disasters to them as the working of the Almighty Righteous God visiting His people[42] with punishment for their sins, and every fresh disaster as a stronger call to repentance.[43] His anger was not turned away,[44] but His arm was stretched out still.[45] Nevertheless, they did discern that behind the anger of God there was compassion and love. If God chastised them it was for their good. These great teachers had dim vision of the Fatherhood of God which Christ perfectly revealed. By sheer genius of spiritual intuition, and not like the Greeks by long process of reason, they came to the truth that creation was a universe ruled by One Supreme Power Who was perfectly righteous and perfectly loving, and they believed Him also to be absolutely all-powerful.

This great faith they clung to in the teeth of awful difficulty. They saw the righteous forsaken and down-trodden, and the ungodly in great prosperity and flourishing like a green bay tree. The Old Testament is full of the pain of this problem of evil which faces us to-day. If God be a righteous and a loving God, and if all disasters and diseases are His punishments for sin, why do they fall so heavily on the innocent, and why do the wicked

---

40 SK referred generically to verses such as 1 Kings 8.37, Jer. 14.12 or Rev. 18.8, where suffering is explained as part of a divine therapy plan.

41 SK seems to have had in mind the vision in Dan. 11.

42 Cf. Ruth 1.6 and Luke 7.16.

43 Cf. Luke 13.3.

44 Cf. Ps. 27.9.

45 Cf. e.g. Ex. 6.6.

prosper? This is the sorrow of the Psalms and the pathetic puzzle discussed in the Book of Job. No solution was forthcoming. It was an utter mystery.

> It is higher than heaven; what canst thou do?
> It is deeper than hell; what canst thou know?[46]

Job is faced in the end with a vision of the power of God which strikes him dumb and brings him to his knees, and the drama ends with an artificial solution in which Job is restored to all his riches and prosperity.[47] The ending refuses to face the facts of the lifelong suffering of the best and noblest men, and the apparent injustice of it, and goes back to the faith that God does punish the guilty and reward the innocent in this world.

There is the beginning of a higher vision which just glimmers through the darkness for men like Hosea[48] and the writer of the fifty-third chapter of Isaiah.[49] They grope after but fail to grasp the truth that there is not only love and anger, but also bitter sorrow in God's heart, and the writer of the great chapter sees that when the innocent suffer for the guilty, such suffering is a

---

46 Job 11.8.

47 This is a summary of the story of Job, which reaches its climax in Job 42.10–17.

48 What SK meant by this reference to Hosea is far from clear; it may be that he was thinking of oracles (13.9–14) in which God's chosen ones have to suffer, but where it appears that this suffering is a stage in their return to God (14.1–5).

49 This reference to 'the writer' of Isa. 53 is an indication of the depth of SK's biblical studies. It was, for many, one of the shocking ideas of the new 'higher criticism' that Isaiah – traditionally read by Christians as a proof text for the life of Jesus – was the work of several hands over a long period. SK knew and accepted this – which was probably not common knowledge among parish clergy – and saw it as just another fact. By his reference to 'Isa. 53' he is actually thinking of Isa. 52.13—53.12, which is the fourth 'Song of the Suffering Servant'. These 'Songs of the Suffering Servant' – to which SK will refer presently – were first identified by the German scholar Bernhard Duhm (1847–1928) in a work of 1902. This is another case of SK wearing his learning lightly.

majestic and adorable thing, and has a power to redeem from sin beyond the power of punishment. It is a marvellous advance in knowledge, and it comes very near the real truth.

But God is still left Almighty and Serene. He inflicts but does not suffer sorrow. It is He that afflicts the suffering servant[50] and lays on him the iniquity of all.[51] He sits on His throne and receives the intercession of the suffering servant for sinners who deserve punishment. The Prophet[52] sees the majesty of suffering love, but does not dare to carry it into the heart of God. He was not ready yet for that, but was getting near. The Old Testament closes with the vision of the Almighty God, half King, half Father, Who punishes the wicked and rewards the innocent in this life, and leaves the mystery of innocent suffering still unsolved in pathetic and painful blackness against the absolute omnipotence of God.

Then Christ comes. He reproduces in every living line the picture of the suffering servant in Isaiah,[53] but He claims to be not the servant but the Son of God,[54] the image of the Father,[55] and one with Him in a perfect unity.[56] He carries innocent suffering into the heart of God, and explains its power to redeem as the power of the suffering Father of Love. There is about Him no

---

50 The Suffering Servant in the four songs (usually identified as 42.1–7; 49.1–7; 50.4–9 and 52.13—53.12) is both a servant and the chosen one redeemed by God, who must suffer and through this suffering bring life to the people.

51 Cf. Isa. 53.6.

52 Note that SK referred to 'the Prophet' rather than identifying that biblical writer by name.

53 This is the traditional reading of the suffering of Jesus as the Chosen One (i.e. as Christ) in terms of the book of Isaiah.

54 SK was contrasting the one suffering in Isaiah, who is referred to as a 'servant', with Jesus, who is referred to as 'the Son of God'. He may have been thinking of such stories as the Parable of the Wicked Tenants (cf. Luke 20.9–19) that utilize that difference.

55 Cf. Col. 1.15 (and also 1 Cor. 11.7; 2 Cor. 4.4).

56 Cf. John 10.30.

trace of human royalty, there is no pomp or pageantry, and no show of force wherewith to drive men to His will.[57] He comes in weakness, the weakness of God which is stronger than men.[58]

History of course repeats itself. The glimmer of truth that had broken upon Isaiah had not penetrated to the minds of the people or their leaders, except a very few. The common people hear him gladly, for there is the magic of perfect love in His words, but they want to make Him an earthly king[59] and arm Him with a sword. That must be His place if He is the Messiah of God.[60] He refuses it with a shudder. He will not touch the sceptre, and He will not wield the sword.[61] God is not like that. He transforms the whole idea of kingship, and reinterprets it in terms of love and not of material power. Because He is a King[62] – the King – therefore He must suffer,[63] must be mocked, spit on,[64] crucified,[65] and tortured as God has been all down the ages. But also because He is the King he must rise again[66] and go on suffering and striving until His task shall be complete.

God is like that. God is suffering, but triumphant, love. The final revelation of God in Christ Who suffered, died, and rose again[67] to go on suffering in His Church, finally tears the Almighty God armed with pestilence and disease from His throne, and reveals the patient, suffering God of love Who endures an agony

---

57 Cf. John 18.36.

58 Cf. 1 Cor. 1.25.

59 John 6.15.

60 Matt. 26.63.

61 Cf. Matt. 26.52–53.

62 Cf. John 18.37.

63 SK was not simply thinking of the facts of the suffering of Jesus – which could be noted from the Passion Narratives in the Gospels – but that this suffering was part of the nature of the case: cf. Luke 24.26.

64 Cf. Mark 10.34.

65 Cf. Matt. 20.19.

66 Cf. Luke 24.46.

67 Cf. 1 Thess. 4.14.

unutterable in the labour of creation,[68] but endures on still for love's sake to the end.[69]

It is the final truth, but it was miles beyond the world of His day, and it is miles beyond us still.

The tragedy of man's inveterate stupidity continues. The crown that Christ rejected here on earth, the throne of material power which He refused to mount, are given Him in heaven. Men were ashamed of the Cross;[70] and they could not see it as God's real throne. They invented the so-called "glorified Christ," Who, with all His sorrows ended and all His struggles won, ascends to share the throne of God Almighty and enjoy His perfect peace.

White-robed angels stand about Him bowing to His least command, shouts of triumph greet His entrance,[71] the mighty gates lift up their heads and the King of glory enters in.[72] All the pageantry of earthly power, all the pomp of courts and kings which He on earth refused, are used to make Him beautiful, forsooth, Who needs no robes of beauty but His sorrow and His love.

Christ is clothed in that omnipotence which has been all down the ages the veil that hid the real glory of the suffering God of love. But the Cross remained. It made its mark, and men could not forget. It is of course God's real throne, the throne of love that lifts Him up, and draws all men to Him at last. The power of the Cross is the power of God.[73] It is not past, but ever present. God has no other, and needs no other, glory but the glory of the Cross[74] – the glory of suffering, striving, and unconquerable love. This glorified Christ in regal robes is a degraded Christ

---

68 Cf. Rom. 8.22.

69 Cf. Matt. 24.13; John 13.1.

70 Cf. Heb. 12.2.

71 SK had a composite of many images in mind, such as John 20.12, Rev. 7.16 and much of the iconography of the Risen Christ that he would have seen in churches.

72 Ps. 24.7.

73 Cf. 1 Cor. 1.18.

74 Gal. 6.14.

reft[75] of real majesty;[76] these baubles are not worthy of the King. The true God is naked, bloody, wounded, and crowned with thorns, tortured, but triumphant in His love. He is God, and when men's eyes once see Him they must worship Him. He possesses them body and soul, and will never let them go. He is coming to His own to-day.[77] The furnace of this world war is burning out the dross of dead conventions from the Christian creed, and showing up the pure gold of the Cross.[78]

All men are learning to worship patient, suffering love, and the muddy bloody hero of the trenches is showing us Who is the real King.[79] The darkness is being cleared away, and men at last are growing proud of the Cross. Beside the wounded tattered soldier who totters down to this dressing-station with one arm hanging loose, an earthly king in all his glory looks paltry and absurd. I know nothing in my real religion of the Almighty God of power. I only see God in Christ,[80] and these men have shown me – *Him*.

I have seen in them His glory, glory as of the Only Begotten of the Father, full of grace and truth.[81]

I am sure of this God. I know Him. I love Him. I worship Him. I would die for Him and be glad.

* * * * *

Doc, I've been dreaming. I'm going up the line now. How's that lad inside? Dead? O God, comfort his mother. I must bury him at once. He was an only son.

---

75 'Reft' is an archaism meaning 'torn from'. The sense here is of 'bereft'.

76 SK was drawing a paradox here with the purple robes in which Jesus was mocked as a false king: Mark 15.17–20; John 19.2–5.

77 Cf. John 1.11.

78 Cf. Isa. 48.10; Ps. 12.6.

79 Cf. John 18.33–37.

80 Cf. Rom. 8.39.

81 John 1.14. SK has personalized the quotation – 'I have seen' rather than the 'We have seen' of the Gospel – and put 'full of grace and truth' at the end rather than at the beginning of the verse.

A chaplain's grave on Messines Ridge.

Clifford Reed was killed on the opening day of the battle and is buried in Oosttaverne Wood Cemetery which itself lies on the line that was the objective for that day. We do not know if he and Studdert Kennedy were acquainted but they had much in common. Both were there that morning, both were with the men they served, and both won the Military Cross for work evacuating the wounded. This grave witnesses that chaplains faced the dangers of war with their men, and that the dangers described by Studdert Kennedy were not simply a literary device. The quotation from Matthew 5.9 on the bottom of the headstone was placed there at his family's request.

V

God and Democracy

IN a tent two days after a big battle. A battalion parade had just been held. The thanks of the Commander-in-Chief had been conveyed to the troops for their gallantry in the recent action, and parade finished with "God save the King."[1]

*   *   *   *   *[2]

I never was thrilled by "God save the King" before. As a rule it leaves me cold; to-day it sent a tingling down my spine and gave me a lump in my throat. I wonder why. I suppose I am a bit upset really; hell is bad for the nerves. The parade was pretty awful too, so many splendid chaps absentees; it gets on one's nerves. I suppose I am a bit windy.[3] We are all in for it again the day after to morrow,[4] and there will be more absentees. "The King" sounded so dauntless and determined. It seemed like the

---

1 Presumably this parade took place just after one of the many assaults in summer and autumn 1917 that are collectively known as the Third Battle of Ypres or Battle of Passchendaele. The parade would assemble the entire battalion, or what was left of it, around three sides of a square and they would be addressed by the commanding officer, probably a major, who would read a message sent to them in praise of their fighting by Field Marshal Sir Douglas Haig, the Commander-in-Chief of the British armies in France and Flanders.

2 SK again denoted a time difference between the scene described and the moment of his reflection.

3 Soldiers' slang for a temporary loss of 'nerve'.

4 They are to return to the front line the next day: 'we are all in for it' is slang that someone knows they are going to encounter costly fighting in the very near future.

73

song of a thousand martyrs on their road to death. *Morituri te salutamus*[5] business, only in a nobler cause. It thrilled one like a great confession of faith. And yet, if there is anything certain, it is that "God save the King" is not the British Army's confession of faith. Conventionally it may be; really it is nothing of the kind. I suppose there are a thousand reasons, good and bad, why these dear chaps come out to fight. Some came because they were not going to stand bullying, and they regard the Prussian as a bully. Some fight because they think liberty as they know it and understand it is at stake; others because they are Englishmen, and they are not going to see their side defeated if they can help it. Some enlisted because their pals did, or their girl said they ought. But I doubt whether any fight as did the Cavaliers of Charles I because they think the English monarchy a divine institution.

The divine right of kings[6] is an idea as foreign to the British soldier's mind as the infallibility of the Pope.[7] To him it is purely a matter of expediency whether you have a king with crown or president with a top hat. He regards them both as public servants, and respects them for the work they do. The British peoples would not tolerate for an instant the pretensions of a king who took himself seriously as an absolute monarch. They will have any king but Cæsar. To us the Kaiser could not be anything but a bad joke.[8]

---

5 'We who are about to die, salute thee!' – the salute given to the Roman emperor by the gladiators before they fought in the arena.

6 It was – and nominally still is – a matter of political doctrine that British monarchs derive their right to rule from the will of God, a belief expressed in the Coronation ceremony involving anointing by the Archbishop of Canterbury.

7 The dogma of the infallibility of the Pope was formally agreed by the first Vatican Council in 1869–70, although it had been widely accepted from medieval times. It only applies when the Pope is speaking *ex cathedra*, formally defining a doctrine about faith or morals applicable to the whole Catholic Church.

8 SK was making a classicist's joke: starting with the biblical declaration

God and Democracy

No; if the BEF[9] were to make a confession of faith, it would be a vague and sketchy thing, and I doubt if the King would have a place in it at all. It would all centre round the ideas of Democracy and Freedom. Everywhere I find among the men of the army that this is the one great thing that touches them and rouses real enthusiasm. They do believe in Democracy. They are not quite sure what it means, but whatever it means, they believe in it. They believe intensely that every man has a right to a voice in the government of his country. This conviction is the only one of an ultimate kind that I find common and intense throughout the British Army. If they have any religion, it is centred in this idea of Democratic Freedom. This is their faith, vague and shadowy, but enormously powerful and big with mighty issues, good and evil, for the days that are to come.

I was driven to this truth about the British soldier by my wanderings as a preacher throughout the bases and the armies in the field,[10] and I was driven against my will, for, in many ways, the prospect frightens me.

Any form of democracy is bound to throw such an enormous weight of responsibility upon the ordinary average man, and he, splendid fellow as he is, seems to be much more alive to his

---

'We have no king but Caesar' (John 19.15 av), he was struck that the 'reconstructed pronunciation' of Latin used then in most schools would have rendered 'Caesar' with the same sound as 'Kaiser' – and SK was all too aware that that Caesar, Wilhelm II, was fond of imagining himself as governing 'by God's grace'.

9 Here, by 'BEF' – the British Expeditionary Force – SK meant all the British forces, which included Australians, Canadians, Indians, New Zealanders, South Africans and many others from the British Empire, fighting on the Western Front (i.e. in France and Belgium). In other contexts, 'BEF' was used to refer only to those forces present in France or Belgium before the end of the First Battle of Ypres in November 1914.

10 SK was deployed in many places along and behind the Western Front during the war, especially during the National Mission of Repentance and Hope in October 1916. See Michael Snape, *God and the British Soldier* (Abingdon: Routledge, 2005), p. 107.

rights than to his responsibilities in the free democracy which is to be.

This much is certain. The pomp and pageantry of kings, the glamour that surrounds a throne, the outward symbols of royalty have lost all power of appeal to the ordinary man. He looks upon them as he looks upon a Lord Mayor's show, as quaint and picturesque relics of antiquity, that give pleasure on a holiday, but have nothing to do with the serious business of life. The sentiment of passionate loyalty to a king does not exist among the rank and file of the army.

It is hard to part with it without regret, for this passion has a glorious history, but a history full of pathos too. Alas! the record of the race of kings is stained with many crimes. Too often have the kings betrayed and traded on the loyalty and faith of men. They have used them as a stalking horse to further their intrigues to purely selfish ends. They have used the doctrine that the king can do no wrong as a public licence to misuse their power. The treachery of kings has had its inevitable result, and men have ceased to trust in them. Even those who still hold that a benevolent despotism is the best form of government will add with a sigh, "given the benevolent despot," and he is so very rarely given.

The average man does not read history, yet history lives in him; each one of us is history incarnate, and history has killed blind trust in kings.

Of course this is not the only, or the chief, cause of the coming of Democracy. The power behind that coming appears to be the power that lies behind the gradual development of man. It is as near to being inevitable as anything can be in a world of men and women whose wills are partly free. In the days when men's light was largely darkness and ignorance was the common lot of most, when they were babes in brain power, they could be treated as such and ruled as such.

States could be ruled as a father rules a family of small children, who cannot question or dispute his right to rule and punish as he wills. When, however, the children grow up and learn, the form of family government must change, unless it is to ruin the children. So with states. If we seriously wish to stop the coming of Democracy, we must at once, and first of all, abolish free and compulsory education.

I have met men who said they would do this if they could, because modern elementary education does more harm than good, giving us that little knowledge which is so dangerous a thing.[11] I think it is only talk. It is easy to see the dangers of the Primary School education, but there is only one way of abolishing it, and that is to put some better, higher form of education in its place. Talk about the abolition of education is just talk for talking's sake. It may turn a point in an argument, but it has no relation to facts. We are going to have more education, not less or none at all. In order to be effective at all, opponents of Democracy ought to be passive resisters and refuse to pay their rates. They would then be splendidly consistent, and to most men irresistibly comic.

No; education has come to stop, and the immediate result of it, however incomplete, is to develop in man the critical faculty. Criticism is easier than construction, and comes first. It is the critical faculty of the people that destroys their faith in kings – absolute kings, or indeed in absolute anythings or anybodies. It has been and will be found increasingly difficult to protect anything or anybody from criticism. As the minds of men develop they become less and less afraid, and more determined to prove all things and hold fast only that which is true. Everywhere this tendency can be traced in history. Combined with a deep and pathetic longing for an absolute authority and an infallible guide, there is this critical faculty which prevents us from resting satisfied with false absolutes. Men tried an infallible Church, and the critical faculty tore it to pieces after the Renaissance; they tried an infallible Bible, and the nineteenth-century science

---

11 SK took this statement – attributed to Alexander Pope (1688–1744) – as a piece of proverbial wisdom.

cast it into a den of critics whose mouths could not be closed.[12] They have tried infallible monarchies again and again, and seen them torn to bits. What France did in the Revolution, what Portugal did yesterday,[13] Russia is doing to-day.[14] All the energy of effort that has been used to protect Church or Bible or Czar from criticism has been in vain, and must be in vain, unless you abolish education.

The Roman Church still tries to keep her absolute authority alive and to strangle the critical faculty of men for men's own good.[15] She is, however, rather like a desperately conscientious policeman endeavouring to stop the march of an army terrible with banners,[16] and she is left, as he would be left, with the helmet of salvation[17] on the back of her head, furiously waving the baton of pomposity (having mislaid the sword of the Spirit[18])

---

12 As we saw in chapter 4, SK was keenly aware how 'the old certainties' about the Bible had been destroyed by the then new biblical criticism. As with the arguments on God and nature in chapter 2, SK believed here was another case where religious people had to 'face facts'.

13 Portugal abolished its monarchy in 1910.

14 The Czar abdicated on 15 March 1917 and Russia became a republic on 15 September; Lenin and the Bolsheviks seized power on 8 November and negotiated an armistice with Germany on 6 December. SK was presumably referring to the arrival of the Russian republic on 15 September, which would fit with this chapter being written during the later stages of the Third Battle of Ypres.

15 SK was probably thinking of the 1907 decree of Pope Pius X (1903–14) known as *Lamentabili*, which condemned 65 'modern errors', amounting to saying that all modern thinking was simply wrong. This marked a return to the 'war on modernity' trope by the Catholic Church that had characterized the time of Pius IX (1846–78), who had condemned 80 'errors' of modern society – including many of the basic assumptions about civil liberty in a democracy – in his 1864 *Syllabus of Errors*. This stance by the authorities led to the condemnation of many theologians – several in England – as 'Modernists' between 1907 and the death of Pius X in August 1914. SK undoubtedly had this cause célèbre in mind.

16 Cf. Song 6.4, 10.

17 Cf. Eph. 6.17.

18 Cf. Eph. 6.17.

and wildly calling upon an incorrigibly progressive humanity to turn back under threat of the Divine displeasure.[19] It is pathetically hopeless!

There is a party, too, of the Church in England which desires and strives to regain the absolute coercive authority of the Church. They are even more pathetic. They are like special constables faced with an army, as powerless as the policeman, but without his dignity, for the great religious policeman is really dignified even in the invidious position in which he is placed.

It is all wrong. You cannot, and of course ought not to, protect anything or anybody from criticism, not even God. It is really all part of the same pathetic fallacy which has been the root of intolerance and persecution all down the ages – the fallacy that the human soul can be driven and compelled. It is false reverence which seeks to protect truth from attack. True reverence only begins when criticism has done its work. The same error which made the inquisitors burn men for speaking against the Church, and made monarchs burn men for speaking against the throne, makes men threaten with future torments those who speak against the creeds. It is all futile. God invites criticism, asks for it, pleads for it. He challenges us with mysteries, and lures us on by mighty questions to find the living truth.[20]

The faculty of faith is not meant to kill the faculty of criticism and the instinct of curiosity, but rather to keep them keen and alive, and prevent them dying of despair. Faith is the mark of those who seek and keep on seeking, who ask and keep on asking, who knock and keep on knocking, until the door is opened.[21] The passive weak-kneed taking of everything on trust

---

19 These condemnations of 'errors' carried with them ecclesiastical punishments, such as 'excommunication', and a vague hint that God would have suitably deserved post-mortem punishments for those who persisted in their errors.

20 Here SK sketched out an important but not very developed theme within his theology: faith/piety was not to be equated with passivity/fatalism.

21 Cf. Matt. 7.7.

which is often represented as faith, is a travesty of its truth. True faith is the most active, positive, and powerful of all virtues. It means that a man, having come into spiritual communion with that great personal Spirit Who lives and works behind the universe, can trust Him, and trusting Him can use all his powers of body, mind, and spirit to co-operate with Him in the great purpose of perfection; it means that the man of faith will be the man of science in its deepest, truest sense, and will never cease from asking questions, never cease from seeking for the reason that lies behind all mysteries. There are, of course, a thousand things that are at present super-rational: not contrary to but beyond reason; but that fact does not call us to cease from reasoning, but rather bids us reason more and more carefully. Faith is not the anchor but the lodestar of the intellect; it bids it follow, and it keeps it true.[22]

The doctrine that the king can do no wrong has been used all down the ages to stifle political criticism, and so stunt social progress. It has been used to kill the hopes and aspirations of the people, and keep them from seeking the better land to which their instincts urged them on. Absolute monarchy has been used to stifle the divine discontent which is the hall-mark of humanity.

The doctrine that God can do no wrong has been used in exactly the same way. God's will has been a shibboleth for those who wished to bolster up the existing social order. God is Almighty, and God can do no wrong, and therefore, whatever is, is right.

The rich man in his castle,
    The poor man at his gate.
God made them high or lowly
    And ordered their estate.[23]

---

22 This sentence is, arguably, the key to this chapter.

23 This is a verse – now almost invariably omitted – from the popular hymn for children, 'All things bright and beautiful', written by Cecil Frances

So we sang with childish lips, and so we were taught and believed until we learned in the school of the world that the rich man often – not always, but often – entered his castle by filthy ways, paved with human miseries and wet with human blood, and that it was often not God but whisky that put the poor man at his gate.[24]

Once the eyes of man are opened to the power and persistence of evil in the world, this pious or impious fatalism becomes impossible; and when men have learned to hate evil with all their hearts, it becomes not only impossible but repulsive and disgusting.

It is this repulsive fatalism, springing from the doctrine of the absolute God, that has embittered many of the noblest social and scientific pioneers against the Christian religion, and embitters them still. It makes a man who has studied modern poverty mad with rage to be told that Christ blessed the poor,[25] and said they would always be with us,[26] and that therefore the social distinctions, as they exist at present, are the will of God.

This vision of God as an Almighty Monarch swaying the world to His will has ruined the religion of some of the noblest souls, and has been productive of evil all down the ages.

God sat upon His throne armed with poverty, pestilence, disease, war, and sudden death in every form, and with these weapons vindicated His majesty upon earth. When a plague of some filthy disease swept over a country, and men lay writhing with pain from some incurable malady, it was the hand of God,[27] smiting them for their good.

Alexander and published in 1848 in her *Hymns for Little Children.* Alexander may have forgotten that the image of the poor man at the rich man's gate was an echo of one of Jesus' parables (Luke 16.19–31), which had a very different message from that of God ordering 'their estate'.

24 SK was appealing to the parable in Luke 16.19–31.

25 Cf. Luke 6.12.

26 Cf. Matt. 26.11.

27 This is more a generic Christian image of God acting in history than

God sent these evils, and God alone could remove them, and so men must betake themselves to prayer. If a volcanic eruption destroyed a village, it was God's vengeance on the sinful inhabitants; if the *Titanic* struck an iceberg,[28] it was God's punishment for the luxury of the dining-rooms. Nay, according to a dignitary of the Anglican Communion, if a European war breaks out, it is God's judgment on the drink bill of England.[29]

From this vision of God the reason of man has revolted. They have determined that these things are evil, and must be abolished. Faced with plagues they have deliberately turned from prayers to sanitation, with marvellous success. Faced with disease they have rejected resignation to the will of God and have betaken themselves to scientific research with great results. Practically speaking, men have decided that there is much in the world that is not God's will, but is wrong, and must be abolished. Theoretical religion has lagged behind, and hung on still to the Almighty Monarch to Whom all things do bow and obey. The result is that many of the finest practical people have no use for religion.

The pioneers of social betterment and scientific enlightenment have found themselves opposed or damned with faint praise by the people of God, and so have forsaken God, the conventional God, as decent men were bound to do. So comes about the awful state of things that God's foes are often those of His own household – narrow-minded, ignorant, conventional Christians – while His firmest friends are too often found among men outside the pale who do not call upon His Name.[30]

---

an echo of the Bible, but the image does have biblical roots, as in its use in 1 Sam. 5.11.

28 This happened on the night of 14–15 April 1912.

29 This is most probably a reference to Arthur Winnington-Ingram, Bishop of London from 1901 to 1939. He frequently complained about the national 'drink bill', was a keen total-abstainer and a tireless campaigner on many moral and social issues.

30 Cf. Isa. 12.4.

That God can do no wrong is indeed the truest of all truth; but that does not mean that there is no wrong, but that wrong is against God's will, that He hates it, that it thwarts and tortures Him, that He is constantly and actively striving to overcome it, and is overcoming it, and finally that He calls upon us, not for passive resignation, but for fierce and strenuous opposition in His Name.

I believe in God the Father Almighty is not a statement of fact but a confession of faith.[31] It does not declare the existence of an absolute Almighty Monarch Who sits upon a throne and moves the world by His nod: it professes our faith in suffering, striving, but all-conquering spirit of perfect love, Who through pain and tribulation, which torture Him, now is working His purpose of perfection out. The first clause of the Creed is not a cold, theological statement of fact, it is a warrior's battle-cry. It is said by the soldiers of God, standing at attention with their faces turned toward God's altar and the dawn of better days.

In those splendid words we declare our faith that the victory of God is as sure and surer than the rising of to-morrow's sun. God is suffering His agony now, but the day will surely come when His agony and ours will be ended, and we shall sing our song of praise to the triumphant God of Love.

The day of the absolute monarch is passing in politics – passing in tears and terror. We are burning that effigy in the hell flames of this cruel war, whose worm dieth not and whose fire is not quenched.[32] His day is done, and with him must pass all the metaphors and symbols, both symbolic words and symbolic ideas, which are drawn from the throne of earthly tyrants and applied to God.

---

31 'I believe in God the Father Almighty' is the opening line of the Apostles' Creed, which was used on many occasions in Anglican liturgy at the time.
32 Mark 9.48.

The Hardest Part

We must learn afresh what spirit we are of. When the Sons of Thunder[33] called on Christ to vindicate His majesty by burning the Samaritans with fire from heaven, Christ rebuked them, saying that they knew not the Spirit of God, Who came to save and not destroy;[34] and as He rebuked them, so would He rebuke us for our conceptions of God.

One of the ablest and most energetic of our bishops at the outbreak of the war started a campaign, the watchword of which was "The majesty of God."[35] God was King, and by the horrors of Pentecostal calamity strove to turn men back to Him.[36] Men had neglected His worship, despised His commandments, rejected His Kingdom, and this was the vindication of His majesty.

At the time, staggered by the immensity of the evil, I simply did not think; I submitted. Now, after three years of it, I believe that this teaching is liable to be utterly misunderstood, and does but give occasion to the enemies of the Lord to blaspheme. Never again, I believe, will men bow down and worship this majestic tyrant who sits upon a throne and wields as weapons pestilence, disease, and war. Such a vision of God rouses in the

---

33 An allusion to Mark 3.17, where two of the twelve apostles, James and John, are referred to as 'the Sons of Thunder'.

34 Luke 9.52–56, where it was James and John who wanted Jesus to consider sending down fire from heaven to consume those Samaritans who refused to receive them.

35 In 1915 the Bishop of London, Arthur Winnington-Ingram, addressed all the clergy of his diocese, telling them that the world had been losing sight of the Majesty of God. See A. F. Winnington-Ingram, *The Potter and the Clay* (London: Wells Gardner, Darton & Co., 1917), p. 15.

36 SK appears to be using the imagery of Pentecost (Acts 2) to describe the cacophonous experience of combatants on the Western Front. In 1918 a writer in *The Musical Times* wrote: 'Everything has been peaceful up to now – peaceful that is for the Front. . . . Then, without warning . . . the storm bursts, *ffff*. The Pentecostal calamity is at hand, with its mighty rushing wind and tongues of riotous fire.' The irony of likening the horrors of battle to the gift of the Holy Spirit was no doubt intentional. See Cecil Barber, 'Battle Music', *The Musical Times* 59:899 (1 January 1918), pp. 25–6.

best of men, not reverence, but revolt; not loyalty, but contempt; not love, but bitter hatred.

The Church lives on its vision of God. No perfection of organisation, no multiplication of effort, is of any real good apart from vision. I believe that if she goes forth to meet the world armed with the vision of God upon a throne, she will die. If she goes forth in any power but the power of the Cross she will die.[37]

She lives and works now, so far as she has real life and energy, and thank God she still has much of both, because she holds up before men for their worship and adoration, not God Almighty seated on a throne, the Lord of all power and might, but Jesus Christ, naked, bleeding, but unbeaten on the Cross, the Lord of all courage and love. Though we do our best to cloud the splendid sorrow of this vision by frantic efforts to reconcile it with the serene, omnipotent, passionless monarch on a throne, still through the clouds of our stupidity the Cross finds way into the heart of man, because it is God, the living God, Whose light is shining there.

Men, I believe, have done for ever with crowns of gold. They do not respect, but despise them. Most decent men, looking upon the tattered, muddy, bloody khaki of a procession of wounded that comes in after a battle would say, "Solomon in all his glory was not arrayed like one of these."[38] In their hearts all true men worship one God – the naked, wounded, bloody, but unconquered and unconquerable Christ. This is the God for Whom the heart of democracy is longing, and after Whom it is blindly, blunderingly, but earnestly groping.

The heart of the common people is near to the heart of Christ in its view of royalty. "The kings of the Gentiles," He said, "exercise lordship over them; and they that wield this power are called benefactors. But it shall not be so with you; but he that is

---

37 Cf. 1 Cor. 1.17.
38 Matt. 6.29.

greatest among you shall be as the younger; and he that leadeth as he that doth serve."[39]

So Christ pronounced the doom of Kaiserism, and it is being wrought out. No superiority of breeding or of brains, no pre-eminence of social position, no power of wealth, appeals to us apart from service. An idle duke is frankly disreputable, and infinitely inferior to a working dustman. The dustman may per-haps die a pauper, but that is nothing to the disgrace of living as a parasite. A man possessed of great powers must be either a devoted public servant or a damned nuisance. Service is the only thing we can respect, and suffering service is the only [thing] that we can crown.[40]

We have come to see the hollow mockery of power that is not love. This is the truth which is dawning rapidly upon the heart and head of modern democracy. It is, of course, only a great ideal still. Demos still has idols, and there its danger lies. We still bow down and worship the gods of wealth and position. Fine clothes still cover as great a multitude of sins as charity. To be respectable still means to have a banking account. We have amongst us still, snobs and sycophants, to whom a title is a real triumph and a coronet a halo that outshines the glory of a saint. Snobbery and servility of this kind are common in every class, commoner perhaps among the common people than they them-selves are ready to allow. Nevertheless, this is not our real faith. We may still worship idols, but in our hearts we despise them, and despise ourselves for worshipping them. The only thing we can respect, and remain self-respecting, is loving service. The worship of idols is rooted in fear, and the progress of man is the conquest of fear. Perfect love casteth out fear.[41] So, at last, the great suffering, striving God of service and of love is coming to His own, and as He comes into His own, so the High and

---

39 Luke 22.25–26.

40 The theme of the Suffering Servant from the book of Isaiah explored in chapter 4.

41 1 John 4.18.

Mighty Potentate, King of kings and Lord of lords, Almighty God, powerful, passionless, and serene, is being deposed from His throne in the hearts of men, and in His place there standeth one amongst us Whom we knew not,[42] with bloody brow and pierced hands, majestic in His nakedness, superb in His simplicity, the King Whose crown is a crown of thorns.[43] He is God.

His coronation by mankind is drawing nearer through the clouds of battle smoke that hide the inner thoughts of men in the Europe of to-day. He is revealing Himself to men out there in a thousand different ways. He is calling to His service men of every sort, and among them many to whom the name of Christ, and the idea of the Christian Church, mean nothing or worse than nothing. Men are turning to God in Christ, even as they curse the Christian God. They do not, and will not, believe in the monarch on the throne; they do, and will, believe in the Servant on the Cross.

"Every inch a king." So the Kaiser was described by a journalist who saw him at a great military review before the war. Power perfectly personified he was, with his thousand different uniforms and endless royal robes, mounted on his charger, reviewing the greatest and most perfect army in the world. An impressive personality. A wretched withered anachronism, all the more wretched, and all the more withered to us now that we know what he meant. We despised him when we thought he stood for nought but empty pomp and show of power. We despise him much more now we know that he stands for the brutal reality of loveless power. We despise him, as free men despise all tyrants. We can no longer interpret ultimate reality in the terms of absolute monarchy if we are to reach the heart of men. Christ has come so far into His own that He has slain Caesar. The danger is lest the people go out and away toward Christ beyond the Church, and she proves helpless to aid them with the problems they must face. The British Demos is

---

42 Cf. John 1.26.
43 Cf. Matt. 27.29.

astoundingly Christian, but it is exposed to awful dangers as it advances in freedom and takes up the inevitable burden of responsibility.

A free democracy must have a living religion if it is to live. I love the Church of England, and am proud to be her priest, but, O God of sorrow, love, and service, open her eyes that she may see and live. The people perish now,[44] to spite their wonderful hold on truth, because they want a guide to lead them higher still – and the Church lags behind, and sits upon a fence, because her vision of God is dim.

* * * * *

Perhaps, after all, I ought to be thrilled by "God save the King." Our English kings are public servants now. The King of the British is a monarch of free men. A patient, painstaking, public servant upon whom great burdens of responsibility rest. If any king survives it will be ours, for he is very nearly a "Christian king."[45] The crown of our British kings is a crown of golden thorns. Perhaps our English "God save the King" is a fit song for the Army of the Free. I think I will always love it more since I have heard it sung by men who stood at attention with death behind them and death before.

---

44 Cf. Prov. 29.18.

45 This was the honorary title used by French kings before the French Revolution. Note also SK's earlier reference to the 'divine right of Kings'.

VI

God and Prayer

IN the trenches during a heavy bombardment.[1] *It lasted over two hours. We could do nothing but sit still and wait. A sergeant on one side of me swore great oaths and made jokes by turns. A man somewhere on the other side kept praying aloud, in a broken and despairing kind of way, shivering out piteous supplications to God for protection and safety.*[2]

* * * * *

I wish that chap would chuck that praying. It turns me sick. I'd much rather he swore like the sergeant. It's disgusting, somehow. It isn't religion, it's cowardice. It isn't prayer, it's wind. I'd like to shut him up. He probably seldom, if ever, prayed before, and now he substitutes prayer for pluck. I wouldn't mind if he'd pray for pluck, but it's all for safety. I hate this last resort kind of religion; it's blasphemy. The decent men all despise it. Look at the sergeant's face. That other chap keeps banging into his mind a connection between Christ and cowardice. That's where the blasphemy comes in. There is not, and there cannot be, any connection between Christ and cowardice. I wonder who is to blame for this miserable caricature of Christian prayer. Is it the

---

1 As with the previous chapters, we assume this was somewhere in 'the Salient' during the Third Battle of Ypres.

2 The aphorism that 'there are no atheists in foxholes' dates from the Second World War. However, the phenomenon that in the face of death, even nominal Christians would turn to God as a last resort, praying for survival, was widely recognized in the First World War.

A chaplain leads a service in a field in France.
One of the most visible duties of the chaplain was to lead public acts of worship, such as seen here, in the field. Studdert Kennedy saw this as part of his normal work and it formed the background to much of what he wrote in the book. However, in addition to this he asked questions about the nature of the activity, about prayer, about the nature of the group assembled, about what being a member of the Church means and about its purpose – and, from those reflections, developed his thinking on the relationship of God to the world.

chap himself? Is it just common blue funk,[3] or are his teachers partly to blame, who lead him to suppose that God could and would hearken to this piteous wailing? I wonder is there something wrong in the way men learn to pray?

"Whatsoever ye ask in My name, I will do it for you."[4] It is a sweeping kind of promise, and easily misunderstood. Lots of Christians seem to think it means that prayer is a kind of magic cheque upon the bank of Heaven, only needing the formal endorsement with Christ's name to make it good for anything.

Of course it does not come off. Millions of such cheques are dishonoured every day. When the war broke out there was

---

3 Army slang for crippling and disorientating fear.
4 John 14.13 (and cf. 16.26).

a regular run upon the bank of God, and our churches were thronged with distracted people waving cheques for protection, duly endorsed "through Jesus Christ our Lord,"[5] and still the German host swept on and trampled helpless Belgium underfoot. I suppose there must have been millions of German and Austrian prayer cheques presented at the same time. They soon got sick of it of course, and fell away. In a dim way they realised that it was useless, and a waste of time.[6] I believe we parsons were, and are still, much to blame. We have not told people the truth about prayer for fear of hurting their feelings or discouraging them in their prayers. We went on the theory that any kind of prayer is better than no prayer at all. A chaplain said that to me the other day. "Don't discourage last-resort religion; it is better than no religion at all." I don't agree. It's worse than no religion; it's a base and superstitious form of idolatry.

I think there can be little doubt that we have encouraged this magic idea by the monotonous and formal ending of our prayers with the sacred Name, as if the name had power in itself.[7] Of course prayer in Christ's name means prayer in Christ's spirit. The greatest of all prayers does not contain the Name, but is drenched with the spirit.[8] What is Christ's spirit? In a word, "heroism." God and my duty first – a long way first. God's will above and beyond all other things. My pals and other people second. Myself and my own desires last, and a long way last, almost nowhere. That is Christ. Now what's this poor devil thinking about? Not his duty, not his pals; he's forgotten all about them. His whole mind is filled with one idea; the safety

---

5 The standard liturgical conclusion to Christian prayer; SK would have used it many times in every service he led using the BCP.

6 SK again appealed to the actual experience of people as a basis for their religious positions.

7 SK was thinking of such formulae as 'we ask through Christ our Lord' or 'we ask this in Jesus' name' attached to the end of petitions.

8 The Lord's Prayer does not conclude with 'through Christ our Lord' but with a note of praise 'For thine is the kingdom, the power and the glory. For ever and ever.'

of his own skin. Well, don't be hard on him. Perhaps he has a wife and a kiddie at home, like your Patrick.[9] I don't want to be hard, but I must be Christian. Christ said, "He that hateth not father and mother,"[10] and other fierce, hard sentences. He made it plain that in big things, when God's will was made clear to us, we must put Him and duty out away beyond even the wife and kiddies. It may be hard, but it is Christian. This is not prayer at all. Cowardice has turned it into sin. It is sin, not prayer. To think of one's own skin now, to pray for one's own safety, is sin. There is no such thing as selfish prayer. There is no such thing as prayer which does not put God first. That is the essence of it. That is the spirit. The name without the spirit is as futile as the mumbo-jumbo of a conjuror. This chap's prayer is much more sinful than the sergeant's swears. There is love in the sergeant's blasphemy. He may not be thinking about God, but he is thinking about his platoon. He may not be a Christian, but at any rate he's not a coward.

I suppose he has the ordinary brave man's idea about death and danger. He's a fatalist. "If it's coming, it's coming; if it ain't, it ain't; and any'ow, I can't 'elp it." That's what he'd say. "If the bullet or the shell is made that has my name on it, then I'm for it any'ow." It isn't the Christian way. It isn't the noblest way. But it's a brave way. It resists the temptation of fear. It crushes down this cursed terror that takes your spirit by the throat and drives it into selfish cowardice – the cowardice that will not let you do your job with all your heart and soul, and think of comrades first. It means, at any rate, that the spirit holds its own even if it can't attack.[11]

---

9 SK brings his argument back to himself, his lived reality, his own wife and son.

10 Luke 14.26.

11 The fatalism SK described was most probably the dominant attitude of ordinary combatants in the conflict. It was preferable to seeing oneself at the mercy of the randomness of the trajectory of an artillery shell or, alternatively, subject to the whim of an all-controlling God who decided where the

Of course the Christian spirit rips through that and goes out beyond it. It is not merely fatalistic in that dull sort of way; it is utterly and joyfully reckless. Danger doesn't matter, death doesn't matter; only God and the job matter at all. The Christian spirit despises death and laughs at danger, if they be on the road where duty leads.[12] It does not merely face the shadow of death,[13] it sees through it into the life beyond; it does not merely withstand fear, it tramples it underfoot,[14] it kills it, and leaps out to find the courage of the Cross. The Christian spirit is the spirit of positive, powerful, and infectious heroism. It is not content with refusing to let pals down, it seeks to encourage, inspire, and uplift them. It is the spirit of that supremest kind of moral courage which includes physical courage, and transforms the splendour of the bull-dog into the splendour of the Christ. The British Army is full of splendid bull-dogs like this old swearing sergeant, and they make it glorious. But, dear God, what an army we would have if every soldier prayed, and, through prayer, caught up the spirit of the Christ! An army of British Christians would take the Kaiser in its stride, and beat the devil himself.

I see Gethsemane;[15] I always see it these days. Christ Himself was once in danger of losing that splendid spirit. He is faced with the agony of the Cross. The sickening feeling that men, who have stood as we stand now, know something of sweeps over Him. It is worse for Him; how much worse we cannot altogether understand. He was alone for one thing; that made it

shells fell or whom the bullets hit. See Stuart Bell, *Faith in Conflict: The Impact of the Great War on the Faith of the People of Britain* (Solihull: Helion, 2017), pp. 76–84.

12 SK may have been thinking of the motto on the badges of the Royal Artillery: *Quo fas et gloria ducunt* ('to where duty and glory lead').

13 Ps. 23.4.

14 Ps. 91.13.

15 SK combined the accounts of the scene known as 'the agony in the garden of Gethsemane' from Matt. 26.36–46, Mark 14.32–42 and Luke 22.39–46 in the memory that inspired this reflection.

worse. God, how I hate being alone with darkness and the fear of death. One pal makes all the difference. He had no chance either; there was no hope of a blighty one,[16] and then home. It is certain death, and certain torture. He is in the grip of terror. We see Him alone in the garden, praying. Three times the horror of the Cross wrings from His lips the human cry, "If it be possible, let this cup pass from Me."[17] Let Me off, O God; let Me off, I cannot bear it. That is not His prayer, that is what He is praying against, that is the expression of the terror He has to fight. But each time the prayer follows, the real prayer, with power that receives immediate answer: "Nevertheless, Thy will be done."[18] That is the real prayer. They ruined it all for me as a child; they told me that God's will was the Cross. God wished Christ to be crucified; He wished Judas to be a traitor, Pilate a coward, the priests to be fiends, and the crowd to be cruel and fickle-hearted. It was all part of His plan.[19] Of course that is impossible. God cannot plan treachery and murder. They told me that when Christ realised that His prayer could not be answered, He meekly bowed His head to God's plan, and said, "Thy will be done."[20] The cry of agony was the prayer,[21] and "Thy will be done" an act of meek submission. It is the topsy-turvy kind of interpretation that arises from the Almighty Monarch on the Throne

---

16 A 'blighty' was the slang for an 'ideal wound' in the minds of many soldiers – one that would not disfigure or permanently maim but was serious enough to mean one would be moved to a hospital in Britain (i.e. Blighty) and then be granted a discharge on medical grounds, or at least several months' leave.

17 Matt. 26.39.

18 Matt. 26.39.

19 The logical deduction from a belief that nothing happens without it being God's will is that the sequence of events leading up to Christ's crucifixion must have been ordained by God. SK railed against this argument.

20 SK interpreted Matt. 26.39 as a variant of the line of the Lord's Prayer (Matt. 6.10).

21 Luke 22.44 – this verse is omitted in many modern editions of the Gospels.

idea of God, Who wills both good and evil. But it is madness. God could not will the Cross. It must have been utterly abhorrent to Him. God's will for Christ was that He should live the perfect life, bear witness to the final truth, and bear the torch of perfect love undimmed through everything. That was God's will, and Christ's work; and if it was to be done, it must mean that the Cross be carried, and all it meant endured, to the very end. That was necessary because of sin. So in His agony Christ prays "Thy will be done." The prayer is immediately answered. The angel of God appears to comfort Him.[22] Terror dies within His soul, hesitation disappears, and with His battle prayer upon His lips, "Thy will be done," He goes out from the garden[23] in the majesty of manhood to bear such witness to His truth, to live in death so fine a life, that He becomes the light in darkness of every age, and the deathless hope of a dying world.

The great truth is that "Thy will be done" is the real prayer of Gethsemane. It is the prayer, and not an afterthought of sad submission in case God cannot answer the prayer to be let off.

Too often we model our prayers upon the false interpretation of Gethsemane. Our prayers are too often either a wail of agony or a kind of indent upon God for supplies[24] to meet our needs, with "Thy will be done" put in at the end in case God cannot take away the pain we plead against or grant us the supplies we need. "Thy will be done" ceases to be the great prayer, and becomes the necessary apology for praying.

It becomes an act of passive submission instead of an act of positive and powerful aspiration.[25] Much of our war prayer in churches at home, and much of our peace prayer too, is rendered

---

22 Luke 22.43 – this verse is omitted in many modern editions of the Gospels.

23 The traditional identification of Gethsemane as a garden is based on John 18.1 – SK took this for granted.

24 The 'indent' was the normal method of obtaining supplies in the army.

25 As noted in the previous chapter, SK was insistent that piety was not to be confused with passivity/fatalism.

futile by this false conception. We parsons are to blame. We have been kind to be cruel because we were afraid of being cruel to be kind; we have failed to be Christian because we tried to be kinder than Christ. We have not called upon our people for heroism in their prayers. We have accepted the lower standard, and excused it by saying that it is human. Of course it is human, but religion must be more than human or else it must be vain. We have allowed our people, and even encouraged them, to fill our churches with cries of agony for those they loved, "Let this cup pass from them,"[26] and have allowed them to believe that it was prayer, provided they would add the great submission, "Thy will be done."

We have failed, in fact, to put first things first. The first thing, by far the first, that every Christian mother should learn to pray for her son, and every Christian wife for her husband, is that by him and through him, at whatever cost, God's will may be done. We must learn to leave the matter of life and death entirely in God's hands, and pray that in life or death our men may keep their manhood clean from every spot of cowardice or sin.

Especially must we teach our children this. The first prayer I want my son to learn to say for me is not "God keep daddy safe," but "God make daddy brave, and if he has hard things to do make him strong to do them." Life and death don't matter, Pat, my son; right and wrong do. Daddy dead is daddy still, but daddy dishonoured before God is something awful, too bad for words. I suppose you'd like to put in a bit about the safety too, old chap, and mother would. Well, put it in, but afterwards, always afterwards, because it does not really matter near so much. Every man, woman, and child should be taught to put first things first in prayer, both in peace and war, and that I believe is where we have failed.

We have taught our people to use prayer too much as a means of comfort. Not in the original and heroic sense of uplifting,

---

26 Cf. Matt. 26.39.

inspiring, strengthening, but in the more modern and baser sense of soothing sorrow, dulling pain, and drying tears. The comfort of the cushion, not the comfort of the Cross. Because we have failed in prayer to bear the Cross, we have also failed to win the crown.

From the soldier's point of view the condemnation of such prayers begins with the conviction, bought by bitter experience, that they do not work. Religion as an insurance policy against accident in the day of battle is discredited in the army. The men have lost what faith in it they ever had. Just as the rain descends upon the just and the unjust,[27] so do the shells, and good and bad, praying and prayerless, are shattered into bits. It is terrible, but it is true; as terrible and as true as life. The flying death that shrieks in a shell is as impartial as an avalanche or a volcano. It is as inevitable as the Cross. Though in their agony men cry to God if it be possible to let it pass, it will not pass if the laws by which it flies must bring it to your feet. As God did not quench the fires that burned the martyrs or close the lions' mouths before they tore them limb from limb, so God does not turn aside the shell that flies shrieking out the call to martyrdom for me or for my son. Even as I pray now I may be blown to bits, as Christ, still praying, suffered on the Cross, and as His followers all down the ages have died the death with prayers upon their lips. Christ never promised to those who prayed immunity from suffering and death.

Well, then, what use is praying? What answers do we win? We win the only answer worth having, the power to pass through danger and through death with a spirit still unbroken and a manhood still unstained.

In all these things we can be more than conquerors through Him Who loves us,[28] because through prayer He can pour into us the gift of the splendid spirit. And it does not end there, for having poured it into us, He can, through our prayers for

27 Matt. 5.45.
28 Rom. 8.37.

others, pour it through us into them. The splendid spirit can run through the men who really pray, like a stream of living fire, out into the world of men and women who need just that, and only that, for with that comes all that's best worth having in this world.

A shell is just an iron sin, like the nail that pierced His feet.[29] It is just sin wrought into metal. Sin can be worked into any form. It is just a gift of God misused. Sin takes form and substance in a million ways: it pours forth in speech, it is painted in colours, it is built into bricks and mortar, it is carved into marble. Wherever a gift of God is misused sin takes form. It took the form of a wooden cross and crucified the Son of God; it takes the form of an iron shell and kills God's children by the score. War is just sin in a million forms in a million of God's gifts misused. God cannot deal with war in any other way than that by which He deals with sin. He cannot save us from war except by saving us from sin.

How does God deal with sin? By what way does He conquer it? By the way of the Cross, the way of love. He suffers for it; He takes it upon Himself, and He calls on us to share His burden, to partake of His suffering. He makes an army of the Cross, an army of men and women who pledge themselves to fight with sin and gladly suffer in the fight, that by their strife and suffering the power of evil may be broken and the world redeemed.

Prayer is the means of communication by which the suffering and triumphant God meets His band of volunteers and pours His Spirit into them, and sends them out to fight, to suffer, and to conquer in the end.

Prayer will not turn away the shell from my body; it will not change the flight of the bullet; but it will ensure that neither shell nor bullet can touch me, the real me. Prayer cannot save me from sorrow, but it can draw the sting of sorrow by saving me from sin. And in the end, through prayer and the army of those

---

29 Cf. John 20.25.

that pray, God will reach down to the roots of war and tear them from the world. When at last through prayer the stream of the Spirit has flowed out to all, men will look upon their guns, their bombs, their gas cylinders as mad monstrosities, and will take the metal from the earth to mould and beat it, not into engines of death, but into means of beauty and of life.[30]

Prayer, true prayer, will bring us victory. For victory comes at last to those who are willing to make the greatest venture of faith, and the supremest sacrifice. By prayer we can reach Berlin. But more than that, by prayer we can conquer war itself, and march at last into the New Jerusalem of God.[31]

* * * * *

I mustn't curse this poor beggar. He's just gone under. He's lost the spirit. I was nearly as bad, for I had nearly lost it too. I must not curse him. I must pray for him. Probably I'd better begin with a fag. Have a fag, lad? I think it's dying down now. Yes, I've got a light.[32] Christ the God the only God come down into his soul, and make him brave. Good God Almighty, what is that? Are you there, sergeant? Well, pull me out, will you. That chap's got it bad; I'll go for stretcher-bearers. This lad's dead, and he never lit that fag. The cup could not pass. I hope he had braced himself to stand before the Christ . . .[33] It must have been one of our own trench mortars, that.

---

30 Cf. Isa. 2.4; Joel 3.10; Mic. 4.3.

31 This reference to the 'New Jerusalem' was not for SK an invocation of a utopian human society – as used by William Blake – that was the outcome of social progress, but the eschatological image of the universe as the heavenly city when all has been brought to fulfilment. The roots of the image are to be found in Gal. 4.25–26; Heb. 12.22; Rev. 3.12 and 21.1—22.5.

32 SK was known as 'Woodbine Willie' because he gave the troops cigarettes ('fags', of which the preferred brand was 'Woodbine'), together with copies of the New Testament.

33 Cf. Rom. 14.10.

VII

God and the Sacrament

On the morning before the battle of June 7th, a large number of
officers and men attended the Holy Communion.[1] *I noticed one*
corporal in particular whom I had never known to attend before. I
remember thinking what a splendid young body his was as I said the
words, "Preserve thy body and soul unto everlasting life".[2] *Three*
days later I buried his body, terribly mutilated, in a shell hole just
behind the line.

* * * * *

I wonder why you came that morning, and did not come before.
I wonder what you thought about this Service of the Broken
Body and the Blood outpoured.[3] I am sure you had the ordinary
man's respect for it. You had a kind of feeling that it was a very
special kind of service, not to be treated lightly or approached
without thought.[4] You probably felt that you were not and could

1 For the context, see the notes to chapter 1.

2 The prayer from the BCP uttered by the officiating minister as each
member of the congregation is given a fraction of the broken loaf at what
was invariably called, in 1918, 'Holy Communion'.

3 SK referred on at least six occasions in this chapter to the Eucharist as
'the Broken Body and the Blood outpoured'. Later in the chapter the image
blurred with the broken bodies and pools of outpoured blood SK saw on the
battlefield around him.

4 This phrase echoed the 'warning' to be given 'before the Celebration of
the Holy Communion' in the BCP that reads:

my duty is to exhort you . . . to consider the dignity of that holy mystery,
and the great peril of the unworthy receiving thereof, and so to search

British soldiers receive Holy Communion before battle.
This official postcard describes the scene simply as a 'church service' but it is clearly a celebration of Holy Communion and is similar to the liturgies described in this chapter. Studdert Kennedy would, on the basis of this experience, produce what is now a familiar eucharistic theology, but which was then quite startling.

———————

and examine your consciences, and that not lightly . . . but . . . as worthy partakers of that holy Table.

This warning approach was so effective that most preferred not to participate in Holy Communion by 'receiving' (see Frances Knight, 'From Diversity to Sectarianism: The Definition of Anglican Identity in Nineteenth-Century England', *Studies in Church History* 32 (1996), pp. 377–86). It is this phenomenon, which is theologically self-contradictory (as SK noted), that stands behind both his comment about the corporal as an instance and, more generally, his eucharistic theology in this chapter. The corporal's participation is a starting point for complete critique of the warning approach to the Eucharist, common across all the Western churches for centuries, which was predicated on the notion of God as a dangerous potentate who punished his subjects after the manner of a fear-inspiring king. St Paul's warning in 1 Cor. 11.27 was also highly influential.

not be good enough to come very often. It was to you a service for the very good – for men who never swore, never drank too much, and never did a lot of things that you had done and might do again. You had the ordinary man's idea of goodness, the purely negative idea of not doing wrong, and so, because you knew that you often did wrong, and would probably keep on doing it, you did not come very often. The other day you were up against it; you were faced with death. You were not really frightened, but you were dead serious, and you came. I wonder did you dimly hope that it might shield your body in the battle. Did you take the great words "Preserve thy body" literally? Maybe you did. Superstition dies hard. I find it lingering in men's minds still, and in the minds of the most unlikely men, especially on religious subjects which they do not try to think about much. Was it thoughts of home that brought you? Your mother would like to know that you had been. Your sweetheart always goes, and wanted you to go. Sentiment plays a large part in the ordinary man's religion. I've often known men come rather from love of mother or Mary, the girl, than from any conscious love of Christ. God bless them. I don't think Christ minds. Many a man finds God mainly through good women. It is a common road to Christ.

It was not a bad motive for coming, but it was not the best. The Sacrament evidently did not mean to you what it should mean, or you would have come more often. It would have been your food, and not your medicine. You are just typical of the rank and file of the British. Your religion was made up of some superstition, more sentiment, and something else which you did not understand; but it was there, and was very like the real thing.

I wonder why we did not succeed, we who teach, in making the Sacrament mean to you all that we believe it was intended to mean. I think it is quite evident that in a large number of cases we have not succeeded. I wonder why.

For some years now the teaching of all the Churches, Catholic and Nonconformist, has been increasingly strong on the Sacrament.[5] We all agree now, far more than we did, that it is the sum and centre of Christian worship.[6] I have been much struck with that in talking to ministers of the English and Scottish Free Churches.[7] The Roman Catholic Church has, of course, never abated her emphasis upon its absolute necessity, and her children are evidently much more devout in their attendance at it, and more regular.[8] Yet neither we nor they have much ground for real satisfaction.[9] In every Church there is a body of regular

5 SK was aware that since the late nineteenth century, interest in the Eucharist as a phenomenon of Christian life was spreading within Christian theology far beyond its traditional haunts in Catholicism and the High Church party within Anglicanism. This new interest was possibly a result of the prominent place of the Eucharist in an early Christian document known as the *Didache* and first published in 1883, which showed the practice of the Eucharist to have been both a regular and normal part of very ancient Christian life. SK's awareness of these developments is another indication that this book was the result of a long period of research and gestation rather than something that just sprang to his mind in a moment.

6 This is one of the more remarkable sentences in the book, in that it was echoed almost verbatim, albeit in Latin, in the documents issued by the Roman Catholic Church during the Second Vatican Council (1962–5); see *Sacrosanctum Concilium* (1963), n. 10 and *Eucharisticum mysterium* (1967), 1, B. The similarity is, moreover, not simply verbal, in that both SK and the Council viewed the Eucharist as a moment in the pilgrim eschatological journey of the Church.

7 This is one of the explicit pieces of evidence that SK was developing his theological position over time by discussing matters with others.

8 Actual participation in terms of 'receiving Communion' would not, in 1917, have been much higher among Roman Catholics than among Anglicans. Both used a warning theology, and this was compounded for Catholics by the fasting regulations which, though often suspended in wartime, were so ingrained as to make such dispensations meaningless.

9 SK viewed ecumenism and the union of Christians not as a reunion – looking backward to a common mother Church that is 'rejoined' – but as an eschatological project. Each denomination had to work towards it, and all of them, even the Church to which one gave allegiance, needed to change for a better future. This would have raised questions about identity, links to a perfect past and orthodoxy of which few theologians at the time were aware and even fewer were willing to acknowledge; see Tom O'Loughlin, 'Divisions

communicants surrounded by a larger body of occasional and irregular communicants, surrounded again by an enormous body of non-communicants who would still claim to be called Christians.[10]

Perhaps that must always be so to some extent. It is the natural order in which the leaven would work in the lump.[11] But I think we would all agree that the inner circle is far too small, and the two outer ones far too large. The inner circle is far too small, and too often, I fear, it is composed of the wrong sort of people. Too often, I am afraid, we find at our altars as regular communicants rather the comparatively little tempted than the actively and positively good. Many old and middle-aged women, some young girls, and a few very respectable men. I don't mean to despise or disparage them. Far from it. Probably England owes them more than she will ever know, but it does seem as though those who come to Christ's banquet are those who need it least. That is not good, is it?

We must not, on our peril, break down the barriers of instinctive reverence that surround the Altars and Communion Tables of our churches.[12] We must make them stronger still. I think

in Christianity: The Contribution of "Appeals to Antiquity"', in S. Oliver, K. Kilby and T. O'Loughlin (eds), *Faithful Reading: New Essays in Theology and Philosophy in Honour of Fergus Kerr OP* (London: T. & T. Clark, 2012), pp. 221–41.

10 This imagery of concentric circles with fuzzy boundaries between them may seem a commonplace to us, but it was a radically new way of thinking of church membership in the early twentieth century, when most theologians, and virtually all pastoral theology, thought of belonging to the Church in binary in/out terms. SK's use of it was not sloppy thinking but a consequence of his theology of the incarnation, which only becomes fully realized, and 'visible', at the eschaton.

11 Cf. 1 Cor. 5.6 and Gal. 5.9. SK's language of the leaven and the lump may derive from part of Edward Talbot's charge to the Diocese of Rochester in 1903, when he spoke of committed Christians as the 'leaven' in the 'lump' of the wider constituency of those who professed belief without practising it. See G. Stephenson, *Edward Stuart Talbot, 1844–1934* (London: SPCK, 1936), pp. 157–9.

12 A debate raged since the sixteenth century as to whether the object

once more that we are agreed upon that. We must not make the great Food cheap, and yet we must not suffer those who really need it to starve their souls for lack of it.

I wonder if in our teaching about it we have not tended to make the Sacrament an end in itself rather than a means to an end, the great end of Christ-like life. It has seemed to the man in the street that we were trying to persuade him that regular and frequent attendance at this Service would of itself avail to save his soul, and secure him entry into heaven hereafter. We have failed, in fact, to connect the Sacrament with life. There is a great gulf fixed between the altar and the street,[13] between the sacred and the secular. The man in the street feels instinctively that this is wrong. He feels that salvation depends upon character and not upon ceremonies. He has at last outgrown magic and mechanical religion. He regards it with the deepest suspicion. He may not be a good man himself, but he is quite sure that religious people ought to be good, positively and pre-eminently good. He will have nothing to do with religion which does not make character, and show itself a means to that end. He is sure that the Sacrament was made for man, and not man for the Sacrament.[14] In this respect he is more Christian than the Church appears to be. Of course in theory we are just as much opposed to anything in the nature of magic and mechan-

of furniture used at the Eucharist, which is physically a table, should be interpreted as a 'Table' (emphasizing the notion of the Christ's welcoming banquet) or as an 'Altar' (emphasizing the notion of the sacrificial death of Jesus). This was one of the points of contention between the various parties in the Church of England at the time, and SK, being of High Church leanings, would usually have used the word 'altar' – as he did on several occasions in this chapter. But by using both words here he was deliberately seeking to move beyond both the sectarian divisions and the limitations of any one theological explanation of the actual event.

13 Cf. Luke 16.26.

14 This was an appeal to an often-forgotten principle of traditional theology: *sacramenta propter homines* ('significant rituals are there for the sake of humans'), which appealed in turn to Mark 2.27.

ical religion as he is, but in practice and in much of our teaching we sail very close to it. The Churches tend to become ends in themselves. We reckon our prosperity by the number of our communicants and the filling of our churches. The Churches war against the chapels, and in the struggle tend to lose sight of the end in view.[15] The greater our reverence for the Sacrament, the stronger is the temptation to make it an end in itself, and insist upon it as a means not to fine life, but to salvation undefined.

Because we aim at filling our churches we empty them, and because we aim at crowding our Altars they are comparatively deserted. We have our small band of devotees, but the great tide of restless, vigorous life sweeps by our doors and finds outlet in a thousand other ways. We have been calling men to services when what they wanted was the call to service and to sacrifice. I think there is something in that, and other things have followed as a result of it. The Sacrament which was meant to be the centre of our Christian unity has become the source and centre of a most unchristian strife.[16] The chorus of united praise that should have risen round our altars is broken into discords by our party cries. Our different ways of thinking about the Sacrament, and of interpreting our experience of it, have destroyed our unity and turned the Church into the warring Churches.

The great word Catholic has been degraded from its high estate and has become a party shibboleth. It has become associated with certain forms of ritual, and certain dogmatic expressions of Christian experience, and with a protest against all others. It has become the catchword of unchristian parties rather than the war-cry of the Christian Church. It has, in fact, completely changed its meaning. The real duty of a good Catholic is not to wear vestments and hate Nonconformists, but

---

15 At the time, Nonconformist places of worship were invariably termed 'chapels'; thus SK was referring to rivalry between Anglicanism and Nonconformity.

16 Again, SK used the expression of the Eucharist being 'the source and centre', which will be found in Vatican II.

to love everybody and wear Christ.[17] How utterly bewildering to the ordinary man all this division must be. Our interminable disputes on ritual questions and the method and meaning of the Real Presence, and the bitterness which they create – what is he to make of them? "I cannot make it out," he says; "aren't we all making for the same place?" "Making for the same place" is the phrase which the bewildered man in the street uses to dismiss from his mind the problem of divided Churches. It is a vague loose phrase which the apostles of what is called definite religious teaching (generally, I'm afraid, their own) are never tired of carping at, but it contains a truth which we would all do well to keep in mind. The truth is that our divisions are largely caused by the fact that we are not all "making for the same place," striving for one end, but each for our own end, which is really not an end at all, but a means disguised as one.[18] There is a truth behind H. G. Wells' bitter charge, "The Churches with their instinct of self-preservation at all costs."[19] We have come to care more for our Churches and our parties than we care for our God. We have not kept ourselves from idols. Idolatry always divides and destroys where the worship of God would unite and create. The very centre of our idolatry is, to our shame, be it said, the Sacrament itself. That great gift more than others has tended to become an idol, as the Sabbath did to the Jews.[20]

---

17 One of the flashpoints of conflict between various church parties and theologies at the time was on whether the minister should or should not wear vestments, and if so, which ones.

18 SK put forward a view of Christian unity that was based in the future – each party recognizing the common destiny of all, coupled with an awareness of the weaknesses of every group in the present; and most unusually for the time, he linked the issue of the unity of Christians with the Eucharist. In both he can be considered a harbinger of much later theological developments.

19 Efforts to identify this quotation, including consultation with experts on the corpus of H. G. Wells, have been unfruitful. It may be from a newspaper article, or else should be understood as a summary of Wells' argument in, for example, *God, the Invisible King*.

20 Cf. Mark 2.23–28.

The one thing that matters in the Sacrament, as in everything else, is God. Of itself and in itself the going to the Sacrament could no more save us than going on a pilgrimage to Mecca. There is nothing magic or mechanical in it.[21] It is nothing unless it is a means of revealing God to human souls, whereby He comes to dwell in us and we in Him.[22] That is what It ought to be to all Christians, and what It is to those who have found Its secret. Why do so many neglect and forget it? I fear it is because we have made the commandment of God of none effect through our traditions. We have either made attendance at the Sacrament an end itself to which our people came in blind obedience, trusting It would save their souls, or else we have obscured its simple truth by complex interpretations. Broken bread and wine outpoured, quite simple things, what do they mean? Is it not plain in the light of the Cross. The Sacrament is just the continual representing of the Cross. Coming to the Sacrament is coming to the Cross, and coming to the Cross is coming to God, the only God, Whose body is for ever broken and Whose blood is ever shed, until the task of creative redemption shall at last be all complete. The Cross is not really past, but present, ever present, and the Sacrament is the means of making its presence, or rather His presence, real to ourselves. It is a simple thing we do in remembrance of Him,[23] out of love for Him; and just because we do it out of love for Him, It makes Him real to us in a very special way.

---

21 Behind this statement stands a long-running late-medieval/Reformation debate about 'sacraments'. Do they 'effect by the action' (*ex operate operato*) or 'effect by the intention of those performing them' (*ex opera operantis*)? This debate was interminable because its premises were badly defined in relation to one another. SK not only sidestepped the debate, he rendered it redundant by an appeal to sacramental finality: 'the one thing that matters in the Sacrament . . . is God.'

22 Cf. John 1.14 – SK will appeal to this more explicitly a little further along in the chapter.

23 Cf. 1 Cor. 11.24–25; Luke 22.19.

God and the Sacrament

It is all quite simple, but how complex we have made it, when we have tried to explain it at all, and have not been content to leave it as a mystery unexplained. Our dual vision of God has once more led us into endless complications. The Old Testament has again obscured the New. We have read into the Sacrament the Father on His throne accepting the sacrifice of the Son upon the Cross. We have made an absolute necessity of the Old Testament metaphor of sacrifice, and have clung to it as essential part of the truth. Our doctors have compiled a complicated theology which, amidst much wrangling and dispute, sets out to explain, not the Sacrament Itself, but the Old Testament metaphors used in the Epistle to the Hebrews and the Epistles of St. Paul,[24] to express the inner meaning of the work and person of Christ. The very words in which these writers strove to express the inexpressible have been taken as sacred and essential, and of necessity the only vehicles for the truth in all ages. The splendid, passionate, grammarless rhetoric in which St. Paul splashed out, in his hurried but immortal letters, the truth that burned within him, has been treated as if it were the cold and carefully considered language of an academic professor. The idolatry of the Bible which gave rise to the idea that it was dictated word for word by the Almighty God has made the simplicity of the Sacrament infinitely complex, because we have interpreted the Bible utterances about it according to the letter rather than the spirit.[25] Sacramental controversy has become the delight of theologians and the despair of religious people.

---

24 SK was referring to another interminable wrangle seeking to align Heb. 7.27; 10.11–18 with 1 Cor. 5.7 (and other passages) and later practices. These arguments were also popularized in sectarian squabbles. The debate went round in circles because the unspoken assumptions of all concerned would not let them see that sources did not form a consistent set of premises. It is to be noted that SK – contrary to the still common practice at the time – did not attribute the Letter to the Hebrews to Paul's authorship.

25 Cf. 2 Cor. 3.6.

Of course we could not expect the plain man to understand this infinitely complicated theology, so we said it was unnecessary for him to understand anything at all. He must come and ask no questions, and It would save His soul. We gave him a choice between stark mystery and a mass of complicated dogma. He is not satisfied, and does not come. Can we wonder? There is but one way to understand the Sacrament, the way in which the first Christians understood it. First they saw Him. They beheld His glory, glory as of the only begotten of the Father.[26] In His suffering manhood they saw God, and learned to love and worship. Then, when His Body was taken away from them, they knew Him in the breaking of bread.[27]

The Sacrament was just Jesus Christ to them, and Jesus Christ was God. In Him it began, and in Him it ended. That is the truth, sublime in its simplicity – the Sacrament is Christ, and Christ is God.

If we want our people to come to the Sacrament we must first of all give them the clear and shining vision of the Suffering God revealed in Jesus Christ, and then ask them to come to the service of the Broken Body and the Blood outpoured to meet Him, in order that by communion with Him they may be filled with His Spirit and inspired to suffer with Him, and so help to save and lift their comrades out of darkness into light. We must give them the vision first. The Sacrament was never meant to convert men to God. Conversion is the coming of the vision to the soul, and it must always come through men in whom Christ lives. Once the work of conversion is done, and a man has seen and loved God in Christ, then through the Sacrament the vision can be constantly renewed, and its power strengthened, until the man no longer lives, but God lives in Him through Christ.[28] But the work of conversion comes first, and that is not the work of the Sacrament but of the prophet of God. No exaltation of

26 John 1.14.
27 Cf. Luke 24.35.
28 Cf. Gal. 2.20.

the Sacrament can do away with the vital necessity of inspired
men and women through whom the vision of the Suffering God
can shine into the souls of men whose minds are still in the
dark. The priest is not a substitute for the prophet. The prophet
sows the seed, and the priest feeds the tender plant that springs
up from it. Both are vitally necessary. Perhaps that is what our
Nonconformist brethren have to teach us.[29] They do realise
more than we do that men need real prophets, real preachers.
I hope when this business is over we shall each learn our lesson
from the other, and go out together in the power of the Suffering God, speaking a simple Gospel with tongues of flame,[30] and
bearing a simple Sacrament with hands that tremble for the
greatness of the precious thing they hold.

I think this mutilated body, and the thousand others like it,
have taught me more of the meaning of the Sacrament than all
the theology I ever read.[31] In the days of peace the Broken Body
and the Blood outpoured seemed to have so little to do with
ordinary things in life. But here, broken bodies and pools of
blood are the most ordinary things in life. So ghastly ordinary,
always bodies, broken battered bodies, and always blood. Is it
wrong to see in them His Body and His Blood – God's Body,
God's Blood? They are His; He is their Father, their Lover, and
His Heart must bleed in them. Surely it is the simple truth of
life and death. God suffers in man's suffering, and man, if he
be man, suffers with God, and the world is saved by the suffering of God in man. The Cross, the Sacrament, the battlefield,

29 The notion that various Churches can learn from one another, each
recalling an aspect of the mystery more distinctly than others, and that
through this process they progress towards the union for which Jesus prayed
is, today, a commonplace, often labelled 'receptive ecumenism'. However, in
1918 most Christian thinkers were happy to imagine that there was a single
true way and that others were afflicted with various degrees of confusion,
error or heresy. SK's approach here was very much ahead of its time.

30 Cf. Acts 2.3.

31 SK was rarely as explicit about the existential starting point of his theology.

there is the vision of God in them all – God with outstretched, bleeding, pleading, patient hands calling for volunteers. These are they who answered the call, who have drunk God's cup, and been baptized with His Baptism,[32] the dead who died for Right. These are men, and in them one sees the meaning of manhood.

To be a man means to be a thinking creature, filled with the spirit of suffering and creative love which made him. The Sacrament is the means by which we become filled with that spirit. It is the heart, the blood centre, of the great army of men who, having seen and loved God in Christ, are resolved to fight for and suffer with Him unto death and beyond it. It is the appointed means and method of meeting God. We are ready to have our bodies broken and our blood shed in the great Christian warfare against wrong, and we come for the refreshing of our spirits that we may not shrink. That bread is the ration of a fearless, fiercely fighting army. That wine is the stirrup-cup of a band of knights who ride out to an endless war. Salvation is not a matter of the future, but of the present.[33] Eternal life is here and now, and unless it is here and now, it cannot be hereafter. A famous soldier, speaking to troops on Whit-Sunday, said that he only wanted the soldier's virtues, and it would not matter to him if there were no Holy Spirit, so far had religion in his mind become divorced from life.[34] There is but one Holy Spirit, the Spirit of Christ, and that is the most perfect soldier spirit in the world, the spirit of Divine heroism.

---

32 Cf. Mark 10.38–40.

33 This approach to the Christian 'future' – that it is already present – is often today referred to as 'realized eschatology'; SK was probably the first theologian to adopt this approach in English.

34 The irony of this story is that Whit Sunday – the Sunday the fiftieth day after Easter Sunday and today more commonly referred to as Pentecost – is the day when Christians celebrate as a festival the giving of the Holy Spirit to the Church; this is a theme that has appeared on several occasions already in this chapter, as when SK referred to his hope that after the war Christian ministers would learn to speak with 'tongues of flame'. Efforts to identify this 'famous soldier' with any degree of certainty have not been successful.

God and the Sacrament

I wonder if you felt that dimly, Corporal.[35] I wonder if you really came because you wanted to do your duty even to death,[36] and wanted strength to do it. Did there flash into your mind the vision of heroic unselfishness, and did you love it, and come there to meet it? If you did, then no theology can make you wiser and no dogma clear your vision. You may have been a Wesleyan, a Baptist, a Unitarian,[37] but you ate the Body of the Lord and drank His precious Blood. You knew the truth. I wonder will your mother learn that truth through you. I wonder when she goes to bring her burden of sorrow before God, and kneels at the Altar rail, will she have strength to say:

Dear Lord, I hold my hand to take
    Thy body broken here for me;
Accept the sacrifice I make,
    My body broken there for Thee.

His was my body, borne of me,
    Borne of my bitter travail pain,
And it lies broken on the field,
    Swept by the wind and rain.

Surely a mother understands
    Thy thorn-crowned head,
The mystery of Thy pierced hands,
    The broken bread.[38]

---

35 SK now addressed the dead corporal directly. This was more than a literary device: the corporal had done his duty, united his sacrifice with that of Jesus, and so was now risen in Christ.

36 Cf. Matt. 26.38.

37 The sweep of SK's ecumenism is significant: many Anglicans at the time would not have considered Unitarians to be Christians.

38 This is SK's poem 'A Mother Understands', first printed in his *Rough Rhymes of a Padre* (London: Hodder & Stoughton, 1918).

Mothers and sons are learning the sternly simple truth of the Sacrament in a harder school than the Church, and from better masters than the priests. They know what it means, and we must learn from them and with them, or the nation will be more Christian than the Church. We must cut ourselves adrift from the entanglement of needlessly complicated theology that has grown up around us in the course of the years, and must return to the stern simplicity of the truth.

Corporal, I wish you could come back, take up again your broken body, and tell us what you know. You would be wiser than the wisest of us. Perhaps we could not understand you if you did. Perhaps we know all we need to know. God suffers and God conquers, and calls on us to suffer and to conquer with Him. By this simple act, which Christ bade us perform,[39] if it be done for love of Him, we can draw near to Him. He can speak to us and we to Him. He can fill us with His Spirit. That is all we want to know, that is all we want to do – do This in remembrance of Him[40] Who is our God.

"O God of love and sorrow, relieve us of this weight of pride and prejudice which drags us down, and keeps us from Thee and from one another.[41] We have degraded Thy Sacrament by pride of intellect and stubbornness of will, but by all these broken bodies, and by all this blood outpoured, bring our souls to Thy simplicity and the naked truth of Thee."

When this mad muddle is over and the days of peace return, there is a greater warfare still to wage. Still we must fight and still must suffer for the truth. God turn the Church from an

---

39 Cf. 1 Cor. 11.24–25; Luke 22.19.

40 Cf. 1 Cor. 11.24–25; Luke 22.19.

41 SK, having spoken directly to the dead corporal, then moved to a direct address to God in prayer. He prayed on behalf of all ministers/theologians who had 'degraded Thy Sacrament' by using the mystery of the Eucharist to reinforce divisions, or had made it alien to Christians by their theological complexities.

ambulance[42] into an army, and make it really militant on earth. Let us give up quarrelling with one another about the non-essentials, and leaving men large freedom about dogma and ritual, let us get to the real war with evil, and go in to win. Let us cease to dream of uniformity and strive for unity. One thing only matters. Do we love God? Do we love the suffering God, and do we want to suffer with Him? Do we find Him in the Sacrament? Ritual does not matter; the manner of the Presence does not matter; the validity of orders does not really matter.[43] They are not essentials. Nothing really matters but the love of God in Christ. That we must have. In all these non-essential matters let each Church be free to follow its custom and its bent, but let us endeavour to keep the unity of the spirit, the splendid spirit which is the only bond of peace.[44]

*   *   *   *   *

---

42 By 'ambulance' SK was not thinking of a vehicle that transports a casualty to a hospital, but using it in the technical sense used by the army in 1917: the 'field ambulance' was a medical unit manned by the Royal Army Medical Corps. Each ambulance would in theory be able to deal with 150 casualties at any one time, through a series of posts along the evacuation chain, starting around 600 yards behind the regimental aid posts.

43 This was not a random list but identified the major sources of division and bitterness within the Church of England and between it and other Churches over the Eucharist to which they all paid lip service as 'the sacrament of unity'. The place and nature of 'ritual' – such as what vestments should be worn by clergy or what liturgical practices to be found in the Catholic Missal should be practised in Anglican churches – was a major source of conflict within the Church of England. Every Church argued about how to explain the 'presence' of Jesus either in the bread or in the community (e.g. was it by 'transubstantiation' or 'consubstantiation'?), and SK's reference to 'the validity of orders' recalls that in 1896 the Roman Catholic Church had issued a formal statement that Anglican priests were not really priests; that is, 'their orders were not valid', hence their celebrations of the Eucharist were only a sham. In this single sentence SK was declaring that the entire edifice of bitter and vigorous controversy was a waste of time.

44 Cf. Eph. 4.3.

Good-bye, Corporal. I'll write to mother for you. Thank you for dying for me, and teaching me so much. I will try to carry it out. The Church will, too. She is learning from the men that die. She will be more simple in the future. Christ is greater than the Church, and He can use her still, and through her revival He can save the world.

VIII

God and the Church

WANDERING in the Ypres salient about dawn on June 9th, 1917, I came across the body of a British soldier. He was still kneeling up on one knee in a shell hole, grasping his rifle, with his face turned to wards the Green Line which two days before had cost our battalion many lives to win.[1] His forehead was pierced with a bullet which had evidently killed him instantly. His identity disc bore the name of Pte. Peter——[2]

*   *   *   *   *

Poor old Private Peter. Damn this war. I must get to work and bury him. Good thing I brought the shovel. I thought I'd find some one. Here's his pay book[3] and a photo of his wife and kids.

---

1 The context makes it clear that SK was in the southern part of 'the Salient' in the land just captured in the assault on Messines Ridge (see chapter 1), and it is just after that battle. The 'Green Line' was one of the objectives the troops had to reach, and was called this because it was originally drawn with a green pen on a map. That this soldier was facing that line meant that he was killed facing the enemy.

2 Military identity tags, usually made of metal or compressed fibre, were discs designed to be worn at all times and to record an individual's identity. The British Army introduced them in 1907. They were produced within each unit and stamped with key information: typically service number, surname and initials, regiment and sometimes battalion and rank. Religion was also indicated. Chaplains were very often responsible for gathering and burying human remains, and then notifying families of their loss; in this task the identity tags were invaluable.

3 The soldiers' pay-book was a logbook of personal details, ranks, awards,

To bury the dead.
*One of the chaplain's duties was to lead the prayers for the dead – we hear
Studdert Kennedy refer to it often – and to try to record where burials took
place. This official postcard shows a chaplain tending a grave with a shovel to
the left. 'To bury the dead' was seen as the final Christian duty owed by one
Christian to a brother or sister. Studdert Kennedy added such a shovel to his kit
so that he could bury the bodies of men he encountered on the battlefield.*

Four of 'em. I must write to her. He couldn't have died better,
anyhow. Evidently rose to advance and got it clean through the
head. It's a fine fighting face; no saint, but a fine man. A gentle-
man in his own way, as every British Tommy is.[4] If faces go for
much he was no saint. Heavy fighting jaw; thick sensual lips;
deep lines round the eyes and mouth. They all tell the same
tale. This was man Peter – fine man, Peter, but no Saint Peter. I

---

charges, sickness, pay, next of kin and the bearer's Will. It was to be carried
at all times.

4 'Tommy' – or 'Tommy Atkins' or 'Thomas Atkins' – were colloquial collective nicknames for every British soldier. Usage dates from the middle of
the eighteenth century, though the precise origin is disputed. It is particularly
associated with the First World War – hence the marking of the death of the
'last Tommy', Harry Patch, in 2009.

should not think he was a pillar of the Church.[5] Not the sort of stuff we build them of. Yet, I don't know.

I wonder what sort of a man Saint Peter was before he met Christ. He could curse and swear; we know that. He evidently went back to the old days on the lake of Galilee when that maidservant tripped him up.[6] He was married,[7] and knew a man's passion. He had a nickname, too; that always means a lot. Christ called him "Rocky,"[8] as soon as He saw him almost. It must have been a joke on his appearance. He wasn't much like a rock really. You never knew quite where you had him; he was swearing fidelity one minute, and denying it the next.[9] Now ready to die for Christ in the garden,[10] a sword in his hand and battle in his eyes;[11] now creeping away into a corner, afraid of jeers and jokes and the chaff of a silly girl.[12] Half a hero, half a sheep. He brings joy to the eyes of Jesus by a splendid confession of faith,[13] and the next moment makes those same eyes flash fire by crass misunderstanding.[14] Blessed art Thou Simon, Bar-Jonah . . .[15] Get thee behind me, Satan.[16] Heaven and hell, God and the devil, rolled in one and forever at war. That was Saint Peter. That was Private Peter too. You can see the traces of the struggle written deep into his face.

------

5 The image of a regular churchgoer as 'a pillar of the church' is proverbial, but SK would have known that the image is derived from Gal. 2.9.

6 Cf. Matt. 26.69–71.

7 Cf. Matt. 8.14.

8 Cf. Matt. 16.18.

9 Cf. Matt. 26.33–35, 70, 72, 74.

10 Cf. Matt. 26.35.

11 Cf. Matt. 26.51, read in conjunction with John 18.10.

12 Cf. Matt. 26.75.

13 Cf. Matt. 16.16.

14 Cf. Matt. 16.22.

15 Cf. Matt. 16.17.

16 Cf. Matt. 16.23.

The Hardest Part

Why shouldn't Private Peter be a stone in the foundation of the Church?[17] Why did Christ choose Saint Peter for one? Of course the great promise was partly a joke.[18] I am sure it was said with a smile. The play upon the name is full of that splendid humour which is made up of love and faith in human greatness and sorrow for its faults. It was a joke, but it was more. Why did He choose Peter? Was it because he was an exceptional man? Was he the greatest and the strongest of that little band? I doubt it. There's not much sign of it that I can see. One can't help loving Saint Peter; he was so human, so weak, so strong, so great, and so small. He was just a splendid specimen of the average man, the incarnate paradox of God. That's why he was chosen, I believe. Not because he was exceptional, but because he was good average. Found an empire on a strong man's strength, and it will die when the strong man dies; found an empire on a weak man's faith, and it will last forever.

The secret of victory lies in the spirit of the rank and file. The Kingdom of God is within you.[19] Christ knew that; He was the leader of men. Peter was a splendid specimen of the rank and file, and when he grasped the truth and sprang to it, Christ cheered, because He knew the job was done. Christ in the soul of the average man is the rock foundation of the Church. St. John and St. Paul were exceptional men. They build the towers and the turrets of the Church, but the foundation is laid in the heart of St. Peter, the private in the Army of the Cross. That is why the history of the Church is so like the history of an ordinary man. It is full of splendid deeds and sordid crimes; full of glorious aspirations and silly sinful futile failures. An infallible Church is as hard to conceive as an infallible man.[20] It simply couldn't happen.

---

17 Cf. Matt. 16.18.

18 Cf. Matt. 16.18.

19 Cf. Luke 17.21.

20 This is an allusion to the Roman Catholic doctrine of the infallibility of the pope that had been made an article of faith – something Catholics had

Look at the life of the average man with the eyes of love, and you can see God. You cannot see God Almighty Whose will works out perfection without a struggle or a hitch. You cannot see that even in the saint. But in the saint and in the average man you can see God in an agony of creative effort, God cruci- fied, but conquering, Christ.

Look at the history of the Christian Church, and you see the same vision. The Church is the broken, battered, bleeding, but deathless body of the suffering God revealed in Christ. How often have men cried out that the Church was dead, that the body was putrified, corrupt in every part, stinking of avarice and deceit, eaten up by the worms of political intrigue, torn by factious pride and petty personal ambition, a useless carcase, only fit for burial in the grave of a disreputable past. How often has the cry seemed to be justified by facts. Yet the Church does not die, it turns in its death-sleep like its Master in the tomb, and rises again, still bearing in its hands and feet the signs of suffering, but alive with a deathless life. Church history makes the Christian now bow his head in shame, now lift it up in pride; but once he sees its story not as the history of a Society or even of the Society, but as the history of his God at war with evil, the very shame that stains its annals makes him love it all the more. The Church is a failure. Men keep shouting that out. Of course it is. All great things are failures; only little things succeed. The Church fails as God fails, as Christ failed upon the Cross, and it succeeds with His success, the success of the Crucified. When most the Church is beaten, when her standards are mocked, despised, and trampled under foot, when she is harassed most

---

to believe or face expulsion from the Church – in 1870 and which was used by Catholics from that time until the mid-twentieth century as an argument that their Church was infallible, the only true Church and uniquely under divine protection. Already in chapter 5, SK had linked such notions of an interventionist God to dated ideas like the divine right of kings: 'the divine right of kings is an idea as foreign to the British soldier's mind as the infalli- bility of the Pope'.

by spies and traitors from within and enemies without,[21] then is her appeal for loyalty most strong and her real power appears.

Her real power appears, and shows itself to be the appeal of the suffering God revealed in Christ to the heart of the average man.

But this vision of God is obscured by that other vision which we set up beside it, the vision of the regnant God upon a throne, calm, serene, and passionless, ruling the world with a wave of the hand. How can men see that God in the Church? How can you expect men to look at the wounded, crippled, crucified Church as she is at present, and as she has been in the past, torn by a thousand factions, cut into a thousand silly sects, bound hand and foot and hanging helpless on the cross of a world-wide war, with her voice drowned by the roar of guns and the groans of dying men how can they look at her and see God Almighty? The ordinary man has this vision of the Almighty God and looks for it in the Church. Can you wonder that he is at once puzzled and disappointed? Is it not St. Peter over again? He had it of course. He got it from the Old Testament; that was why he was puzzled to death when Christ told him that the Son of God must be mocked and spit on, tortured and killed.[22] He could not understand the suffering God; he shrank from that terrible truth. "This be far from Thee, Lord," he cried,[23] and Christ recognised the enemy, and hissed out "Satan" at him.[24] It was the ancient enemy.[25] Men will make God an earthly king. The

---

21 In the situation in which SK wrote, there was a constant watch for spies and traitors, who would gather information for the enemy or go over to them with it. Indeed, in 1917 the hunt for spies, especially in France, amounted to paranoia; *the* sensational court case of 1917 had been that of the (Dutch) *femme fatale* 'Mata Hari' (Margreet MacLeod), who was executed by the French as a spy on 15 October 1917.

22 Cf. Matt. 16.21; read in conjunction with Matt. 27.29–30, and a preliminary to the crucifixion.

23 Cf. Matt. 16.22.

24 Cf. Matt. 16.23.

25 Cf. Gen. 3.15.

natural man cannot see the King upon the Cross. Peter found that the hardest of all lessons to learn, and men have shared his feelings ever since. St. Peter did learn it. He learnt it through tears, and terror, and fires of shame that were not quenched. That made him the rock indeed at last.

I don't think Private Peter learnt it. I think he died without seeing it – died without seeing it after two thousand years of Christ. Why? Whose fault was it? Was it his own? Well, partly for sure. I know men too well to be humbugged by the sickly sentimental "John Bull" idea of the perfect hero touch. I think he failed to be a pillar of the Church partly because he was a pillar of the "Pig and Whistle." But was it all his fault? I don't think so. It was partly my fault, and the fault of those like me whom Christ sent out to teach him. We did not teach him right. We did not give him the true vision of God; we had not got it ourselves. We, too, feared to face the facts, and to look upon the face of the suffering God. We sentimentalised the Cross, the greatest fact of all. We dared to glorify Christ with our earthly glory, which is a heavenly shame.[26] We were Satan to a million Peters, because we thought the thoughts of earth and failed to speak the speech of heaven.

Private Peter would have told you that he believed in a Supreme Being. This Being ordered the details of men's lives and arranged the hour of their deaths. He managed everything, and everything that happened was His will. That was the faith that Peter, on being taxed with it, would probably have professed. But it did not interest him or make any difference to him. In truth he did not really believe it in any living sense. It was not his own faith; it was borrowed. Dimly, I believe, he felt that it was absurd in the face of facts. This Supreme Being (which is the plain man's name for "The Unknown God"[27]) was a puzzle which he could not solve. He was there, of course, but He could neither know nor love Him, His ways of working were so weird.

---

26 SK may have had in mind the imagery of Gal. 6.14 and Heb. 6.6; 12.12.
27 Cf. Acts 17.23.

He looked at the mangled body of a pal, muttered "I dunno," lit his fag, took up his rifle, and went out to die, because it was up to him and probably died without the vision of God.

That's a pretty ghastly thought. Peter,[28] old chap, I'm sorry. I'm awful sorry,[29] it was my fault. I should have told you more. We chaps who wear our collars wrong way round as a queer kind of sign that we preach Christ, we should have reached you, and we didn't. We're sorry, and it makes us sick. We're sorry, not only because we love you, but because we love the Church. It's a bad thing when the Church fails to produce great saints, but it is a worse thing when she fails to find the heart of the average man. That she should have no towers or turrets to catch the dawn light of the higher truth is a bad thing, but that she should be shaky in her foundations is a worse one, and her foundations ought to be in your heart and in the heart of those like you.

That's our trouble, Peter, my son; that's our trouble. We are missing the average man. Here I am, digging your grave; it's all I can do, but I wish I could have done more. I'll have to drag you to it, old chap; it's beastly, but I must. I can't lift you up. The dead weigh heavy on the hand, and on the heart. Poor woman, and poor kiddies! When I've finished filling in I'll get a couple of sticks and put up a bit of a cross for you. I don't think you knew what it meant in life, but you have probably found out through death. There, that's finished.

Now for the cross. Lord, I hope they're not going to start shelling. I'm going to put this cross up, anyhow. Here are two bits of wood; I've got some string somewhere, I know. That's the way. The Tree.[30] The Cross of Christ. You did not know it, but

---

28 As in the previous chapter, SK addressed the dead man as one who was still alive in Christ.

29 SK was noted for speaking with an Irish accent and here was one of the places we hear it: 'I'm awful [rather than 'awfully'] sorry' is an Hibernicism.

30 The identification of the cross with a tree is a complex theme in Christian history, first found in Acts 10.39. It draws on the notion of the cross having become the new 'tree of life' (cf. Gen. 2.9) for humanity.

you died for the cause of Christ, in defence of that civilisation[31] which He has slowly and painfully built up in the western world. It's not much of a cross, I'm afraid, but it is more like His, and so more really beautiful, than the gold and jewelled ornaments that glitter on our altars at home. This rough cross, and the million others like it, will be a challenge to the world and to the Church of Christ, calling them out to war for Him. I'll do my best, Peter; I swear by this cross I will. I'll go and tell the other Peters about the suffering God, and how He is crucified afresh every day, and how He needs men like you to come out and share His sorrow and help to save the world. Perhaps they won't fight any better when they know; I don't see how they could; but they will know that they are suffering with God, and will feel that He is near. That's a great thing. I know it is. I've felt it. Men like you must worship Him when they see Him; He would appeal to all that's best in you. Only, you must get the vision. It won't be done by preaching half so much as living, and yet there must be both. Peter, my lad, living is a durned difficult business, much harder than dying. I think I could die for Christ, but living for Him is a struggle. But I will try to live as the servant of the gallant God Who suffers always and is never overcome. I've got to do some of the preaching too. I'm not fit to preach; but who is? That's the awful business. Preaching is so much mixed up with living. How can one put the vision into words?

There is so much barbed wire entanglement to get through before I can hope to get the message to the men I want to reach. The Church herself has done a lot of wiring in her war of the ages,[32] and now she must tear it down. At the beginning the Church beat the world by suffering; later, the world beat the

---

31 It was a commonplace in British political discourse to say that the war was 'being fought in defence of civilization'.

32 The imagery is that of 'No Man's Land' – the area between the opposing front-line trenches – where each side engaged in 'wiring': putting up ever deeper belts of barbed wire so as to impede, entangle and stop anyone who tried to walk or crawl through it.

Church by compromise. The Church borrowed the world's weapons and the world's ideals. She took the sword, and very nearly perished by it.[33] The glory of the world's great kings obscured the glory of the Christ. Men would have no king but Caesar,[34] and the Church, because she feared the world, was feign to Caesarise the Christ. The vision of God which she presented to the world grew dim and distorted. The ordinary man was puzzled. The Almighty Caesar God seated on His throne alternated with the suffering figure on the Cross,[35] and the Peters of the world did not know which was the true God. Later on, the worship of the Bible made it worse. The partial truth of the Old Testament obscured the final truth of the New, because Peter was taught to think of them as equally true. The Bible was an idol, and obscured the truth of Christ which it was written to reveal. The figure of Christ Himself was distorted, and His life on earth misinterpreted in order to reconcile the two visions of God. The glorious rebellion of Christ against evil, the fierce and lifelong war which found its culmination on the Cross, has been distorted into passive submission to the mysterious, and apparently immoral, will of the unknown Caesar God Who planned that men should torture, mock, and crucify the Christ. The foulest, filthiest crime in the world's history has been held up as God's plan, God's chosen method of saving the world, the finest fruit of His absolute omnipotence. Led by this false vision the Church played the world's game. Christianity, which was meant to turn the world upside down, became a means of keeping it wrong way up. Great Christians ceased to be rebels and became policemen – constables of Almighty God.

---

33 Cf. Matt. 26.52.

34 Cf. John 19.15.

35 SK seems to have in mind the great images of the Christ seated on majesty as Pantocrator that are often found painted on the walls, domes and ceilings of church buildings.

Submission to the world order became a Christian virtue, and took the place of that tremendous Christian aspiration which should have smashed the world order into pieces. The Church fought against demands for social justice, and the abolition of social evils. She became other-worldly in the wrong way, and taught men the lesson of indifference not only to sorrow, but to injustice, oppression, and cruelty.

Her rulers allied themselves with the strong against the weak, and devoted their energies to keeping the people quiet. They taught contentment as the chiefest of all virtues. Blessed are they that neither hunger nor thirst after righteousness, for they shall be called respectable.[36] Blessed are the poor in pocket, for they shall be patronised by the rich. Blessed are they who do not mourn for the wrong in the world, for they shall need no comfort. Blessed are they that expect nothing, for they shall not be disappointed. Christianity became static instead of dynamic, because it taught men to worship a passive and submissive Christ, bowing to the will of an incomprehensible God.

---

36 SK assumed that his readers knew 'the beatitudes' (Matt. 5.3–11) almost by heart and so could appreciate this parody:

Matthew 5.3–11	*The Hardest Part*
Blessed are they which do hunger and thirst after righteousness: for they shall be filled. (v. 6)	Blessed are they that neither hunger nor thirst after righteousness, for they shall be called respectable.
Blessed are the poor in spirit: for theirs is the kingdom of heaven. (v. 3)	Blessed are the poor in pocket, for they shall be patronised by the rich.
Blessed are they that mourn: for they shall be comforted. (v. 4)	Blessed are they who do not mourn for the wrong in the world, for they shall need no comfort.
SK was probably thinking of one like: Blessed are the pure in heart: for they shall see God. (v. 8)	Blessed are they that expect nothing, for they shall not be disappointed.

Neither the submissive Christ nor the tyrant God has any appeal to what is best in Peter the average man; they leave him cold. The sporting instinct, the love of fair play, the hatred of injustice, the fine combative instinct, which make up the character of Peter, have remained untouched by this staggering, broken-spirited, submissive figure on the Cross, Who, in the words of a popular mission hymn, "died of a broken heart,"[37] and these same splendid instincts have been actually raised to bitter antagonism by vision of the tyrant God.

So Peter has left the Church, and found what his soul needed in his union, his club, his cause – the cause of the down-trodden and oppressed. This has taken place, and is taking place, not only in England, but in every country in the world. Everywhere the followers of Christ are found outside the Church. The Church of Christ has ceased in these days to be the pillar of cloud and fire[38] which leads the pilgrim Peter along the way of social righteousness, and has become a weak and inefficient ambulance brigade which picks up the wreck and ruin of a cruel and mechanical civilisation. That's all I am, Peter, an informal and incompetent undertaker, with tears in my eyes and sorrow in my heart, and I'm very like the Church I represent. We dig men's graves when we ought to save their souls, because we have, and give to others, a distorted vision of God.

But that is not the whole truth, Peter. There is another side. Christ has used the Church, and spoken through her in spite of her stupidity and sin. Some of your comrades found the truth in her, and loved her. To some she brought the strength to suffer and to fight for right. Crippled, tortured, crucified as she is, she has the root of the matter in her. Christ still uses her.

---

37 SK seems to have had in mind the early twentieth-century hymn by Thomas Dennis, 'Have you read the story of the cross', which used the notion of the death of Jesus as being a substitute for human sins appeasing the divine desire to punish creatures.

38 Cf. Exod. 13.21.

And believe me, Peter, she is going to do better. She knows her weakness, and that means much; she knows she has betrayed her Lord, but at any rate in this war she has gone out to weep bitterly.[39]

And let me whisper this, lad: she loves you, she really loves you, she is not the Church of a class any longer at heart. She means to reform. She is not going to read your comrades impossible stories out of the Old Testament on Sundays.[40] She is going to reform her money matters, which have been a scandal.[41] The bishops are very uncomfortable in their palaces. The Prayer Book is going to be revised.[42] The parson is going to stop being God Almighty in a little narrow world and become brother-man. Please, Peter, poor old dead Peter, the man with his collar wrong way round is very sorry, and is going to do better, and show your comrades Christ, the suffering, conquering Christ, Who calls us out to the glorious war with evil that is

---

39 Cf. Matt. 26.75.

40 This is an aspect of the liturgical renewal – the reform of the lectionary – that SK had already mentioned in chapter 4.

41 This is a reference to the growing problem of great differences between the value of different 'livings' – the annual income of parish incumbents (rectors and vicars) – and the related crisis of clergy poverty, especially among incumbents with poor livings and curates who were paid by their incumbent. Many wartime church newspapers carried appeals for funds in support of poverty-stricken clergy.

42 By the time of the First World War, many of those involved in the specialist study of liturgy were aware that most of the liturgical books produced in the sixteenth century, such as the BCP, despite attracting fierce loyalty were not actually fit for their intended purpose. Consequently there was a movement for 'the reform of the prayer book', which would present a new format to the House of Commons in 1927 (when it was rejected). SK and many other chaplains aligned themselves with this movement, which would lead to revisions to the BCP across the Anglican Communion and, decades later, within the Church of England itself. For the context of SK's position, see R. C. D. Jasper, *Prayer Book Revision in England 1800–1900* (London: SPCK, 1954).

not fought with guns – calls us to enlist in the ever-fighting army of the suffering God.

* * * * *

There, that will do. It's a poor show of a cross, but you know what is meant. I hope old Boche won't knock it down before we get a stronger one. "O Christ my God, my only God, Eternal Spirit of strong love, give unto Thy Church a fuller measure of Thy Spirit, that for the sake of such as these she may sanctify herself."

Good-bye, Peter, old chap; I'll write to the missus, and I'm going to follow Christ.[43]

---

43 This final comment was both a word of farewell and a statement of SK's own theology of discipleship: one encounters each moment with its reality as part of a greater movement – the pilgrimage of following which SK rejoined once he had finished this particular task of burying Peter.

IX

God and the Life Eternal

On *the last Sunday in June 1917*[1] *the Advanced Dressing Station in which I was working was blown in, and every one in it killed except the doctor, two stretcher cases, an R.A.M.C. sergeant,*[2] *and myself. Among those killed was Roy Fergusson, my servant,*[3] *a splendid lad of nineteen years, with whom I was great friends.*[4] *He went out after the first shell had broken the end off the station to guide some walking wounded to a place of safety and was killed instantly. I found him*

---

1 24 June 1917. Although the 'battle' of Messines Ridge was officially over, there was constant shelling in the area around Ieper and consequently there was continual 'wastage' as men were killed and wounded. It was the constant attrition – particularly in vulnerable places like 'the Salient' around Ypres – of men being killed without it being part of a battle that led Erich Maria Remarque to name his novel *All Quiet on the Western Front.*

2 RAMC = The Royal Army Medical Corps, a specialist corps of the British Army founded in 1898. Under the Geneva convention it was and is a non-combatant unit, and members of the RAMC may only use their weapons in self-defence. As such, many members of the Society of Friends (Quakers) and also some clergy of various Churches enlisted in the RAMC during the First World War.

3 Every officer – and chaplains ranked as officers – had a servant, sometimes referred to as his 'batman'. This chapter is the only one with any reference to SK's servant. Many other chaplains' diaries are similarly silent about their servants, which may suggest that their existence was thought unremarkable.

4 Private Duncan Roy Fergusson, aged 19, 49893, 1st Battalion, Royal Fusiliers, now has no known grave and is commemorated on the Menin Gate, and these details are recorded in the Book of Remembrance there: 'Son of Martha Fergusson of 23 Milton St, Barrow-in-Furness, and the late William Fergusson.'

The crater in Railway Dugouts Cemetery today.
This cemetery, maintained by the Commonwealth War Graves Commission, is located just south of Ieper (Ypres) between a farm and the railway line. One can still visit the very place that Studdert Kennedy mentions in the text. These references to exact locations in The Hardest Part *are more than touches of local colour. They are to convey to the reader that theology must be based in the actual experiences of human existence moment by moment – and for Studdert Kennedy this approach was a consequence of his central belief that God had entered human history in the life of an individual, Jesus, who lived, suffered, died and was buried.*

leaning against a heap of sandbags, his head buried in his hands, and a great hole in his back.

*　*　*　*　*

Poor old Roy. I thought I had saved his life when I sent him on that job. There seemed a decent chance of getting through, and it looked a dead certainty that we should all be killed within a few minutes. There must have been a chance. All the walking wounded apparently got through, and he alone was killed. He probably warned them and took it himself. It would be like him. He looks as if he were saying his prayers. I must get the body carried across to the cemetery near Railway Dugouts, and bury it at once.[5] It will probably be unburied again before the morning if they start shelling again. That cemetery is an awful sight, with half its dead unburied; but it is the only place. I must give the body Christian burial somewhere, even if it is blown up again. His mother will surely want to know where he rests. Mothers always want to know that first. I wonder why. Do they think that this same broken body will break the earth above its grave and rise again to become once more the temple of the spirit[6] that has passed on? Do they think that it matters in the resurrection where the body lies, or is it just a natural longing, an echo of Mary's exceeding bitter cry beside the empty tomb, "They have taken away my Lord, and I know not where they have laid Him."[7]

The first Easter Day should have hushed that cry forever and turned its sorrow into joy,[8] but it has not done so for many who love and follow Christ. Still men and women seem to seek the living midst the dead,[9] and to think of their dead as lying in their graves. They always want to know where the dead are buried. It may be natural sentiment, or it may be false religion. Anyway, that's not my business now. Sentiment or religion, the desire is there, and I must do my best to satisfy it. A Padre out here has got to be an amateur undertaker. So ghastly amateur, that is the worst of it. We cannot hope to bury half the dead. Many a mother's aching heart must go uncomforted because we know not where we have laid him. No one knows. Some are

---

5 This cemetery is just south-east of Ieper and is now cared for by the Commonwealth War Graves Commission. The special monuments in this cemetery, and the fact that Roy Fergusson has no known grave, bear out what SK wrote here about the dead there being 'unburied' and 'blown up again'.

6 Cf. 1 Cor. 6.19.

7 John 20.13.

8 Cf. John 16.20.

9 Luke 24.5.

not buried, because there is nothing to bury but scraps of flesh
and clothing. Some are buried, and then blown to pieces out of
their graves. There is an enormous crater in the middle of the
cemetery, and the bodies are not; that's all that can be said. But
where Christian burial can be given, it must be given, if only for
pity's sake.

I say, you chaps, this lad was my servant. Could you help
me across with him to the cemetery. You'll have to lift him very
carefully, he's so badly shattered. That's the way. Now we'll
carry him across and have the service while the lull is on. There
is a grave ready. Would you mind staying while I say the service
over him?[10]

* * * * *

No, you need not stay to fill in, boys. I'll do that.[11] Thank ye
very much. It only saddens them, and what's the use? I wonder
why Christian men and women still think of their dead as lying
in their graves. I suppose the Church is partly responsible.

The burial service, with all its wonderful beauty, is very hard
to understand. It is difficult to gather from it what the Church
does believe about the future of the body it lays in the grave. It
consigns it to the earth as ashes to ashes and dust to dust, and
then speaks of the resurrection in which Christ shall change our
poor bodies that they may be like unto His glorious body.[12] It

---

10 SK had a keen interest in the role of liturgy within the Christian life,
and this meant that he viewed this action of burying Roy's body as an action
of the community of the Church – hence his request that these soldiers stay
there and form such a community for the couple of minutes that the service
took.

11 The service was then over and the soldiers had stayed with SK. For the
next task, SK carried on alone, filling in the grave with his shovel.

12 SK was echoing the minister's statement from the BCP that was said
while the grave was filled in with earth:

we . . . commit his body to the ground; earth to earth, ashes to ashes, dust
to dust; in sure and certain hope of the resurrection to eternal life, through

seems to mean that this same body will some day break the earth that covers it, and rise to life again. Our hymns contain the same idea:

> For a while the tired body
> > Lies with feet toward the morn.
> Till that last and greatest Easter
> > Day be born.[13]

And that astounding verse:

> Days and moments quickly flying,
> > Blend the living with the dead;
> Soon will you and I be lying
> > each within his narrow bed.[14]

It is poor poetry, and I cannot help feeling that it contains really false teaching. Neither you nor I nor any one else will ever lie in any narrow bed. Our bodies will for a time, and will then rot, and, decomposing, will become part of the earth. It is, I take it, dead certain that this sad wilderness of war will one day be clothed with a festive robe of living green,[15] decked with daisies, and that the life that weaves this robe will spring from the bodies of our British dead. They will give life to the dying seed, and

---

our Lord Jesus Christ; who shall change our vile body, that it might be like unto his glorious body, according to the mighty working, whereby he is able to subdue all things to himself.

13 This is the third stanza of Sabine Baring-Gould's (1834–1924) hymn 'On the resurrection morning', published in 1866. The full first verse of the opening stanza explains why it came to SK in this context: 'on the resurrection morning soul and body meet again'.

14 This is the opening stanza of a hymn by Edward Caswell (1814–78). He became a Roman Catholic in 1849 and this hymn was published in his 1858 collection *Masque of Mary, and other Poems*.

15 SK seems to have in mind 'the best robe' of Luke 15.22.

produce the fields of golden grain[16] from which the new France will gain its strength.[17] This will be the resurrection of these bodies buried here.

We cannot now believe that there will ever come a time when these same bodies will burst their graves and rise from broken trenches and from shell holes, living men.[18] If men ever believed it, we cannot believe it now. In face of facts out here the attempt to believe it can only lead to bewilderment. What a picture it would be! – when the dead who followed Napoleon stand up with those who followed Joffre; when the French who cursed the British with their last breath stand up with these brave Poilus[19] who blessed us as they died – the last roll-call when all shall answer, Present, and friend stand side by side with foe. What a picture for a poet or a painter! but it is only an imaginary picture; nothing more. It could never be a fact. I don't suppose that any one who thinks and faces facts believes it now, yet, on the surface at any rate, much of our Church teaching seems to contemplate it. The creed in the Baptism Service contains "The resurrection of the flesh."[20] It is a great question which St.

---

16 The imagery draws upon 1 Cor. 15.37–38.

17 SK was actually a few kilometres inside Belgium at this point!

18 SK took issue with a very common reading of the notion of 'the resurrection of the body' – a phrase used in the creed – that looked to such biblical verses as 1 Cor. 15.22. The power of this image was not only its literal simplicity but its visual effect in a long tradition of Christian iconography that showed resuscitated bodies leaving their tombs on the Last Day. Hence the common understanding that bodies were simply waiting there until that time. SK's subsequent references to 'pictures' show that he was thinking of this iconographic tradition.

19 The colloquial name French soldiers gave to themselves, the equivalent in the French army of 'Tommy'.

20 This is a variant translation of 'the resurrection of the body' mentioned in an earlier note, when the underlying Latin text – the Apostles' Creed – was presented to those at the baptism in the BCP in the form of questions: 'And dost thou believe in the Holy Ghost; the holy Catholic Church; the communion of saints; the remission of sins; the resurrection of the flesh; and the life everlasting after death?'

Paul's objector asks, and is called a fool for asking, "How are the dead raised up, and with what body do they come?"[21] St. Paul's answer is by no means clear. It is glorious in its conviction that the spirits of those who die in Christ survive death, and are clothed by God with a body; but as to the nature of that body and its connection with the flesh that is buried, it is distinctly vague.

The first part of the answer is quite intelligible and satisfactory. The resurrection body is related to the fleshly body as a flower to its seed, *i.e.* it is the same body only in the sense that it is the clothing of the same life.[22] In appearance and in actual composition, I suppose it is entirely different. That is quite clear and helpful. He goes farther, and definitely states that the two bodies must of necessity be different. "Flesh and blood cannot inherit the Kingdom of God; neither doth corruption inherit incorruption."[23] That is exactly what we feel in the present day. Then a sense of difficulty seems to come over his mind, and he cries, "Behold I show you a mystery,"[24] and there breaks upon us once again something very like the gloriously impossible picture. There is the blare of the trumpet, the whole air quivers with expectation, the graves slowly yawn, and the dead are raised[25] – all the countless millions who have stood on earth and looked upon the sun. It is a wonderful passage, and has gripped the imagination of men for nearly two thousand years. But what does it mean? It seems to contradict the other more reasonable statement. Corruption puts on incorruption, and mortal puts on immortality, and the dead are raised incorruptible.[26] What does it mean? Is it poetry or prose? Is it emotional allegory or literal statement of fact?

---

21 1 Cor. 15.35–36.
22 1 Cor. 15.37–44.
23 1 Cor. 15.50.
24 1 Cor. 15.51.
25 1 Cor. 15.52.
26 1 Cor. 15.53.

The Hardest Part

I feel sure it is the usual outburst of splendid spiritual emotion which sooner or later always bursts through the bounds of the Pauline arguments, and shattering all syllogisms, breaks into a song of certainty which soars above reason into fields of faith.[27] These outbursts are what make the Pauline Epistles immortal, and men will thrill to their music when the arguments of Paul the learned Pharisee[28] leave them unconvinced and cold.

St. Paul's answer seems to mean that there are more things in heaven and earth than are dreamed of in the very narrow philosophy[29] of the man who refuses to believe in the resurrection because of the difficulty of the visible decomposition of the flesh.[30] "Leave it to God," he says in effect; "leave it to God Who raised up Christ." Who raised up Christ – that is the one root-fact which inspires this chapter. Christ was dead and is alive again. That is the one vivid certainty which shatters all doubts for St. Paul. He has no real theory of the resurrection body to give us, and no real answer to the question "How are the dead raised up, and with what body do they come?"[31] He has only a vivid intuitive conviction that, as Christ conquered death and rose again, so the man who lives in Christ and in whom Christ lives can conquer death, and live on hereafter with a full embodied life,[32] and not in any shadowy kind of existence which the heathen as a rule believed to be the state of the dead.[33]

---

27 SK here identified Paul's religious vision with his own: in neither case, SK argued, could the religious insight be caught in prose. Prose and systematics were but an attempt *post factum* to explicate the intuitive certainty. As the chapter progresses, this aspect of SK's thinking will come more to the fore and be given more explicit attention.

28 Cf. Phil. 3.5.

29 An allusion to Hamlet's comment to Horatio in *Hamlet*, Act 1, scene 5.

30 SK returned to 1 Cor. 15.35.

31 1 Cor. 15.35.

32 Cf. 1 Thess. 4.14.

33 SK was thinking of classical images of Hades.

That seems to be the real point of the great funeral chapter.[34] It all turns and hinges on the fact of Easter Day.[35] There is in all the letters of St. Paul a continual confusion between physical and spiritual death, and it is very hard at times to tell which he means.[36] I suppose the reason of that confusion is that, to him, there is only one kind of death worth bothering about, and that is spiritual death, which is the climax and final result of sin. Physical death was only death to him when it was the material expression of this spiritual death. That, I think, is the great truth. I have seen physical death which was real death, the last and bitterest enemy of man.[37] That death was defeat, defeat and disaster: a broken, peevish, sordid spirit reluctantly hounded out of a body which it had weakened by disease and defiled by misuse. That is real death, the saddest and most repulsive thing on earth. From such a death may God deliver me and all I love.[38] But that death and this boy's splendid exit are two quite different things. There is something triumphant about this. It has no connection with disease or decay. A young spirit quivering with life and energy has, in an act of supreme sacrifice, thrown off its earthly raiment and leaped glad and naked into another world

---

34 That is, 1 Cor. 15.20–58, which is set out as the Lesson in the Burial Service in the BCP. This reading was one of those pieces of Scripture that would have been heard most often on the Western Front, and this familiarity no doubt explains why it is so prominent in SK's mind and reflection. In this chapter of *The Hardest Part* he offered what was, in effect, a theological exposition of that reading from St Paul.

35 That the whole of early Christian proclamation should be seen in relation to the 'Easter event' may now be a standard element in Christian theology, but in 1918 this was not a widely held position or even one that was widely known.

36 SK correctly identified the fact that Paul referred on many occasions to death – and he very often linked this to 'sin' and that 'the Spirit of life in Christ sets' the human being 'free' from this connection of 'sin and death' (cf. e.g. Rom 8.2). Paul never saw any need to be clear about the connection between death as a physical fact and death as a spiritual calamity.

37 Cf. 1 Cor. 15.26.

38 Cf. Pss. 56.13; 116.8.

to receive the best robe of sonship from the Father God.[39] It is true there is no sting in this, because there is no sin.[40] This is not defeat, but victory through Jesus Christ our Lord.[41]

Roy was a fine Christian. What about men who aren't? There are many men who die fine deaths who have no faith, or at least no conscious faith, in God or Christ as Son of God. How about them? Well, God is greater than the Churches.[42] He is the source, and the only source, of all fine life of the spirit. If a man dies for duty's sake a death which is for his spirit not defeat but victory, he dies in Christ. That is how it looks to me. Christ is the Lord of all good life. He is the only source of the splendid life of the spirit which turns defeat in death to victory. This gift of the "life eternal"[43] is indeed poured out upon men through the Church and the appointed means of grace, but we cannot confine God to His covenants. The river of eternal life breaks through a thousand channels and finds the soul of man.

I don't mean by that to subscribe to the rather sentimental idea that every man who dies in battle attains automatically to the perfection of eternal life.[44] God only knows how each man

---

39 Cf. Luke 15.22, where the generous father wants 'the best robe' for his returned son.

40 Cf. 1 Cor. 15.55–56.

41 1 Cor. 15.57.

42 SK here restated in explicit terms the universalism he saw as corresponding to the universality of the divine love he had explored in the previous chapter.

43 This phrase is used on nearly a hundred occasions in the New Testament (e.g. Matt. 19.16) as a name for that which humans most desire from God. SK assumed his readers would recognize it as such.

44 The idea that death in the cause of God, King and country ensured the soldier's eternal salvation, irrespective of his faith or lifestyle, became commonplace during the conflict. As A. F. Winnington-Ingram, the Bishop of London, famously put it: 'As I have said a thousand times, I look upon it as a war for purity. I look upon everyone who dies in it as a martyr.' For a discussion of this attitude and responses to it, see Stuart Bell, *Faith in Conflict: The Impact of the Great War on the Faith of the People of Britain* (Solihull: Helion, 2017), pp. 100–6.

dies.[45] There may be real death on a battle-field as well as in a sick-room.

Two bodies may lie side by side upon the same battle-field, both shattered by the same shell, and their two spirits may stand in the other world in utterly different states, one weak and wounded, defiled and defeated by sin, and the other strong and radiant, having conquered death in the spirit. It is not the act of death which counts, but the spirit of it. That seems to be St. Paul's idea, and I believe it is profoundly true.

A critic might suggest that it was all emotional assumption, without any solid basis of fact. It is not really that. It is based upon the fact of Christ and the revelation of God that fact contains. It is true that the vivid certainty which makes the fact of Christ for Christians the crowning fact of life, is the direct result of spiritual communion with God in Christ, and that this communion is an act, not of the intellect, but of the spiritual faculty. Nevertheless, the intellect plays its proper part in the mind of St. Paul and of other thinking Christians. The intellect cannot give certainty in anything except purely abstract sciences like mathematics; its normal function is to provide probability as a basis of intuitive certainty, and to follow faith, which is its lodestar, along the paths of mystery which lead to real truth.[46]

---

45 Here we see an important nuance in SK's thinking: it is not simply that a way of life does not matter – 'God will save all in any case' – but that the extent of salvation cannot be constrained within human categories such as 'only those who confess Jesus as Lord will be saved' or 'outside the church there is no salvation'. Rather, he acknowledged that only God knows the destiny of his creatures. This idea, rarely spelled out in 1918, would find expression in Roman Catholic liturgy after Vatican II, when praying for the dead included 'all those whose faith is known to you [God] alone'. This was subsequently influential in other communions.

46 This and some other comments in this chapter constituted SK's position on the relation of religious knowing and human rationality. While one can detect many overlaps of his thought with such thinkers as John Henry Newman (1801–90) and Henri Bergson (1859–1941), SK did not adopt

It plays this proper part both for St. Paul and for us in our faith concerning eternal life. St. Paul believed that Christ conquered death and rose again on historical evidence which was sufficient to satisfy his intellect. He goes through this evidence at the beginning of the chapter, recounting the appearances of Christ to trustworthy witnesses after death.[47] This evidence, combined with certain facts which he himself had observed – the sublime heroism of St. Stephen and the calm conviction of many Christian men and women whom he himself had put to death for Christ's sake struck his mind,[48] and, thinking on it, prepared the way for the vivid spiritual vision of the risen Christ which was the basis of his whole Christian life.[49] The intellect provided the living and disturbing probability as a basis for the glorious intuitive certainty which was his inspiration.

That is always the way with thinking Christians. For us to-day there is the disturbing probability of the resurrection which rests on facts. There is for us a larger fact of Christ, which in honesty we ought to face. There is not merely the story of His death and resurrection as told in the Gospels, which, isolated and of itself, would not perhaps be convincing, but there is the fact of what Christ has done. There is the history of Western civilisation, with the risen Christ at its core and centre. Men say that this civilisation has broken down and been destroyed, but that is shallow talking. It never was so strong as it is to day in the hearts of the Allied nations; it is so strong that men by millions prefer death to life without it. Never were sane men so certain of the truth of Christ as they are when they see it against the background of this insanity of barbarism.

European history, and indeed the history of the world, is to me an insoluble riddle apart from the resurrection of Christ.

---

any one position but rather distanced himself from any form of rationalistic propositionalism.

47 Cf. 1 Cor. 15.4–8.
48 Cf. 1 Cor. 15.9; Acts 7.54–58.
49 Cf. 1 Cor. 15.3, 8.

When one tries to picture the death of Christ upon the Cross as the end of His story, one is left staring at history in a state of utter bewilderment, as one would stare at an effect which appeared without a cause. Thus we have our basis of intellectual probability, but it is only a basis. The mere intellectual assent to the fact of the risen Christ could not of itself inspire a man with certainty and a sense of victory over death. That certainty can only be provided by spiritual communion with God through Christ, and that communion is an act, not of the intellect, but of intuition or faith. Of course this business of separation between intellect and intuition is, as usual, a process of convenient but impossible abstraction, but it is almost necessary for thought. Bergson taught me much.[50] What a comic combination Bergson and Boche bombardments make! It comes back to this: The only source of a living certainty and a sense of victory over death is a vision of God. Where there is no open vision, the people perish,[51] and faith in the life thereafter grows dim; where the vision of God is unclouded, faith rises supreme and triumphant over death. Once more we find it true. It is God that matters. God alone can give the victory over death. Everything depends upon a man's vision of God.

But then, in battle men go mad; they have no vision of anything: they see red. Every man who dies in a bayonet charge dies mad – what about them? If madness means anything it means that a man's actions have no moral or spiritual significance

---

50 The French philosopher Henri Bergson was at the height of his fame in Britain just before the war. In 1913 he had been elected president of the (London) Society for Psychical Research and in the spring of 1914 had delivered the Gifford Lectures in Edinburgh. His 1907 book, *Creative Evolution*, appeared in English in 1911, and it contained many of the ideas on the role of intuition we see in this chapter. That the cleric in Worcester was reading and assimilating Bergson's work is another indication that *The Hardest Part* represents SK's careful reflection and that – as we have seen already – it is a work deliberately engaging the great issues of faith in the theological culture of its time and not merely some rough notes of a padre.

51 Cf. Prov. 29.18.

whatever, but are just mechanical results of his surroundings. In their case the act of death can have no spiritual meaning. Quite so; but the spiritual act took place before the madness.[52] There is a Gethsemane before every Calvary,[53] and there the cup is either taken or refused.[54] The soldier can say with St. Paul, "I die daily";[55] and as he faces the daily death of ever-present danger, so he will face the real shadow when it comes.

As a matter of fact, almost every man who dies in battle dies under a natural anaesthetic of some sort. If nature had not a supply of anaesthetics the finest battalions would turn and run. Flesh and blood could not stand it unless our sensibilities were deadened, but the nature of the anaesthetic is largely determined by a man's character and convictions. It may be the madness of excitement, or the dullness of despair, or the numbness of extreme terror, or it may be the splendid recklessness of sacrifice based upon entire devotion to duty and to God; but in every case it is a man's daily life that determines the spirit of his death, and his vision of God that determines his daily life.

There may be apparently sudden conversions on the battlefield as there are on death-beds, but in both cases they are probably the result of a change that has been gradually coming over a man's spirit. Real conquest over death can only be obtained by real redemption from sin.

---

52 The notion that the last moment before death was *not* what was determinative of one's post-mortem destination was radically new in 1917. (It was, after all, this notion of the last moment that inspired much battlefield pastoral practice, such as 'absolution' for Roman Catholic troops just prior to battle.) SK's insight would re-emerge later in the twentieth century in the related notions in practical theology of 'fundamental option' and 'anonymous Christianity' put forward by theologians who, like SK, took an existentialist approach to faith.

53 Cf. Matt. 26.36; Luke 23.33.

54 Cf. Mark 14.30; Luke 22.42.

55 1 Cor. 15.31.

'Hope' by George Frederick Watts (1817–1904).
Painted in 1886 and presented to the Tate in 1897, this picture – this
'symbol' in Watts' terminology – is intended to be read as an allegory
for part of the human condition. That Studdert Kennedy asks his
readers to reflect on this image, and to read it in terms of both their
faith and their experience, can be seen as an aspect of his sacramental
approach to Christian life.

The measure of a man's victory over death is the measure
of his victory over sin.[56] No amount of purely intellectual conviction of immortality could or would accomplish a man's
redemption from death. "If they believe not Moses and the

---

56 Cf. 1 Cor. 15.56–57.

prophets, neither will they believe though one rose from the dead."[57] The living hope of life eternal must be founded on faith in God.[58] Faithless hope is as sad and as weak as despair. That is what Watts would teach us in his picture of Hope.[59] He depicts the rationalistic nineteenth century seated on the summit of the world, and commanding a view of the whole universe from those dizzy heights of material knowledge which progressive science has enabled her to climb. All her knowledge cannot comfort her soul. She cannot bear to look upon the picture it opens out to her, and so she blinds her eyes and strains her ears to the one unbroken string from which music can be wrung, the string of hope. "If in this life we have only hope in Christ, we are of all men most miserable."[60] That is the correct translation of that text, and it is a profound truth. Positive and powerful hope can only spring from faith and in communion with the suffering, but deathless and conquering, God Who reached the soul of St. Paul with a cry of splendid agony, "I am Jesus Whom thou persecutest."[61]

We need such positive hope to-day as we never needed it before. We must have it if we are to rise as a nation from our present sorrow, having won from it new life and power. We are now bearing our burden very largely on the false stimulant of drugs – the common drugs of drink, vice, pleasure-seeking,

---

57 Luke 16.31.

58 Cf. 1 Pet. 1.3.

59 This is a painting from 1886, now in the Tate Britain gallery in London, by the 'symbolist' artist George Frederick Watts (1817–1904). The painting was inspired partly by Heb. 6.19.

60 1 Cor. 15.19; the AV reads: 'If in this life only we have hope in Christ, we are of all men most miserable.' SK adapted the translation, but the underlying Greek can support either translation; in his own scholarly judgement, his is 'the correct translation'. That SK was considering such points of textual precision shows, once again, that the thinking behind *The Hardest Part* was not some momentary reflection but the work of long hours of careful study brought to fruition in the shock and ghastliness of war.

61 Acts 9.5; 22.8; 26.15.

self-deception, and wilful blindness to the facts. The nation too often turns for refuge from the hideous facts of war, not to its higher but to its lower self, and tries to drown its sorrows in the waters of Lethe.[62] Our aim is to forget, because we dare not remember. God forbid that I should condemn wholesale the spirit of my people, or fail to appreciate their splendid heroism – I too have longed to forget, craved for an anaesthetic, and have taken them in hours of weakness – but I believe there is real danger lest we fail to reap the fruits of this purgatory of pain because we seek not to remember but to forget, and, unlike Christ, Who turned His head away and refused the myrrh and wine,[63] drink deep and eagerly of any drug that deadens pain.

The nation needs this hope now, and it will need it always. Nations cannot keep their heads on earth unless their hearts are fixed in heaven. They inevitably suffer from the madness of materialism unless they have the living hope of life eternal which puts our earthly life into its true perspective as something, not indeed unimportant, but certainly not all important, or even of the first importance. The comparative failure in modern times of real hope of life eternal is largely responsible for the insanity of dreary materialism which has issued in a temporary throwback into barbarism and the outbreak of this cursed conflict.

The only way in which this hope can be quickened and revived among men is by giving them an open vision of God, a vision which can be seen by men without a wilful refusal on their part to face in their fullness the darker facts of life. Everything which obscures the vision of God weakens faith in life eternal. It is because the Church persists in presenting to men to-day a vision of God which the facts of life as men know them now render impossibly obscure and incredible, that she is failing to satisfy their hunger for this living hope. They are turning away

---

62 In Greek mythology the Lethe was one of the rivers in the Hades that produced forgetfulness (*amnesia*) of earthy life, and so oblivion, for those who passed through it.
63 Cf. Mark 15.23.

from her in bitterness and disappointment, because she has no food to offer which will appease the hunger of their hearts. And because they must have something, they are seeking for comfort in Spiritualism and the discoveries of those engaged in psychical research.

Psychical research is a perfectly legitimate study and was bound to be taken up by man.[64] The evidence for the survival of the human personality after death accumulated by men like F. W. H. Myers[65] and Sir Oliver Lodge[66] is legitimate evidence, and contains its measure of comfort for the troubled intellect. It can, however, never take the place of the lively hope[67] which comes of faith in and communion with God. I am grateful for all such evidence; it helps to satisfy my intellect when it is inclined to doubt, because it provides new facts which are very difficult, if not impossible, to account for on a materialistic basis; but of

---

64 Bergson had been made President of the Society for Psychical Research in 1913 and his Gifford Lectures (1914) were on the topic of 'the problem of personality'. SK's passing reference here shows that he took these investigations seriously. They would fit with his empiricism, reluctance to accept conclusions on the basis of syllogisms from a priori doctrinal positions, and his general fear of believers avoiding difficult facts by 'blinking'.

65 Frederick W. H. Myers (1843–1901) was the founder of the Society for Psychical Research, and did much to promote the notion that individual personality survived death and that this was empirically verifiable through the use of mediums.

66 Oliver Lodge (1851–1940) was an eminent physicist who was also interested in spiritualism and telepathy (which he combined with Christianity), and held that human immortality could be demonstrated by contact with the dead. He had been President of the Society for Psychical Research from 1901 to 1903, and SK no doubt knew his writings from before the war. However, Lodge came to new prominence after his son, Raymond, was killed in battle in 1915, leading to Lodge writing *Raymond; or, Life and Death* (London: Methuen, 1916), giving accounts of his visits to psychics in order to contact his son. Many who would not have known Lodge's earlier writings would have known *Raymond*, for Lodge was just one of many, such as Sir Arthur Conan Doyle, who had recourse to mediums in the aftermath of the death of sons in the war.

67 Cf. 1 Pet. 1.3.

and in itself it would not satisfy the needs of my nature in regard to immortality. It is not a source of spiritual vital energy, and has no power to inspire me with a sense of victory over death and give me the lively hope,[68] not merely of existence, but of fuller and more splendid life beyond the grave. What we need is moral and spiritual energy, and this is what these studies cannot supply; indeed, the study of psychic phenomena, as experience shows, is dangerous for any but healthy and well-balanced minds, and would be a disastrous substitute for ethical religion.

Such evidence as it affords does not in any way contradict the faith of Christians. Christ told us practically nothing about the conditions of the life hereafter, beyond the plain fact that our fate there depended upon the use we made of our powers here. The reason of this reticence I believe was that, if He had told us, we could not have understood, having no faculties for such understanding. This appears to be confirmed by the meagreness of the communications which the dead are able to make with us, and the fact that their ability to communicate becomes less by lapse of time.[69] There are no words and no method of speech by which we can be made to understand the conditions of life in the other world. The evidence seems to support the idea of a kind of purgatorial progress after death. This has always been the Christian teaching. The abolition of purgatory was one of the temporary absurdities due to the reaction of the Reformation against abuses.[70] The ideas of progress and purification

---

68 Cf. 1 Pet. 1.3.

69 SK's empiricism allowed him to take the findings of those involved in the Society for Psychical Research at face value, but then to note – as he had in chapters 2 and 3 – that such evidence, based within the creation, should not be confused with the divine.

70 One of the classic ways of presenting purgatory was that the completion of conversion (*metanoia*) would have to be processual if the freedom of the individual was to be respected by God. Note that this, in turn, assumes an adherence to the notion of the *potestas ordinata Dei*, to which SK has referred repeatedly. Thus, the movement of the Christian life would continue post-mortem, assisted by the prayers of the Church. SK here explicitly

are essential to our thought about the hereafter. Eternal life, as
St. John says, is progressive knowledge of the only true God,
and Jesus Christ Whom He has sent.[71]

The turning to Spiritualism is sad, because it will ultimately
fail to satisfy the real needs of man. At best it can give only hope,
hope that is based not on faith, but on doubt and despair, and
that does but make us the more miserable.[72] We come back to
the bed-rock truth. The sting of death is sin,[73] and real redemption from death is just redemption from sin. God alone can go
to the root of the trouble and conquer death by pouring life
into the soul. To the man who has learned the secret of the love
of God in Christ, death has only the uncertainty of a glorious
adventure. He does not know the way by which he will climb
after death, and he neither expects nor desires to know it. It
is enough for him that he knows and trusts his guide. He will
in this life be "steadfast, unmovable, always abounding in the
work of the Lord,"[74] because he knows through Christ that his
"labour is not vain in the Lord."[75] I am sure we have obscured
the vision of God because we feared to face the facts of life.
We have been ashamed of the Cross and have shrunk from the
suffering God. This is what men need, the love of the suffering

---

adopted this view of purgatory as the 'completion of metanoia', but we
should note that it takes him into direct opposition to Article 22: 'On Purgatory' of the (1562) Thirty-Nine Articles of Religion of the Church of England.
For how that Article was interpreted within the Church of England in the early
twentieth century, see E. Harold Browne, *Exposition of the Thirty-Nine Articles,
Historical and Doctrinal* (London: Longman, Green & Co., 1850–3, and many
later editions) on Article 22. This work was the standard textbook in Anglican
theological colleges until well into the twentieth century. Its insistence on the
rejection of praying for the dead would be overturned by the practices that
across the Church of England had become widespread though still contested
before the end of 1914. See Bell, *Faith in Conflict*, pp. 109–15.

71 John 17.3; but slightly expanded by SK.
72 Cf. 1 Cor. 15.19.
73 1 Cor. 15.56.
74 1 Cor. 15.58.
75 1 Cor. 15.58.

God of God in Christ; then, and only then, all things are theirs
– the world, and life and death and things present and things
to come; all things are theirs, for they are Christ's and Christ is
God's.[76]

Red with His blood, the better day is dawning;
　　Pierced by His pain the storm clouds roll apart;
Rings o'er the earth the message of the morning,
　　Still on the Cross the Saviour bares His heart.

Passionately fierce the voice of God is pleading,
　　Pleading with men to arm them for the fight;
See how those hands, majestically bleeding,
　　Call us to rout the armies of the night.

Not to the work of sordid selfish saving
　　Of our own souls to dwell with Him on high;
But to the soldier's splendid selfless braving,
　　Eager to fight for righteousness and die.

Peace does not mean the end of all our striving,
　　Joy does not mean the drying of our tears;
Peace is the power that comes to souls arriving
　　Up to the light where God Himself appears.

Joy is the wine that God is ever pouring
　　Into the hearts of those who strive with Him,
Light'ning their eyes to vision and adoring,
　　Strength'ning their arms to warfare glad and grim.

Bread of Thy Body give me for my fighting,
　　Give me to drink Thy Sacred Blood for wine;
While there are wrongs that need me for the righting,
　　While there is warfare splendid and divine.

---

76 Cf. 1 Cor. 3.22–23.

The Hardest Part

Give me for light the sunshine of Thy sorrow,
  Give me for shelter shadow of Thy Cross,
Give me to share the glory of Thy morrow,
  Gone from my heart is the bitterness of loss.[77]

*   *   *   *   *

Good-bye, Roy, old chap. I will write to the mother and tell her not to think of you as lying in a grave, but as standing to attention, glad and full of life, before the great White Captain of all souls. Some day we shall meet. Some day she and I will recognise you in a new and glorious body, quite different from this poor broken flesh, and yet in difference still the same, because there will be shining in it and through it the gallant, splendid spirit that is Roy, best of soldiers, best of servants, best of pals.

---

77 These are the closing verses of SK's poem 'The Suffering God', published in *Rough Rhymes of a Padre* (London: Hodder & Stoughton, 1918).

Postscript[1]

A REPLY TO SOME CRITICISM AND A FEW WORDS TO ANY
READERS WHO MAY BE HURT BY WHAT I HAVE WRITTEN

SOME very wise and good people have been hurt by what I have written when they read it in printers' proof. There may be many like them. As my object is to help and not to hurt, I would humbly beg my readers to take into account some of the following considerations before they pass final judgment on a very poor attempt to express the inexpressible.

This is not a theological essay. I doubt if I could write one, and I am sure that no one would read it if I did. This is a fairly faithful and accurate account of the inner ruminations of an incurably religious man[2] under battle conditions. I think this accounts for many things. It accounts for what my critics have called a "lack of balance" which runs through it, the predominance of the one idea. Battles do not make for carefully balanced thought. There is one main idea in what I have written, but I believe that it is a true idea. We must make clear to ourselves and to the world what we mean when we say "I believe in God the Father Almighty."

---

1 From internal evidence we know that this Postscript was written after 15 May 1918.

2 The use here of the phrase 'incurably religious man' shows that SK was reading the literature on the anthropology of religion of the time. 'Religion' in this view is neither an external fact imposed on humanity – the prevalent view in the theological orthodoxy of the time – nor a pathology, but rather arises out of the very situation in which the human being finds her/himself.

The Hardest Part

The conditions under which these meditations were made account for the repeated and constant denial of the popular conception. I may have railed at that conception very fiercely, but my raillery is mild and good-natured compared with the outspoken comments of the guns. This also accounts for the style. Good people have told me that it is crude and brutal. I would remind you that it is not, and it could not be as crude as war, or as brutal as a battle. I have not really violated what John Oxenham has finely called "the most loving conspiracy of silence the world has ever known,"[3] or torn aside the veil of noble reticence behind which our soldiers seek to hide the sufferings they endure. I would not if I could, and I could not if I would. I would not if I could, because it would be cruel. I could not if I would, because the brutality of war is literally unutterable. There are no words foul and filthy enough to describe it. Yet I would remind you that this indescribably filthy thing is the commonest thing in History, and that if we believe in a God of Love at all we must believe in the face of war and all it means. The supreme strength of the Christian faith is that it faces the foulest and filthiest of life's facts in the crude brutality of the Cross, and through them sees the Glory of God in the face of Jesus Christ. Thousands of men who have fought out here, and thousands of their womenkind who have waited or mourned for them at home, have dimly felt that the reason and explanation of all this horror was somehow to be found in a Crucifix – witness the frequent reproductions of wayside calvaries in our picture papers and the continual mention of them in our soldiers' letters home. Yet when you talk to soldiers you find that the Calvary appeals

---

3 In newspapers on 15 May 1918 there was this statement: '"The reticence of our soldiers on the horrors they experience is the most loving conspiracy of silence the world has ever known" said Mr. John Oxenham at the London City Temple recently.' 'John Oxenham' was the pseudonym of William Arthur Dunkerley (1852–1941), a poet, hymn-writer, journalist and novelist. The soldiers' reticence to talk about the horrors of their experiences is universally recognized.

to them rather as the summary of their problems than their solution. They feel that it is like life, but has no light to shed upon life's mysteries. It is to them a thing of the past, a tale of long ago, and except that it seems natural to them now, as it stands in the midst of a battered village among broken, tired men, it has no relation to their present problems or their present needs. Their only comment, seldom spoken, but often thought, is, "He died to save us from our sin, and there is this, only this, after so many years." But all the pondering about life which has been done out here has been slowly bearing fruit, and a fresh light is beginning to glimmer through the darkness.[4] Men are beginning to see a fresh vision of God in Christ. If I believed that the point of view expressed in this book was peculiarly my own, and was in that sense original, I would not have bothered to write it down. But I don't, I believe it is in the minds of thousands who have neither time nor words to express it. It is in the air. It is the vision of God that war has shown to many. This fact does not guarantee its truth, but gives to it a value.

"But that is just the weakness of it," some of my critics have said. It is a partial theology, a distorted truth which appeals to men in the awful conditions of War, but the return of Peace and Peace conditions will make it seem lopsided and absurd. I do not think so, unless Peace brings in the Millennium,[5] and though I am an optimist I do not anticipate that. The Vision of the Suffering God revealed in Jesus Christ, and the necessary Truth of it, first began to dawn on me in the narrow streets and shadowed homes of an English slum.[6] All that War has done is

---

4 Cf. John 1.5.

5 This is a reference to 'the thousand years' of Rev. 20 – the end of an apocalyptic time, after which there will be a Christian perfection.

6 It is clear that SK's 'meditations' as found in this book had a long gestation in both experience and study. Here SK rejected the notion that the war was the great exception to human experience. Rather, he saw the war as an intense form of the human dilemma. The implication is that one cannot place his own theological approach within a box as if it is only meaningful in relation to wartime conditions.

to batter the essential Truth of it deeper in, and cast a fiercer
light upon the Cross. A battlefield is more striking, but scarcely
more really crude and brutal than a slum. Only we have all
been suddenly forced to realise war more or less, while it has
taken God centuries to make some of us recognise the existence of slums. Soldiers are not the only people who have their
conspiracy of silence. Scientists, doctors, travellers, and social
workers have their conspiracies too, which decency forces them
to observe. Yet facts are none the less facts because they are
beastly, and though we may not talk about them we must take
them into account. The more deeply you delve into the facts of
life the more utterly incredible the idea of absolute unlimited
Omnipotence becomes. The burden of crude brutality which
is laid upon God in this book is as nothing to the awful burden
God has to bear.

My critics have some of them said that the Church as a whole
has never taught this doctrine of Omnipotence absolute and
unlimited.[7] It is difficult to discover anything beyond the simple
Christian facts which the Church as a whole has always taught
her children. The facts remain constant, the interpretation of
them changes. This much, however, is certain – that, whether
the Church has taught it or not, thousands of her children have
learnt the conception of God as One who can do anything He
likes whenever He likes, and the effort to square that conception
with facts is wrecking their faith.[8]

---

7 Here SK used a technical term from theological debate that contrasted
the 'absolute power of God' (*potestas Dei absoluta* – there is nought God
cannot do for to assert such would be to deny the nature of deity) with the
'ordered power of God' (*potestas Dei ordinata* – God's power is only known
in terms of its ordered use within the creation). For the origins and ramifica-
tions of this debate, which continued in some circles well into the twentieth
century, see Lawrence Moonan, *Divine Power: The Medieval Power Distinction
up to its Adoption by Albert, Bonaventure and Aquinas* (Oxford: Oxford University Press, 1994).

8 Here we see another aspect of SK's existentialist approach to 'facts': it
is no use asking what should have been taught or what should have been

It is true that the doctrine of free-will has been constantly preached, and men taught to recognise that this limited the power of God for good. But this great Truth has been taught as a "self-limitation" of God, as if God could have made men perfect without it, but chose to give it them, thus casting back upon God the moral burden of its misuse. Moreover, it has been taught as if it accounted for all the evil in the world, and it doesn't. It fails to touch the misery that is caused not by knaves but by honest fools, and that is great. It fails to account for the changing standards of right and wrong in different ages, and different countries. It has nothing to say to the cruelties of nature, to disease, insanity, idiocy, which are hidden by the world's great conspiracy of silence about unpleasant things. It has to be modified to allow for the enormous and inevitable influence of heredity and environment upon the will, and so upon conscience and character. To say that a man born in a slum or in Berlin is entirely responsible for his actions is to go beyond the obvious truth, while to say that he is not responsible at all is to fall disastrously short of it.

This sketch of a book is palpably inadequate. It just takes a truth and hurls it at your head as the guns hurled it at mine, only it is comparatively gentle hurling. But a greater "Hardest Part" could be written by a worthier brain and hand which could make the Truth inevitably clear and cogent. All the more clear and all the more cogent when placed in its proper relation to the rest of Truth, and not isolated as it stands here.

One great objection remains. Does not the solution of the whole problem lie in the mystery of time? We are creatures of time and God is eternal and beyond time, we cannot hope to understand His ways or judge them by our puny human standards. This sounds the wise, large-minded, and reverent thing to say. But alas! it goes too far, and proves too much. If

understood – for these approaches are only in touch with an ideal world – but rather one must start with the 'fact' of what has been perceived. This is the reality of the human being's relationship with God.

I cannot judge God's ways by human standards, that is by the standard set by Christ for men, then I cannot judge my own ways by God's standards, since I am, and must be, ignorant of what they are.[9] If that is true there is an end to ethical religion. If the eternal standards of Right and Wrong differ from the temporal standards revealed to us by Christ, then I am making an empty statement when I say that God is good. If that statement is empty, then life is empty and I have no religion, for I cannot worship any God who is not good in the Christian sense. Therein lies the point and poignancy of the whole problem. It is not an intellectual but a moral problem. The popular conception of omnipotence sets up an opposition between our religion and our highest moral values, an opposition which is disastrous to both. This worship of a God so great that He is above Right and Wrong has already led to two terrible but common results. It has led to the easy tolerance by Christian people of social wrongs which are a burning disgrace because they sacrificed their moral standards to their religion, and it has led to the abandonment of religion by many noble souls who sacrificed their religion to their moral standards.

It amounts to this. Religion is impossible when we try to do without or go beyond the Incarnation.[10] Metaphysical speculation which tries to go beyond the God in man and find the God Absolute is valueless from a living and religious point of

---

9 SK took as a datum that one can only speak the truth, however partial, by relating to one's own conscious perception of the situation; anything else is merely to repeat words. In refusing to accept the 'it is all mysterious' trope, SK challenged preachers and theologians to speak honestly from their situations – as he was forced to do when sharing a bunker under shell-fire in chapter 6 – or remain silent.

10 This is the closest SK came to identifying his most central theological base: a belief in the incarnation. It is only from his 'high theology' of the incarnation – witness his many appeals to John 1 – that he could come to the conclusion to which he came.

view. The Rock of Ages[11] is the Divinity of Christ, and in Him
there lies the solution of our problems, and the inspiration of
our lives. He can bear all the weight we can throw upon Him,
and does bear it, for He is God. I go back to the Cross with the
Empty Tomb behind it, and there I find a satisfying and inspiring answer to it all.

Thou who dost dwell in depths of timeless being,
    Watching the years as moments passing by.
Seeing the things that lie beyond our seeing,
    Constant, unchanged as aeons dawn and die;

Thou who canst count the stars upon their courses,
    Holding them all in the hollow of Thy hand,
Lord of the world with all its million forces,
    Seeing the hills as single grains of sand;

Art Thou so great that all our bitter crying,
    Sounds in Thine ears as sorrow of a child?
Hast Thou looked down on centuries of sighing,
    And, like a heartless mother, only smiled?

Since in Thy sight to-day is as to-morrow,
    And while we strive Thy victory is won,
Hast Thou no tears to shed upon our sorrow?
    Art Thou a staring splendour like the sun?

Dost Thou not heed the helpless sparrow's falling?
    Dost Thou not mourn the lost and wandering sheep?
Canst Thou not hear Thy littlest children calling?
    Dost Thou not watch above them as they sleep?

---

11 An allusion to the 1775 hymn 'Rock of ages', by Augustus Toplady
(1740–78).

Then, O my God, Thou art too great to love me,
  Since Thou dost reign beyond the reach of tears,
Calm and serene as the cruel stars above me,
  High and remote from human hopes and fears.

Only in Him can I find Home to hide me,
  Who on the Cross was slain to rise again,
Only with Him my comrade God beside me,
  Can I go forth to war with sin and pain.[12]

There is the real God. In Him I find no metaphysical abstraction, but God speaking to me in the only language I can understand, which is the human language, God revealed in the only terms I can begin to comprehend, which are the terms of perfect Human Personality. In Him I find the Truth that human sin and sorrow matter to God, nay, are matters of life and death to God, as they must be to me. In Him I find the Truth that the moral struggle of man is a real struggle because God is in it, in it and beyond it too, for in the Risen Christ who conquered death and rose again I find the promise and the guarantee that the moral struggle of the race will issue in victory. In Him I still can stand and say my Creed from the bottom of my heart.[13]

---

12 This is SK's poem, 'The Comrade God', from *Rough Rhymes of a Padre* (London: Hodder & Stoughton, 1918). In his first published work – his chapter 'The Religious Difficulties of the Private Soldier', in F. Macnutt (ed.), *The Church in the Furnace* (London: Macmillan, 1917) – SK had written: 'God suffers now, and is crucified afresh every day. God suffers in every man that suffers. God, the God we love and worship, is no far off God of Power but the comrade God of love' (p. 391). The concept of a 'comrade God' was intended to offer a stark contrast with the traditional ideas of a God remote from human suffering. He continued: 'God is not a bad Staff Officer, but a gallant and fatherly Colonel who goes over the top with His men.'

13 This point would be taken up in detail after the war when, in 1921, SK wrote *Food for the Fed-Up: An Exposition of the Christian Creed*; in that work several of the implicit themes of this work are brought out for a more thorough exploration.

For there is a sense in which I believe more firmly than I ever did before that God is Almighty. I can still stand facing East whence comes the Dawn, and say "I believe in God the Father Almighty,"[14] and in those glorious words confess my faith that the final Victory of God is as sure, nay, surer than the rising of to-morrow's sun. God is suffering His agony now, but the day will surely come when His agony and ours will be ended, and we shall sing our song of praise to the triumphant God of Love (cp. pp. 91, 92).[15] Sin and sorrow, though real, are only temporary, the results of temporary and contingent necessities inherent in the task of creation, but they will pass away, and God will prove Himself Almighty in the end.

I have shouted out the negative "Not Almighty" again and again against the popular conception because life in Peace and War shouts it out at me. But the negative is only important so far as it clears away the clouds that hide the great Positive of the All-conquering God revealed in Christ.

In conclusion, my friends have been grieved because I made jokes about serious subjects and serious people. In such matters one should be "dead serious" I have been told. That is a point of view which it is difficult for an Irishman to understand at any time, but is doubly difficult for one who has served with the armies at the front. Out here making fun is the most serious business of our lives.[16] I doubt if it is possible, and I am sure it is not wholesome for any living man to be "dead serious." To lack a sense of humour is one of the most terrible handicaps in life for anyone, and is a disaster in a writer or a preacher who wants to help. I have often suspected that what Mr. H. G. Wells really lacks is a genuine loving sense of humour. He thought he

---

14 The opening line of the Apostles' Creed.

15 SK's cross-reference related to his reflection in chapter 5 on his statement: 'I believe in God the Father Almighty is not a statement of fact but a confession of faith.' See p. 83.

16 Frank Richards summarized his coping strategy in *Old Soldiers Never Die* (London: Faber & Faber, 1933) as 'you must not take this war too seriously!'

had dismissed Bishops when he said they were "jokes."[17] But if a Bishop is a good joke, he may be still one of the best and lightest things in the world. I have made fun of the Archbishop of Canterbury, but I firmly believe that he is one of the rightest and best people in England. Christian laughter always hovers just on the brink of tears, for God in Christ has redeemed them both and wedded joy to sorrow, and real peace to pain.

If anything I have said sounds like contempt or disrespect to the English Church or her teachers, it is not so meant. Honest criticism and difference of opinion is not disrespect, and that is all I have meant to express.

It is all very poor and incomplete. But better and wiser men than I will put that right by picking it to pieces, if they think it worth their while. So Truth grows stronger, and that is all that matters.

I wish I could write it over again, but it would be worse next time. Anyhow, kind reader, think again before you cast it out.

G. A. STUDDERT KENNEDY,
Army Infantry School,
B.E.F.

---

17 In his novel, *The Soul of a Bishop* (London: Cassell, 1917), H. G. Wells told the story of the 'Bishop of Princhester', a man assailed by doubt and perceived irrelevance whose drug-taking led to mystical visions. Reviewers have seen in the bishop's disillusionment with the Church and its clergy many of Wells' own views, as the brief period of his 'resort to God' (as Wells himself put it), typified by his novel *Mr. Britling Sees It Through* (London: Cassell, 1916), came to an end.

**A crucifix that now stands outside
St Paul's Church, Worcester.**
*This was the Church where Studdert Kennedy
ministered before and after his service as a chaplain.
The crucifix – as distinct from a cross on which
there is no image of the crucified Jesus – was quite
rare in Britain until the First World War. Studdert
Kennedy saw it not only as the central image of
Christianity but as the key to the relationship of the
compassionate Father to the suffering of an evolving
humanity. The crucifix as a theological key features
in every chapter of* The Hardest Part *and in the
final section Studdert Kennedy saw its recovery
as a religious icon as part of a new Christian
consciousness.*

I wonder how much this beastly thing would stand. I guess that it would come in with a 5.9. That's a near 'un. Somebody light the candle. I wish we could have got some of them. It was rotten missing all three, & that poor chap all blown to bits. To be wounded is bad enough, but to left out two days & then blown up in the end, that's the limit. What a perfectly filthy business this war is. And it is not as if this were the only War. It is not as if war were really abnormal & extraordinary. In England just before the war, we'd got to think it was. We read the great Illusion & we said that war was an anachronism in a civilised world. We'd got past it. It would not, could not come again. I still think it is The Great Illusion I still think its an anachronism in a civilised world. But it has come again all right. Shut that door the light

The opening page of the notebook in which Studdert Kennedy wrote an early version of Chapter 3.

The re-discovery of this manuscript, written in pencil, in 2017 confirmed that, contrary to first appearances and the genre he adopted, The Hardest Part *was not just the jottings of a moment or random reflections, but a carefully developed argument for a different way of viewing the relationships between God, the creation, evil and suffering.*

Appendix 1: An Early Manuscript Version of Chapter 3

In the archives of the Museum of Army Chaplaincy is a type-written letter accompanied by an exercise book containing handwritten text. The letter was written by the Revd P. T. Kirk, director of the Industrial Christian Fellowship, the organiza-tion of which Studdert Kennedy was a 'missioner' at the time of his death in 1929. Written later that year, it acknowledged a gift for the Studdert Kennedy Memorial fund and, appar-ently in response to a query raised by the recipient of the letter, T. A. Roche of Rosemary Lodge, Felixstowe, suggested that he should keep a manuscript written by Studdert Kennedy. Kirk's vague comment that 'It was probably rewritten either in the same or some other form' suggests that he did not recognize the handwritten pages as being an early version of chapter 3 of *The Hardest Part*, and the exercise book remained unidentified in the archives until the summer of 2017, when a chaplain recognized the textual similarities. The draft chapter and the published text are shown below.

God in History

Draft manuscript of chapter 3	The published text
	In a German concrete shelter. Time, 2.30 a.m. All night we had been making unsuccessful attempts to bring down some wounded men from the line. We could not get them through the shelling. One was blown to pieces as he lay on his stretcher.
I wonder how much this beastly thing would stand. I guess that it would come in with a 5.9. That's a near 'un. Somebody light the candle. I wish we could have got some of them. It was rotten missing all three, and that poor chap all blown to bits. To be wounded is bad enough, but to [be] left out two days and then blown up in the end, that's the limit.	I wonder how much this beastly shanty would stand. I guess it would come in on us with a direct hit, and it looks like getting one soon. Lord, that was near it. Here, somebody light that candle again. I wish we could have got those chaps down. It was murder to attempt it though. That poor lad, all blown to bits – I wonder who he was. God, it's awful.

	The glory of war, what utter blather it all is. That chap in the "Soldiers Three" was about right:
	    Says Mooney, I declare,
	    The death is everywhere;
	    But the glory never seems to be about.
	War is only glorious when you buy it in the *Daily Mail* and enjoy it at the breakfast-table. It goes splendidly with bacon and eggs. Real war is the final limit of damnable brutality, and that's all there is in it. It's about the silliest, filthiest, most inhumanly fatuous thing that ever happened. It makes the whole universe seem like a mad muddle. One feels that all talk of order and meaning in life is insane sentimentality.

What a perfectly filthy business this war is. And it is not as if this were the only war. It is not as if war were really abnormal or extraordinary. In England just before the war, we'd got to think it was. We read the [G]reat Illusion and we said that war was an anachronism in a civilised world. We'd got past it. It would not, could not, come again. I still think it is The Great Illusion. I still think it's an anachronism in a civilised world. But it has come again all right.	It's not as if this were the only war. It's not as if war were extraordinary or abnormal. It's as ordinary and as normal as man. In the days of peace before this war we had come to think of it as abnormal and extraordinary. We had read *The Great Illusion*, and were all agreed that war was an anachronism in a civilised world. We had got past it. It was primitive, and would not, could not, come again on a large scale. It is "The Great Illusion" right enough, and it is an anachronism in a civilised world. We ought to have got past it; but we haven't. It has come again on a gigantic scale.
Shut that door the light can be seen.	I say, keep that door shut; the light can be seen. I believe they are right on to this place. There was a German sausage up all day just opposite, and they must have spotted movement hereabouts this morning. There it goes again. Snakes, that's my foot you're standing on. Anybody hurt? Right-o, light the candle. It's no fun smoking in the dark.
And war is not really abnormal or extraordinary. It's as normal and as ordinary as sin. The history of man is the history of War as far back as we can trace it. It's all wars. Calvary made no difference to that. Christ could not kill the God of War. Men simply turned and waged them in His name. The head of the Church made wars. There's a war on now – and there have not been in the history of	Yes, war has come again all right. It's the rule with man, not the exception. The history of man is the history of war as far back as we can trace it. Christ made no difference to that. There never has been peace on earth. Christ could not conquer war. He gave us chivalry, and produced the sporting soldier; but even that seems dead. Chivalry and poison gas don't go well together. Christ

the world three consecutive years when their[1] has not been a war on somewhere. That much the militarist historians have got in their favour. Progress has been everywhere and at all times accompanied by war. That is not a theory that's a fact – as certain as my mother's mangle.

As the longwinded Johnnies would put it Progress and War are invariably concomitant Phenomena in human history and what is it that chap on the train said Invariable concomitance is incompatible with complete causal independence.[2] Which means that if war and progress always go together, either war must cause progress or progress must cause war, or they must act and interact like drink and poverty. It sounds to durn reasonable for words. But I'm not sure it's true.

Himself was turned into a warrior and led men out to war. Few wars have been so fierce and so prolonged as the so-called religious wars. Of course a deeper study of history reveals the fact that they were not really religious wars. Religion was not the real, but only the apparent cause of them. They were just political and commercial struggles waged under the cloak of religion. I don't believe that religion had anything to do with the Inquisition, it was a political business throughout. Still these struggles, with all their sordid brutalities, proved Christ helpless against the God of War. He is helpless still. God is helpless to prevent war, or else He wills it and approves of it. There is the alternative. You pay your money and you take your choice.

---

1 SK was of course well educated; the occasional minor errors of grammar or spelling here are testimony to the pressures under which this was drafted. We have taken the liberty of correcting 'silently' in a few very minor instances and inserting suggestions in square brackets in some cases where words were missing or unclear. The few crossings-through are SK's.

2 This seems ultimately to derive from the psychologist and philosopher James Ward's *Naturalism and Agnosticism: The Gifford Lectures Delivered Before the University of Aberdeen in the Years 1896–1898* (Cambridge: Cambridge University Press, 2011), p. 24: '. . . invariable concomitance and absolute causal independence are incompatible positions'.

	Christians in the past have taken the second alternative, and have stoutly declared that God wills war. They have quoted Christ as saying that He came not to bring peace upon the earth, but a sword.
	Bernhardi did that quite lately. Luther did it too, I believe. If you cling to God's absolute omnipotence, you must do it. If God is absolutely omnipotent, He must will war, since war is and always has been the commonplace of history. Men are driven to the conclusion that war is the will of the Almighty God.
It's got an enormous lot to say for itself. I guess Mr Treitsch[k]e has said it about as well as it can be said. He has the whole Darwinian theory of evolution as expounded by Ha[e]c[k]el behind the struggle for existence and the survival of the fittest. He can go back to the amoeba and show that the struggle has been the cause of progress right away down – or at any rate that they have always gone together. He can bang away at Christianity with a battery of perfect reason and perfect logic. The philosophy of militarism like the logic of determinism is perfect – it is the most impressive intellectual edifice ever constructed. And if God is Almighty – if the way the world has grown has been in continual accordance with his will [–] I don't see how we can escape it. It is irresistible. God is on the side	

of the Big Battalions, and the man
or nation who can conquer is the
chosen of God. Might is right –
and war is God's method – God's
appointed medicine for the healing
of the nation's ills. The militarist
philosophy of history is absolutely
sound – and Prussian ~~action is~~
practice is the logical outcome of
Prussian theory. The one duty of
the state is to be strong and he
who will not face that fact must
keep his hands off politics. The
Prussian Kaiser is not a hypocrite
when he speaks of God as his ally
– his chief supporter – he is not
a hypocrite – he is perfectly sinie
[*sic* – meaning 'sincere'], perfectly
logical – and perfectly damnable
Prussian frightfulness also is
perfectly logical – perfectly sincere
– and perfectly damnable.

We cry out against it – I cry out
against it – I hate it – I am ready
– quite ready to die – fighting it.
That's why I'm here. I'm not here
because I'm a patriot. I don't care
a hang for England apart from
what I believe England stands
for. I've not got an ounce of loyal
sentiment in me. I respect King
George because I believe him to be
an honest – painstaking – public
servant – and a suitable head of
the Anglo Saxon republic of free
nations. If he were not a decent
man – and good public servant – I
would want to kick him out – the
history of Kings makes me sick
– and I believe the sentiment of
loyalty to a King whether good or
bad to be false – and vicious.

I don't care twopence about
England's commercial supremacy
or her prestige – or her naval
supremacy – or any of this
solemn clap trap of self interested
diplomatic circles. It's all bosh
to me like the German clap trap
about her place in the sun. It is all
cant – silly puerile cant. This race
for commercial supremacy is the
silliest thing that ever happened.
The people of Denmark or
Belgium or Sweden are not a bit
less really prosperous – a bit less
really strong because they are not
commercially supreme. It does
not matter a pin whether nations
are commercially supreme or not
so long as they are free. Every
argument in the [G]reat Illusion
is as sound today as ever it was,
the only mistake he made was to
underestimate the sin and folly
of man. ~~But~~ Every justification of
this war on any ~~but the~~ grounds
but that it is war against the theory
that might is right is rotten and
inadequate. If this war is not a war
to end war then it's just another
damned scandal.

But Almighty God – there's
the rub – Almighty God ordering
history in accordance with his will
– history full of Wars. What are we
to make of that. Look ye we can
only make one thing out of it. God
is Love – He is the author of Peace
– and the Lover of Concord – and
all progress – all true progress is
caused by God – and leads toward
God.

Love – Unity – Concord is the
only real power in the world – the
only cause of real progress. Only
as we progress toward Unity and
Concord do we really progress at
all. Either the Christian religion
means that or it means nothing –
and as old Von Treit[s]ch[k]e said
has no place or application to the
progress of the world of nations.
Now can you see the Spirit of
Unity and Concord – the Spirit of
Love working in History. Yes you
can. You can see it working far
back in the union of the mother
with the child against the world.
You can see it expanding into the
union of the family – from the
family to the clan – from the clan
to the nation – from the nation
to the Empire of free nations.
You can see it working in the
million efforts mens has made at
brotherhoods – societies – unions.
Above all you can see it working
in that great dream which filled
the heart and soul of S. Paul – and
has filled the heart and soul and
genius all down the ages – the
Catholic Church – the universal
brotherhood – breaking down all
barriers of class – and sex – and
nationality – that the world may be
one as God is one.
I see it working everywhere – and
it is God – but nowhere do I see
in the workings of that Spirit – any
trace of Omnipotence. Always it is
striving – struggling – apparently
defeated – yet painfully and slowly
victorious.

If it is true, I go morally mad.
Good and evil cease to have any
meaning. If anything is evil, war is.
It is supposed to be a blessing to
the nations by those who advocate
or apologise for it. It is supposed
to make them virile and strong. It
is a strange method of doing it, to
take all your finest physical and
spiritual specimens and set them to
kill one another by thousands, and
leave weaklings alive to breed the
race of the future. It is the best and
most direct way of securing the
survival of the unfittest. Specially
under modern conditions, when
by mechanical contrivances
weaklings can slaughter splendid
men by scores with shells hurled
at them from miles away. War is
evil. It is a cruel and insane waste
of energy and life. If God wills
war, then I am morally mad and
life has no meaning. I hate war,
and if God wills it I hate God,
and I am a better man for hating
Him; that is the pass it brings me
to. In that case the first and great
commandment is, "Thou shalt
hate the Lord thy God with all thy
heart, and Him only shalt Thou
detest and despise."

Then I give it up. I can't see
God, and I can't love Him. I turn
back to Christ. I can see Him and
love Him. He could not will war.
He brought strife upon earth,
because He roused the powers
of evil by challenging them; but
He did not will strife: He suffered
agony and death because of it, and

pleaded with men to conquer evil and learn to live at peace.

This is the only attitude I can accept without degradation, and if that is not God's attitude, if God does not suffer agony because of war, and if He does not will that men should live at peace, then I cannot and will not worship Him. I hate Him. This is not merely an intellectual alternative, it is a moral one. It lives and burns. It is a matter of life and death which side you take. If it were merely intellectual it would not matter.

Intellectually the Almighty God Who wills war has a lot to say for Himself. Heinrich von Treitschke is His prophet, and the Prussians are His chosen people. They have a splendid case. The militarist interpretation of history is an inevitable result of the doctrine of the absolute omnipotence of God.

Progress has everywhere and at all times been accompanied by strife and warfare. It is the eternal law of nature. The struggle for existence and the survival of the fittest are Almighty God's appointed methods of progress. The strong man must survive and the weaker go to the wall. That is the law of nature, and therefore the will of God. How can you argue against that? You can't. You can only oppose sentiment to reason, and that fight is won before it is fought for any reasonable man. This world is not a Sunday School; it is a slaughter-house, and always has been. Peace or war, what does

it matter? There is no such
thing as peace, and never can
be. Competition is just peaceful
war with far more cruel weapons
than either shot or shell. War is
competition stripped of all disguise
– without the velvet glove. Who is
going to deny that competition is
the law of business and the law of
life? A few parsons perhaps, and
some socialists who want what
they have not got. Every sensible
man of the world knows that cut-
throat competition is the law of
life, the cause of progress, and the
only real motive of efficiency and
work.

You cannot kill knowledge
with rhetoric or alter facts by
furious abuse. You may rail at
the Prussian, but at least he is
no hypocrite. He is the honest
man of Europe, or at least he was
until he was beaten and began
to whine. There was no Sunday-
School sentiment about him.
He did not pretend to apply the
teachings of a visionary Christ
to practical politics. He took his
stand on the rocks of natural
fact, and claimed the support of
the Almighty God according to
Whose will the everlasting strife of
history has been the lot of man. It
is absurd to charge the Kaiser with
hypocrisy when he claims that God
is with him. If God be absolutely
Almighty, then He is with him,
and was when he declared war,
it being the will of God that the
strong should seek to conquer the

weak. The Kaiser is right when you look at the thing honestly in the cold light of reason, and refuse to use sentiment and religious soft soap.

The Prussian is the really consistent worshipper of the Almighty God Whom Nature plainly reveals as the Author of life. He believes in power, patiently makes himself powerful, and then puts power to the test. If he loses then, it is because he is not powerful enough, and he must set to work again. In the end power must prevail, for that is God's will in the world. Might is right.

And what about the British? We are the hypocrites. God is Love, we say. Right is might. But do we trust in right, or in Love? Not much.

Let us have done with this nonsense. Let us have a bit of Prussian honesty. They are the sincere and consistent worshippers of the Almighty God of strife Whose will has always swayed the world, and led it on and upwards to its appointed end.

It is a great argument, it makes one feel angry and helpless. One feels that it is all wrong; but if God is Almighty, how can it be wrong? It is utterly logical and consistent; but one can't accept it because one's soul rebels. The truth is, that history drives one to the knowledge that God cannot be absolutely Almighty. It is the Almighty God we are fighting; He is the soul of Prussianism.

I want to kill Him. That is what I'm here for. I want to kill the Almighty God and tear Him from His throne. It is Him we are really fighting against. I would gladly die to kill the idea of the Almighty God Who drives men either to cruelty or atheism. This war is no mere national struggle, it is a war between two utterly incompatible visions of God. That is what I'm out for. I want to ensure that men do not worship a false God. I want to win the world to the worship of the patient, suffering Father God revealed in Jesus Christ. But can I find any traces of that God in history? Yes, I find Him everywhere.

History's pages but record One death grapple in the darkness 'Twixt old Systems and the Word. Right for ever on the scaffold Wrong for ever on the throne Yet that scaffold sways the future And behind the dim unknown Standeth God within the shadow Keeping Watch above his own.	History's pages but record One death-grapple in the darkness 'Twixt old systems and the Word. Right for ever on the scaffold, Wrong for ever on the throne, Yet that scaffold sways the future, And, behind the dim unknown, Standeth God within the shadow, Keeping watch above His own.

When I read the pages of man's history and try to grasp the nature of that spirit behind it – I cannot see the Almighty Monarch with the Sceptre in his hand. I cannot see him in history any more than I can in nature. History runs red with blood – it rings with the cries of tortured women and suffering children – I shut my eyes and see

again the pictures that my study
of history presents to me – and
much of it – most of it – is dark
with war – strife. But through it
all there runs like a golden thread
the longing after – the striving
after unity – brotherhood – Love –
follow that thread – and I believe it
will lead you straight to the throne
of God – but when you come to
the end – there is no throne – but
only a Cross – and one that hangs
thereon – God not Almighty – but
Splendid – suffering – Crucified –
and Conquering. He is the cause
of all real progress. Progress is
caused by God – who is Love – in
spite of War – in spite of hatred
– in spite of strife – and bitter
competition. The ultimate end
of all war hatred and strife is self
destruction. Love alone creates
and God is Love. This war is not
God's Will or God's Judgment – it
is Recrucifixion – God's defeat
– part of the Eternal Calvary of
God. The crucified Spirit of Love
which is the only God – is calling
us to throw in our lot with him
– share his suffering and help to
save the world. That is the essence
of Christianity. God the Invisible
King is dead – He died with the
Kaiser. God the Eternal Spirit of
Suffering Love is near at hand –
and calls us to follow – to follow of
our own free will.

O Christ my God – my only God
– I see thy face in history's pages as
I saw it in the ~~suns~~ dawning skies
– I see it too in this dark place –
and hear thy voice in the hissing of
shells outside – and it is a voice

shot through with pain – I am
Jesus – whom Thou persecutest
– There is no Almighty Monarch
– and but there is all suffering
Love – and in the end – the victory
will come and at the name of
Jesus every knee shall [bow]. And
meanwhile for every soldier acting
[?] in his name there is in the
midst [of] battle – Peace – in the
heart of sorrow perfect Joy.

God, the Father God of Love, is
everywhere in history, but nowhere
is He Almighty. Ever and always
we see Him suffering, striving,
crucified, but conquering. God is
Love. He is the Author of peace
and lover of concord, and all true
progress is caused by God and
moves toward God, the God of
Love. Only as we progress toward
unity, concord, and co-operation
do we really progress at all. The
workings of God in history are
quite evident and clear. I see the
birth of human unity and concord
foreshadowed far back in Nature
in the union of the mother and the
child. I see it spread out into the
family, from the family to the clan,
and from the clan to the nation,
and from the nation to the empire
of free nations, and I look forward,
and have a perfect rational right to
look forward, to the final victory
and a united world. This progress
is there, and it is the work of God,
but it bears no trace of being the
work of an Almighty God. It has
been a broken, slow, and painful
progress marked by many failures,
a Via Dolorosa wet with blood and

tears. So far as human unity exists to-day, it is, like all other good things in the world, the result not only of the power but of the pain of God. We see the God of Love in all the splendid dreams of and efforts after brotherhood and unity which have marked the course of human history. All of them splendid failures.

Above all, I see it in the splendid failure of a dream which found birth within the brain of Christ, and has won the enthusiasm and life-long devotion of so many noble souls, the Catholic Church. The Church has always been a failure, like Christ; but out of its failure it has won the high success. In it we see the God Father Whom Christ revealed – struggling, suffering, crucified, but conquering still. Men leave Him for dead, and behold He is alive again. They despise His weakness, and then find His weakness strong. They mock at the folly of the Father Who leads but will not drive, and then come to see the wisdom of that folly in the end. For the foolishness of God is wiser than man, and His weakness is stronger than our strength. If the Christian religion means anything, it means that God is Suffering Love, and that all real progress is caused by the working of Suffering Love in the world.

If it means anything, it means that progress is made in spite of, and not because of, strife and war.

Human strife is not God's method, but His problem – a problem that arises from absolute but temporary necessities inherent in the task of creation. Strife and warfare arise from the limitation which the God of Love had to submit to in order to create spiritual personalities worthy to be called His sons. War is the crucifixion of God, not the working of His will. The Cross is not past, but present. Ever and always I can see set up above this world of ours a huge and towering Cross, with great arms stretched out east and west from the rising to the setting sun, and on that Cross my God still hangs and calls on all brave men to come out and fight with evil, and by their sufferings endured with Him help to lift the world from darkness into light.

Always that cry from the Cross is answered; but because of sin, and because we are but children yet, it is only very feebly answered. All nations crucify Him, yet all nations desire Him. All men love Him, and yet, manlike, kill the thing they love because He calls for sacrifice. Longing for Him in our hearts, we deny Him in our lives. We are all hypocrites, and our hypocrisy is our salvation. Honesty would damn our souls to hell, because it could only be Prussian honesty of the lower standard. If we were perfectly honest now, it would mean that we had lost the vision of the Highest which makes hypocrites of all.

We cannot be Christian, but we must be as Christian as we can. We cannot even be human, but we must be as human as we can. We can't be saints, but we must be sportsmen. It is beyond us to turn the other cheek, but at least we must not hit below the belt. That is the form our hypocrisy must take, and it is the only foundation for future honesty. The laws of war, the Geneva Convention and its provisions may be intellectual nonsense, but they are spiritual supersense. They have in them the splendid human inconsistency which is the hall-mark of a man, the super-animal who is always a failure, because his destiny is infinitely high. If one aims at the moon one will not score a bull, but neither will one hit a gooseberry bush.

This is the creed of those who worship the God of Suffering Love, and it is the direct contradiction of the creed of those who worship the supreme untroubled God of power. In this creed, which to men looks like weakness, there lies the source of all true strength. This, I believe, is the real creed of the British Army, if only it could cut itself free from all the complications that have arisen from false teaching in the past.

If we were not fighting this war in order to end all war, and with hatred of war in our hearts, it would be for us, as well as our enemies, another utter disgrace.

	But that is what the heart of the Allies does mean: it means to end war. The heart of the allied nations means it, for the heart of the nations is in their common people, and they all mean it. The heart of the common people knows nothing about God Almighty, except as a puzzle for parsons, but they long for and fight for brotherhood and peace, and therefore, consciously or unconsciously, they long for and fight for the suffering Father God of Love revealed in Jesus Christ.
	* * * * *
The shelling has ceased – come on boys – you did your best. I tried to do mine – we can do no more – let us go home – and sleep. But I will wake in the morning and fight for Love – so let me live and die a decent serving soldier of the Suffering God.	
	Hurrah for the army of splendid human hypocrites who blaspheme the God they die for and kill the thing they love. Here's one of them blaspheming Christ and helping in a wounded Boche. Yes, lad, you can get through now. It's fairly quiet. Follow the white tape and it will bring you through. I wonder, could we carry old Fritz? I bet that foot is giving him what for.

Appendix 2: Author's Preface to New Edition, 1925

I would not have him back, my soldier son,
Though arms and lips are aching for his kiss,
I gave him once for all, my only one,
    But not for this.

This world with sorrow piled upon its sin,
With poverty to crown the curse of War,
With children growing peaked and pale and thin,
    This open sore.

I gave him for his dream of splendid things,
I gave him that a world of men set free
Might seek their God, resurgent on the wings
    Of liberty.

I gave him that his sacrifice might bear
The fruit of growing Peace all down the years;
I gave him that no Mother in despair
    Might weep these tears.

O God, Who tore my heart out by the roots,
I do not ask Thee give him back to me,
I pray Thee, of Thy justice, shew me fruits
    Of Victory.[1]

---

1 This is SK's poem, 'Fruits of Victory', first published in his *Songs of Faith and Doubt* (London: Hodder & Stoughton, 1922).

Author's Preface to New Edition, 1925

Seven years have come and gone since first this book was written and we are still looking for the fruits of victory and finding them in chaos, poverty, disease, and hosts of unemployed.[2] Men said this was a crude and cruel book when it was written, and I replied that it is not as crude or as cruel as the war.[3] I would say now that it was mildness itself compared with the cruelty and brutality of a godless peace.

The soldiers never treated Christ with the cynical brutality of the politicians. Political scheming for narrow ends is the most inhuman and disgusting form of violence, and behind it there is more soul-less unbelief than there is behind the ferocity of war. If the doctrine of the sovereign Kaiser-God was impossible to hold on the battle-fields of Flanders and of France, it is even more impossible in the Europe of to-day. That God is dead, as dead as cold mutton, and even deader, because He can be no longer be used as food even for the poor. Even the most poverty-stricken in mind and spirit have in these days learned to spew out any teaching about God which makes Him less good than Jesus.[4] That is the only good thing, of a positive description, the war appears to have done.

---

2 The disillusionment with the new world that was to come as a result of 'the war to end all wars' and the promises of 'a land fit for heroes' is one of the great cultural themes of the late 1920s. After the suffering, destruction and the orgy of death of the war, 'normalcy' quickly returned and with it not only disappointment but also the economic and social problems that resulted from the war. This was the world in which SK ministered in his work in the Industrial Christian Fellowship. See Gerald Studdert Kennedy, *Dog-collar Democracy: The Industrial Christian Fellowship 1919–1929* (London: Macmillan, 1982).

3 SK's existentialism did not permit him to let this slur go by. To say that a piece of theology is 'cruel' or 'crude' ignored the fact that whatever was found at the level of reflection was secondary to the real cruelty and crudity of actual existence. In fact it is a statement that his critics were not living in the 'real' world but simply engaged in games of words and ideas.

4 Seven more years of preaching and reflection had allowed SK to express one of his central ideas with an explicit sharp clarity that was only implicit in

The Hardest Part

If the revolt against that doctrine of the glorified policeman is crudely stated in these pages I do not feel much inclined to retract it – in some ways, the cruder the statement is, the better. A superstition demands very much the same treatment as a bad smell, and we have had enough disease and fever of the human heart arising directly from this particular blasphemy to make one feel inclined to take to a rat poison to get rid of it. Of course the book won't satisfy theologians, but then it's not written for them to read but for the man who has to earn his bread in the sweat of his brow.

There's a whole lot more to be said on the problems which "The Hardest Part" tries to face, and some of it the author has tried to say in other books.[5] The ultimate problem, the problem of evil, is insoluble; to the writing of books upon it there is no end and the study of them is a weariness to the flesh and the spirit.[6] But our job is not to solve the problem of evil but to destroy evil and blow the problem up, and that can only be done as men learn more and more in spirit and in truth to worship God revealed in Christ and take Him as their Captain and their King.[7]

When they are old enough I am going to read "The Hardest Part" to my sons,[8] and I hope that it will make them uncompromising and bitter rebels against the cruelty and folly and waste of war, and plant in their minds a strong healthy suspicion of the scheming, lying, and greed that bring it about, and most of all that it will help to kill in their minds that power of sickly

---

the 1918 version: what Christians know about God is what we see in Jesus – indeed, in Jesus on the cross.

5 This is an explicit acknowledgement that *The Hardest Part* is not a 'stand-alone' work of the moment but part of SK's more general theological vision. Assessing that vision is a task that is still, after nearly a century, in its infancy.

6 This is an echo of Eccles. 12.12: 'of making many books there is no end; and much study is a weariness of the flesh' (AV).

7 The language of Jesus as 'Captain' and 'King' was very common in the hymnody of the age, not least in the work of Charles Wesley.

8 Alas, SK did not live long enough to do this.

sentimentalism, that idiotic pomp and pageantry of militarism, which provide the glamour and romance for the mean and dirty shambles that are the battle-fields of the world's great wars.[9]

G. A. STUDDERT KENNEDY.

---

9 SK was not among the naïve who thought that there would never again be a war: he seems to have been aware that until the underlying problems were tackled, war would return again to destroy and lay waste humanity.

Appendix 3: Studdert Kennedy's Poems on Divine Suffering

1. The Sorrow of God[1]

A Sermon in a Billet

YES, I used to believe i' Jesus Christ,
    And I used to go to Church,
But sin' I left 'ome and came to France,
    I've been clean knocked off my perch.
For it seemed orlright at 'ome, it did,
    To believe in a God above
And in Jesus Christ 'Is only Son,
    What died on the Cross through Love.
When I went for a walk of a Sunday morn
    On a nice fine day in the spring,
I could see the proof o' the living God
    In every living thing.
For 'ow could the grass and the trees grow up
    All along o' their bloomin' selves?

---

1 First published in *Rough Rhymes of a Padre* (1918). Republished in *The Sorrows of God and Other Poems* (1921), and then with minor textual variations in *The Unutterable Beauty* (1927), which was reprinted as *The Rhymes of G. A. Studdert Kennedy* (1940). The 16th edition of *The Unutterable Beauty* was published in 1961 (all listed here published London: Hodder & Stoughton).

Ye might as well believe i' the fairy tales,
    And think they was made by elves.
So I thought as that long-'aired atheist
    Were nubbat a silly sod,
For 'ow did 'e 'count for my brussels sprouts
    If 'e didn't believe i' God?[2]
But it ain't the same out 'ere, ye know.
    It's as different as chalk fro' cheese,
For 'arf on it's blood and t'other 'arf's mud,
    And I'm damned if I really sees
'Ow the God, who 'as made such a cruel world,
    Can 'ave Love in 'Is 'eart for men,
And be deaf to the cries of the men as dies
    And never comes 'ome again.
Just look at that little boy corporal there,
    Such a fine upstanding lad,
Wi' a will ov 'is own, and a way ov 'is own,
    And a smile ov 'is own, 'e 'ad.
An hour ago 'e were bustin' wi' life,
    Wi' 'is actin' and foolin' and fun;
'E were simply the life on us all, 'e were,
    Now look what the blighters 'a done.
Look at 'im lyin' there all ov a 'eap,
    Wi' the blood soaken over 'is 'ead,
Like a beautiful picture spoiled by a fool,
    A bundle o' nothin' – dead.
And it ain't only 'im – there's a mother at 'ome,
    And 'e were the pride of 'er life.
For it's women as pays in a thousand ways
    For the madness o' this 'ere strife.

---

2 Although Charles Darwin's work had seriously undermined the 'argument from design' for the existence of God, it continued to be widely expressed and apparently accepted in the British churches in this period.

And the lovin' God 'E looks down on it all,
    On the blood and the mud and the smell.
O God, if it's true, 'ow I pities you,
    For ye must be livin' i' 'ell.
You must be livin' i' 'ell all day,
    And livin' i' 'ell all night.
I'd rather be dead, wi' a 'ole through my 'ead,
    I would, by a damn long sight,
Than be livin' wi' you on your 'eavenly throne,
    Lookin' down on yon bloody 'eap
That were once a boy full o' life and joy,
    And 'earin' 'is mother weep.
The sorrows o' God mun be 'ard to bear
    If 'E really 'as Love in 'Is 'eart,
And the 'ardest part i' the world to play
    Mun surely be God's part.[3]
And I wonder if that's what it really means,
    That Figure what 'angs on the Cross.
I remember I seed one t'other day
    As I stood wi' the captain's 'oss.
I remember, I thinks, thinks I to mysel',
    It's a long time since 'E died,
Yet the world don't seem much better to-day
    Then when 'E were crucified.
It's allus the same, as it seems to me,
    The weakest mun go to the wall,[4]
And whether e's right, or whether e's wrong,
    It don't seem to matter at all.

---

3 It was the couplet that gave *The Hardest Part* its title.

4 This expression may derive either from the mediaeval practice that the weak would be allowed to sit on seats around the walls of churches, rather than stand, or else the allowing of the weak to walk next to the walls of buildings on urban streets, rather than near the central gulley – which might well be a sewer.

The better ye are and the 'arder it is,
    The 'arder ye 'ave to fight,
It's a cruel 'ard world for any bloke
    What does the thing as is right.
And that's 'ow 'E came to be crucified,
    For that's what 'E tried to do.
'E were allus a tryin' to do 'Is best
    For the likes o' me and you.
Well, what if 'E came to the earth to-day,
    Came walkin' about this trench,
'Ow 'Is 'eart would bleed for the sights 'E seed,
    I' the mud and the blood and the stench.
And I guess it would finish 'Im up for good
    When 'E came to this old sap end,[5]
And 'E seed that bundle o' nothin' there,
    For 'E wept at the grave ov 'Is friend.[6]
And they say 'E were just the image o' God.
    I wonder if God sheds tears,
I wonder if God can be sorrowin' still,
    And 'as been all these years.
I wonder if that's what it really means,
    Not only that 'E once died,
Not only that 'E came once to the earth
    And wept and were crucified?
Not just that 'E suffered once for all
    To save us from our sins,
And then went up to 'Is throne on 'igh
    To wait till 'Is 'eaven begins.

---

5 A 'sap' trench was dug roughly ninety degrees out from existing trench lines, after which a new trench, parallel to the original, was constructed, thus advancing the front line.

6 John 11.35. Jesus wept at the grave of Lazarus before revivifying him. 'Jesus wept' – in English translation, the shortest verse in the Bible.

But what if 'E came to the earth to show,
    By the paths o' pain that 'E trod,
The blistering flame of eternal shame
    That burns in the heart o' God?
O God, if that's 'ow it really is,
    Why, bless ye, I understands,
And I feels for You wi' Your thorn-crowned 'ead
    And your ever piercèd 'ands.
But why don't ye bust the show to bits,
    And force us to do your will?
Why ever should God be suffering so
    And man be sinning still?
Why don't You make Your voice ring out,
    And drown these cursed guns?
Why don't ye stand with an outstretched 'and,
    Out there 'twixt us and the 'Uns?[7]
Why don't Ye force us to end the war
    And fix up a lasting peace?
Why don't Ye will that the world be still
    And wars for ever cease?
That's what I'd do, if I was You,
    And I had a lot of sons
What squabbled and fought and spoilt their 'ome,
    Same as us boys and the 'Uns.
And yet, I remember, a lad o' mine,
    'E's fightin' now on the sea,
And 'e were a thorn in 'is mother's side,
    And the plague o' my life to me.
Lord, 'ow I used to swish that lad
    Till 'e fairly yelped wi' pain,

---

7 That is, 'Huns' – commonplace propaganda slang for the Germans,
derived from a speech in 1900 in which the Kaiser had called on his soldiers to
suppress the Boxer rebellion in China by replicating the merciless behaviour
of the fifth-century Huns in Eastern Europe, under the leadership of Attila.

But fast as I thrashed one devil out
    Another popped in again.
And at last, when 'e grew up a strappin' lad,
    'E ups and 'e says to me,
'My will's my own and my life's my own,
    And I'm goin', Dad, to sea.'
And 'e went, for I 'adn't broke 'is will,
    Though Gawd knows 'ow I tried,
And 'e never set eyes on my face again
    Till the day as 'is mother died.
Well, maybe that's 'ow it is wi' God,
    'Is sons 'ave got to be free;
Their wills are their own, and their lives their own,
    And that's 'ow it 'as to be.[8]
So the Father God goes sorrowing still
    For 'Is world what 'as gone to sea,
But 'E runs up a light on Calvary's 'eight
    That beckons to you and me.
The beacon light of the sorrow of God
    'As been shinin' down the years,
A flashin' its light through the darkest night
    O' our 'uman blood and tears.
There's a sight o' things what I thought was strange,
    As I'm just beginnin' to see
'Inasmuch as ye did it to one of these
    Ye 'ave done it unto Me.'[9]

---

8 The preceding lines are echoing the widely promoted view of many church leaders in the war that it was simply a consequence of the free will given by God to the human race.

9 Matt. 25.31ff., in which Jesus tells his hearers that, 'Inasmuch as ye have done it unto one of the least of these my brethren, ye have done it unto me' (Matt. 25.40 AV).

The Hardest Part

So it isn't just only the crown o' thorns
    What 'as pierced and torn God's 'ead;[10]
'E knows the feel uv a bullet, too,
    And 'E's 'ad 'Is touch o' the lead.
And 'E's standin' wi' me in this 'ere sap,
    And the corporal stands wiv 'Im,
And the eyes of the laddie is shinin' bright,
    But the eyes of the Christ burn dim.
O' laddie, I thought as ye'd done for me
    And broke my 'eart wi' your pain.
I thought as ye'd taught me that God were dead,
    But ye've brought 'Im to life again.
And ye've taught me more of what God is
    Than I ever thought to know,
For I never thought 'E could come so close
    Or that I could love 'Im so.
For the voice of the Lord, as I 'ears it now,
    Is the voice of my pals what bled,
And the call of my country's God to me
    Is the call of my country's dead.

---

10 A reference to the crown of thorns worn by Jesus at his crucifixion – e.g. Matt. 27.29.

2. Thy Will Be Done[11]

A Sermon in a Hospital

I WERE puzzled about this prayin' stunt,
  And all as the parsons say,
For they kep' on sayin', and sayin',
  And yet it weren't plain no way.
For they told us never to worry,
  But simply to trust in the Lord,
'Ask and ye shall receive,' they said,
  And it sounds orlright, but, Gawd![12]
It's a mighty puzzling business,
  For it don't allus work that way,
Ye may ask like mad, and ye don't receive.
  As I found out t'other day.
I were sittin' me down on my 'unkers,[13]
  And 'avin' a pull at my pipe,
And larfin' like fun at a blind old 'Un,[14]
  What were 'avin' a try to snipe.
For 'e couldn't shoot for monkey nuts,
  The blinkin' blear-eyed ass,
So I sits, and I spits, and I 'ums a tune;
  And I never thought o' the gas.

---

11 First published in *Rough Rhymes of a Padre* (1918). Republished in *The Sorrows of God* (1921) and then with minor textual variations in *The Unutterable Beauty* (1927) and *The Rhymes of G. A. Studdert Kennedy* (1940). It was the only one of Studdert Kennedy's poems about divine suffering to be included in the anthology of prose and poetry, *The Best of Studdert Kennedy* (London: Hodder & Stoughton, 1947). The title clearly derives from the Lord's Prayer.

12 A paraphrase of Jesus' words: 'For every one that asketh receiveth; and he that seeketh findeth' (Matt. 7.8 AV).

13 '(H)unkers' meant 'haunches', so the writer was squatting.

14 'Hun' – see note 7 above on 'The Sorrow of God'.

Then all of a suddint I jumps to my feet,
    For I 'eard the strombos sound,[15]
And I pops up my 'ead a bit over the bags
    To 'ave a good look all round.
And there I seed it, comin' across,
    Like a girt big yaller cloud,[16]
Then I 'olds my breath, i' the fear o' death,
    Till I bust, then I prayed aloud.
I prayed to the Lord Orlmighty above,
    For to shift that blinkin' wind,
But it kep' on blowin' the same old way,
    And the chap next me, 'e grinned.
'It's no use prayin',' 'e said, 'let's run,'
    And we fairly took to our 'eels,
But the gas ran faster nor we could run,
    And, Gawd, you know 'ow it feels
Like a thousand rats and a million chats,[17]
    All tearin' away at your chest,
And your legs won't run, and you're fairly done,
    And you've got to give up and rest.
Then the darkness comes, and ye knows no more
    Till ye wakes in an 'orspital bed.
And some never knows nothin' more at all,
    Like my pal Bill – 'e's dead.
Now, 'ow was it 'E didn't shift that wind,
    When I axed in the name o' the Lord?
With the 'orrer of death in every breath,
    Still I prayed every breath I drawed.

---

15 Strombo horns were alarms driven by compressed air that warned soldiers at the front of a gas attack by the enemy.

16 A reference to the use of poisonous gas as a weapon, most probably mustard gas in this case.

17 Possibly an ornithological reference to a member of the flycatcher family.

That beat me clean, and I thought and I thought
    Till I came near bustin' my 'ead.
It weren't for me I were grieved, ye see,
    It were my pal Bill – 'e's dead.
For me, I'm a single man, but Bill
    'As kiddies at 'ome and a wife.
And why ever the Lord didn't shift that wind
    I just couldn't see for my life.
But I've just bin readin' a story 'ere,
    Of the night afore Jesus died,
And of 'ow 'E prayed in Gethsemane,
    'Ow 'E fell on 'Is face and cried.[18]
Cried to the Lord Orlmighty above
    Till 'E broke in a bloody sweat,
And 'E were the Son of the Lord, 'E were,
    And 'E prayed to 'Im 'ard; and yet,
And yet 'E 'ad to go through wiv it, boys,
    Just same as pore Bill what died.
'E prayed to the Lord, and 'E sweated blood,
    And yet 'E were crucified.[19]
But 'Is prayer were answered, I sees it now,
    For though 'E were sorely tried,
Still 'E went wiv 'Is trust in the Lord unbroke,
    And 'Is soul it were satisfied.
For 'E felt 'E were doin' God's Will, ye see,
    What 'E came on the earth to do,
And the answer what came to the prayers 'E prayed
    Were 'Is power to see it through;
To see it through to the bitter end,
    And to die like a God at the last,

---

18 Matt. 26.39: Jesus praying in the garden of Gethsemane, before his betrayal: 'O my Father, if it be possible, let this cup pass from me: nevertheless not as I will, but as thou wilt' (AV).

19 Matt. 27.33ff.

The Hardest Part

In a glory of light that were dawning bright
   Wi' the sorrow of death all past.
And the Christ who was 'ung on the Cross is God,
   True God for me and you,
For the only God that a true man trusts
   Is the God what sees it through.
And Bill, 'e were doin' 'is duty, boys,
   What 'e came on the earth to do,
And the answer what came to the prayers I prayed
   Were 'is power to see it through;
To see it through to the very end,
   And to die as my old pal died,
Wi' a thought for 'is pal and a prayer for 'is gal,
   And 'is brave 'eart satisfied.

3. The Suffering God[20]

If He could speak, that victim torn and bleeding,
    Caught in His pain and nailed upon the Cross,
Has He to give the comfort souls are needing?
    Could He destroy the bitterness of loss?

Once and for all men say He came and bore it,
    Once and for all set up His throne on high,
Conquered the world and set His standard o'er it,
    Dying that once, that men might never die.

Yet men are dying, dying soul and body,
    Cursing the God who gave to them their birth,
Sick of the world with all its sham and shoddy,[21]
    Sick of the lies that darken all the earth.

Peace we were pledged, yet blood is ever flowing,
    Where on the earth has Peace been ever found?
Men do but reap the harvest of their sowing,
    Sadly the songs of human reapers sound.

Sad as the winds that sweep across the ocean,
    Telling to earth the sorrow of the sea.
Vain is my strife, just empty idle motion,
    All that has been is all there is to be.

---

20 First published in *Rough Rhymes of a Padre* (1918). Republished as the second poem – after the short autobiographical 'Woodbine Willie' – in *The Sorrows of God* (1921) and then with minor textual variations in *The Unutterable Beauty* (1927) and *The Rhymes of G. A. Studdert Kennedy* (1940).

21 While 'shoddy' originally meant low-quality fabric made from waste wool, in general use it meant low-quality, second-rate, inferior etc.

The Hardest Part

So on the earth the time waves beat in thunder,
  Bearing wrecked hopes upon their heaving breasts,
Bits of dead dreams, and true hearts torn asunder,
  Flecked with red foam upon their crimson crests.

How can it be that God can reign in glory,
  Calmly content with what His Love has done,
Reading unmoved the piteous shameful story,
  All the vile deeds men do beneath the sun?

Are there no tears in the heart of the Eternal?
  Is there no pain to pierce the soul of God?
Then must He be a fiend of Hell infernal,
  Beating the earth to pieces with His rod.

Or is it just that there is nought behind it,
  Nothing but forces purposeless and blind?
Is the last thing, if mortal man could find it,
  Only a power wandering as the wind?

Father, if He, the Christ, were Thy Revealer,
  Truly the First Begotten of the Lord,[22]
Then must Thou be a Suff'rer and a Healer,
  Pierced to the heart by the sorrow of the sword.

Then must it mean, not only that Thy sorrow
  Smote Thee that once upon the lonely tree,
But that to-day, to-night, and on the morrow,
  Still it will come, O Gallant God, to Thee.

---

22 In the Bible, Jesus is often referred to as the 'firstborn' – e.g. Rom. 8.29;
Col. 1.15; 1.18; Heb. 12.23.

Red with His blood the better day is dawning,
    Pierced by His pain the storm clouds roll apart,[23]
Rings o'er the earth the message of the morning,
    Still on the Cross the Saviour bares His heart.

Passionately fierce the voice of God is pleading,
    Pleading with men to arm them for the fight;
See how those hands, majestically bleeding,
    Call us to rout the armies of the night.

Not to the work of sordid selfish saving
    Of our own souls to dwell with Him on high,
But to the soldier's splendid selfless braving,
    Eager to fight for Righteousness and die.

Peace does not mean the end of all our striving,
    Joy does not mean the drying of our tears;
Peace is the power that comes to souls arriving
    Up to the light where God Himself appears.

Joy is the wine that God is ever pouring
    Into the hearts of those who strive with Him,
Light'ning their eyes to vision and adoring,
    Strength'ning their arms to warfare glad and grim.

So would I live and not in idle resting,
    Stupid as swine that wallow in the mire;
Fain would I fight, and be for ever breasting
    Danger and death for ever under fire.

---

23 In earlier editions of *The Unutterable Beauty* and in *The Rhymes of G. A. Studdert Kennedy*, these two lines were replaced by 'Swift to its birth in spite of human scorning // Hastens the day, the storm-clouds roll apart.' In later editions of *The Unutterable Beauty* (e.g. the 16th, 1961), the original words were restored.

The Hardest Part

Bread of Thy Body give me for my fighting,
 Give me to drink Thy sacred Blood for wine,[24]
While there are wrongs that need me for the righting,
 While there is warfare splendid and divine.

Give me, for light, the sunshine of Thy sorrow,
 Give me for shelter shadow of Thy Cross;
Give me to share the glory of Thy morrow,
 Gone from my heart the bitterness of Loss.

---

24 A reference to the bread and wine of the Christian service of Holy Communion, Mass or Eucharist, in which they represent the body and blood of Christ in the recollection of the Last Supper of bread and wine he shared with his disciples and the shedding of his blood at his crucifixion.

4. A Sermon[25]

My brethen, the ways of God
　　No man can understand,
We can but wait in awe and watch
　　The wonders of His hand.[26]
He dwells in Majesty sublime
　　Beyond the starry height,
His Wisdom is ineffable,
　　His Love is Infinite.
Before Him all created things
　　Do bow them and obey,
The million stars that night by night
　　Wheel down the Milky Way.
The shrieking storm obeys His Will,
　　The wild waves hear His call,
The mountain and the midge's wing,
　　God made and governs all.
'Tis not for us to question Him,
　　To ask or reason why,
'Tis ours to love and worship Him
　　And serve Him till we die.

---

25 First published in *More Rough Rhymes of a Padre* (London: Hodder &
Stoughton, 1919). Republished in *The Sorrows of God* (1921) and then with
minor textual variations in *The Unutterable Beauty* (1927) and *The Rhymes of
G. A. Studdert Kennedy* (1940).

26 This poem expresses the very common attitude of clergy and others that God's purposes were being worked out in the war, but that God's
purposes and actions are beyond human comprehension. Therefore such
questions about God's action – or rather apparent inaction – should not be
asked. While to the modern reader the poem may appear a gross parody
of sermons expressing that perspective, a reviewer in 1919 stated that 'A
Sermon' 'reproduces one of those gramophone homilies with scrupulous fair-
ness' (A. Hird, in *Aldersgate Magazine*, April 1919, p. 260).

O weeping Mother torn with grief,
  Poor stricken heart that cries,
And rocks a cradle empty now,
  'Tis by God's will he dies.
His strong young body blown to bits,
  His raw flesh quiv'ring still,
His comrades' groans of agony,
  These are God's Holy Will.
He measures out our Peace and War
  As seemeth to Him best,
His judgments are unknowable,
  Remember that – and rest.
For what are we poor worms of earth,
  Whose life is for a day,
Our finite minds that Satan blinds,
  My brethren, what are they?
We are but little children weak
  Who cling to God's right hand;
Just think how wonderful He is,
  And bow to His command.
He has some hidden purpose sure
  For all this blood and tears,
It is His Will – be still – be still,
  He is the Lord of years.
He bids us love our enemies,
  And live in Christian Peace,
'Tis only He can order Wars
  And woes that never cease.
Vengeance is Mine, I will repay;
  Beware! Thou shalt not kill:
Behold the bloody fields of France,
  They are God's Holy Will.
That is what makes Him wonderful
  To our poor human sight;

He only can work miracles
   And turn Wrong into Right.
So bow you down and worship Him,
   Kneel humbly and adore
This Infinitely Loving God
   Who is the Lord of War.
Lift up your hands in ceaseless prayer
   That He will spare your lives,
And let His loving judgments fall
   On other people's wives.
He is a God who answers prayer,
   And alters His decrees,
If only we persistently
   Beseech Him on our knees.
If only we would pray enough,
   My brethren, for our sons,
Then He would save their lives for us,
   And spike the German guns.
Our shrieks of pain go up in vain,
   The wide world's miseries
Must still persist until we learn
   To pray upon our knees.
Upon our knees, my friends, I said,
   And mark well what I say,
God wants to see us on our knees,
   The proper place to pray.
Nought is impossible to God
   In answer to such prayers;
If only we are meek enough,
   He is a God who spares.
Whenever people seek to know
   And ask the reason why
Their sons are swallowed up by wars,
   And called to fight and die,

The Hardest Part

There is one thing I ask, dear friends,
  One thing I always say,
I ask them straight, I'm not afraid,
  I ask them, 'Did you pray?
Did you pray humbly on your knees
  That it might be God's Will
To spare his life and bring him back,
  To spare, and not to kill?'[27]
Then if they still can answer yes,
  And think to baffle me,
I simply answer, 'Bow your head,
  His death was God's decree.'
And who are we to question it,
  Who crawl upon the earth
As insects in His Holy sight,
  Vile things of little worth?
Remember, rather, all your sins,
  And bow to God's decrees.
Seek not to know the plans of God,
  But pray upon your knees.
That you may love with all your heart,
  With all your soul and mind,
This perfect God you cannot know,
  Whose face you cannot find.
You have no notion what He's like,
  You cannot know His Will,
He's wrapped in darkest mystery,
  But you must love Him still,
And love Him all the more because
  He is the unknown God

---

27 A commonplace response to questions about why a prayer – e.g. for
the preservation of a loved one – had not been answered was that the prayer
had not been sufficiently fervent.

Who leads you blindfold down the path
  That martyred Saints have trod.
That is the Gospel of the Christ,
  Submit whate'er betides;
You cannot make the wrong world right,
  'Tis God alone decides.

.   .   .   .

O, by Thy Cross and Passion, Lord,
  By broken hearts that pant
For comfort and for love of Thee,
  Deliver us from cant.

5. The Comrade God[28]

THOU who dost dwell in depths of timeless being,
  Watching the years as moments passing by,
Seeing the things that lie beyond our seeing,
  Constant, unchanged, as æons dawn and die.

Thou who canst count the stars upon their courses.
  Holding them all in the hollow of Thy hand,
Lord of the world with its myriad of forces
  Seeing the hills as single grains of sand.

Art Thou so great that this our bitter crying
  Sounds in Thine ears like sorrow of a child?
Hast Thou looked down on centuries of sighing,
  And, like a heartless mother, only smiled?

Since in Thy sight to-day is as to-morrow,
  And while we strive Thy victory is won,
Hast Thou no tears to shed upon our sorrow?
  Art Thou a staring splendour like the sun?

Dost Thou not heed the helpless sparrow's falling?[29]
  Canst Thou not see the tears that women weep?
Canst Thou not hear Thy littlest children calling?
  Dost Thou not watch above them as they sleep?

---

28 First published in *More Rough Rhymes of a Padre* (1919). Republished
in *The Sorrows of God* (1921) and then with minor textual variations in *The
Unutterable Beauty* (1927) and *The Rhymes of G. A. Studdert Kennedy* (1940).
  29 Luke 12.6: 'Are not five sparrows sold for two farthings, and not one of
them is forgotten before God?' (AV).

Then, O my God, Thou art too great to love me,
   Since Thou dost reign beyond the reach of tears,
Calm and serene as the cruel stars above me,
   High and remote from human hopes and fears.

Only in Him can I find home to hide me,
   Who on the Cross was slain to rise again;
Only with Him my Comrade God beside me,
   Can I go forth to war with sin and pain.

6. High and Lifted Up[30]

SEATED on the throne of power with the sceptre in Thine hand,
While a host of eager angels ready for Thy Service stand.
So it was the prophet saw Thee, in his agony of prayer,
While the sound of many waters swelled in music on the air,
Swelled until it burst like thunder in a shout of perfect praise,
'Holy, Holy, Holy Father, Potentate of years and days.
Thine the Kingdom, Thine the glory, Thine the splendour of
the sun,
Thine the wisdom, Thine the honour, Thine the crown of
victory won.'[31]
So it was the prophet saw Thee, so this artist saw Thee too,
Flung his vision into colour, mystery of gold and blue.
But I stand in woe and wonder; God, my God, I cannot see,
Darkness deep and deeper darkness – all the world is dark
to me.
Where is Power? Where is Glory? Where is any victory won?
Where is wisdom? Where is honour? Where the splendour of
the sun?
God, I hate this splendid vision – all its splendour is a lie,
Splendid fools see splendid folly, splendid mirage born to die.
As imaginary waters to an agony of thirst,
As the vision of a banquet to a body hunger-cursed,
As the thought of anæsthetic to a soldier mad with pain,
While his torn and tortured body turns and twists and writhes
again,
So this splendid lying vision turns within my doubting heart,
Like a bit of rusty bayonet in a torn and festering part.

---

30 First published in *Peace Rhymes of a Padre* (London: Hodder & Stoughton, 1920). Republished in *The Sorrows of God* (1921) and then with minor textual variations in *The Unutterable Beauty* (1927) and *The Rhymes of G. A. Studdert Kennedy* (1940).

31 Cf. Isa. 6.1ff.

Preachers give it me for comfort, and I curse them to their face,
Puny, petty-minded priestlings prate to me of power and grace;
Prate of power and boundless wisdom that takes count of little
    birds,[32]
Sentimental poisoned sugar in a sickening stream of words.
Platitudinously pious far beyond all doubts and fears,
They will patter of God's mercy that can wipe away our tears.
All their speech is drowned in sobbing, and I hear the great
    world groan,
As I see a million mothers sitting weeping all alone,
See a host of English maidens making pictures in the fire,
While a host of broken bodies quiver still on German wire.
And I hate the God of Power on His hellish heavenly throne,
Looking down on rape and murder, hearing little children moan.
Though a million angels hail Thee King of Kings, yet cannot I.
There is nought can break the silence of my sorrow save the cry,
'Thou who rul'st this world of sinners with Thy heavy iron rod,
Was there ever any sinner who has sinned the sin of God?
Was there ever any dastard who would stand and watch a Hun
Ram his bayonet through the bowels of a baby just for fun?[33]
Praise to God in Heaven's highest and in all the depths be praise,
Who in all His works is brutal, like a beast in all His ways.'[34]
God, the God I love and worship, reigns in sorrow on the Tree,
Broken, bleeding, but unconquered, very God of God to me.
All that showy pomp of splendour, all that sheen of angel wings,

---

32 Cf. Luke 12.6.

33 Probably a reference to the atrocities committed by German troops in Belgium in the opening months of the war. While some stories were created for propaganda purposes, many accounts were fully substantiated, and the treatment meted out to 'brave little Belgium' helped to bolster support for Britain's declaration of war and the subsequent costly warfare.

34 These two lines are a parody of John Henry Newman's hymn, 'Praise to the holiest in the height // And in the depth be praise; // In all his words most wonderful, // Most sure in all his ways.'

The Hardest Part

Was but borrowed from the baubles that surround our earthly
  kings.
Thought is weak and speech is weaker, and the vision that He
  sees
Strikes with dumbness any preacher, brings him humbly to his
  knees.
But the word that Thou hast spoken borrows nought from
  kings and thrones,
Vain to rack a royal palace for the echo of Thy tones.
In a manger, in a cottage, in an honest workman's shed,
In the homes of humble peasants, and the simple lives they led,
In the life of one an outcast and a vagabond on earth,
In the common things He valued, and proclaimed of priceless
  worth,
And above all in the horror of the cruel death He died,
Thou hast bid us seek Thy glory, in a criminal crucified.
And we find it – for Thy glory is the glory of Love's loss,
And Thou hast no other splendour but the splendour of the
  Cross.
For in Christ I see the martyrs and the beauty of their pain,
And in Him I hear the promise that my dead shall rise again.
High and lifted up, I see Him on the eternal Calvary,
And two piercèd hands are stretching east and west o'er land
  and sea.
On my knees I fall and worship that great Cross that shines
  above,
For the very God of Heaven is not Power, but Power of Love.

7. The Soul of Doubt[35]

THAT'S it. Doubt's very soul of doubt
Lies here. Is God just faith in God,
Or can God work His will without
Our human faith? Is flesh and blood
Made by, or maker of, the mind
That works upon the mass of things
Inanimate? Has this wild wind
A master, riding on its wings
His chosen way, or is it free
Of any but its own mad will
To sweep in wanton liberty
Over the patient earth, and spill
Destruction, breaking hearts and homes,
A drunken thing without a plan
Or purpose anywhere? It comes
To that at last. Is mortal man
Fated to fight a senseless world
Of blind material force alone,
By its haphazard powers hurled
This way and that, until his own
Small wit in desperation finds
A way to short uncertain Peace?
Around this core of doubt thought winds
Its endless coil, seeking release,
And, finding none, for ever binds
Its meshes tighter round the soul.

.   .   .   .

35 First published in *Songs of Faith and Doubt* (London: Hodder & Stoughton, 1922). Republished in *The Unutterable Beauty* (1927), which was reprinted as *The Rhymes of G. A. Studdert Kennedy* (1940).

The Hardest Part

The preachers blame our lack of faith
For all our human ills, but why?
Does God depend on man? 'Thus saith
The Lord omnipotent,' they cry.
Aye, God for ever says, but we
Must do, and how? We lack the power,
And from the task's immensity
Reel back in fear, as hour by hour
It grows, and frowning peak on peak
The evil mountains rise ahead.
We stumble on bewildered, weak,
Half blind, trusting what we have read
Of God, that legendary Love
Urgent to help us, and redeem
Our souls, a Love we cannot prove,
But shut our aching eyes and dream
It true. Could any God endure
The sight unmoved and silent still?
Would not a real God assure
Our doubts, and work His mighty Will
Without our faith? So many wrecks;
Wrecked faith, wrecked hope, wrecked love, wrecked dreams;
And still we bow our helpless necks
To meet the storm. God's silence seems
Decisive. God is only faith
In God, and when Faith dies, God dies,
And Hope, a homeless weeping wraith,
Beats on her shrivelled breasts, and cries,
Refusing to be comforted,
Because her little ones are dead,
All dead.

And yet – and yet – doubt may deceive,
Joy may give truer thought than grief.
It may be so, Lord, I believe,
In mercy help mine unbelief.[36]

---

36 A reference to the plea of the father of a child brought to Jesus for healing: 'Immediately the father of the child cried out, "I believe; help my unbelief!"' (Mark 9.24).

References and Further Reading

Selected References

Material not directly relevant to SK and *The Hardest Part*, fully identified in the footnotes to the original text above, are omitted. For works by SK, see the section so headed below. An annotated list of biographies of SK then follows.

Bell, G. K. A., 1952, *Randall Davidson, Archbishop of Canterbury*, London: Oxford University Press.

Bell, Stuart, 2012, '"Patriotism and Sacrifice": The Preaching of Geoffrey Studdert Kennedy ("Woodbine Willie"), 1914–1918', in Lyons, William John and Sandwell, Isabella (eds), *Delivering the Word: Preaching and Exegesis in the Western Christian Tradition*, Sheffield: Equinox.

Bell, Stuart, 2013, 'The Theology of Woodbine Willie in Context', in Snape, M. and Madigan, E. (eds), *The Clergy in Khaki: British Army Chaplains in the First World War*, Farnham: Ashgate. (A later version of this chapter formed part of Bell, Stuart, 2017b.)

Bell, Stuart, 2017a, 'From Collusion to Condemnation: The Evolving Voice of "Woodbine Willie"', in Smith, A. K. and Cowman, K. (eds), *Far Beyond the Lines: Landscapes and Voices of the Great War*, London: Routledge.

Bell, Stuart, 2017b, *Faith in Conflict: The Impact of the Great War on the Faith of the People of Britain*, Solihull: Helion.

'Books received', *Anglican Theological Review* 7:3–4, Dec. 1924–Mar. 1925, p. 528.

Brittain, Christopher Craig, 2011, *Religion at Ground Zero: Theological Responses to Times of Crisis*, London: Continuum.

Carey, D. F., 1929, 'Studdert Kennedy: War Padre', in Mozley, J. K. (ed.), *G. A. Studdert Kennedy: By His Friends*, London: Hodder & Stoughton.

Chapman, M. D., 1999, 'King and Kennedy: Two Visions of Ministry for March 8', *The Expository Times* 110:5, pp. 141–3.

Dunn, J. C., 1938, *The War the Infantry Knew: 1914–1918*, London: P. S. King & Son.

Ellis, Robert, 2005, 'Geoffrey Studdert Kennedy: The Pastor and the Suffering God', *Transformation* 22:3, pp. 166–75.

Hastings, J., 'Notes of Recent Exposition', *The Expository Times* 30:3, Dec. 1918, pp. 97–105.

Hermitage Day, E, 'The Editor's Table: The Padre in Evidence', *Church Times*, 15 Nov. 1919, p. 356.

Lodge, Oliver, 1916, *Raymond; or, Life and Death*, London: Methuen.

Madigan, Edward, 2011, *Faith under Fire: Anglican Chaplains and the Great* War, Basingstoke: Palgrave Macmillan.

Martin, A. A., 2011, *A Surgeon in Khaki: Through France and Flanders in World War I*, with an introduction by G. Harper, Lincoln, NE: University of Nebraska Press.

Moltmann, Jürgen, 1974, *The Crucified God*, London: SCM Press.

Moltmann, Jürgen, 1981, *The Trinity and the Kingdom*, London: SCM Press. First published in 1980 as *Trinität und Reich Gottes*. Page references are to the 1993 Fortress Press edition.

Moltmann, Jürgen, 2007, *A Broad Place: An Autobiography*, Minneapolis, MN: Fortress Press.

Mozley, J. K., 1926, *The Impassibility of God: A Survey of Christian Thought*, Cambridge: Cambridge University Press.

Mozley, J. K. (ed.), 1927, *G. A. Studdert Kennedy: By His Friends*, London: Hodder & Stoughton.

Mozley, J. K., 1952, *Some Tendencies in British Theology from the Publication of Lux Mundi to the Present Day*, London: SPCK.

Oden, Patrick, 2011, *Sessions with Moltmann: A Summary of Three Conversations in Tübingen*, retrieved from www.dualravens.com/phd/sessions.pdf and quoted by kind permission of the author.

Pauck, W. and Pauck, M., 1977, *Paul Tillich: His Life and Thought, vol. 1: Life*, London: Collins.

Pythian-Adams, W. J., 'Correspondence: The Padre in Evidence', *Church Times*, 6 Dec. 1918, p. 420.

Ramsey, A. M., 1960, *From Gore to Temple: The Development of Anglican Theology Between Lux Mundi and the Second World War, 1889–1939*, London: Longmans.

Rowell, Geoffrey, 2004, 'Kennedy, Geoffrey Anketell Studdert', in *Oxford Dictionary of National Biography*, Oxford: Oxford University Press.

Snape, Michael, 2005, *God and the British Soldier*, Abingdon: Routledge,

Snape, Michael, 2011, 'Church of England Army Chaplains in the First World War: Goodbye to "Goodbye to All That"', *Journal of Ecclesiastical History* 62:2, pp. 318–45.

Snape, Michael, and Madigan, Edward (eds), 2013, *The Clergy in Khaki: New Perspectives on British Army Chaplaincy in the First World War*, Farnham: Ashgate.

Studdert Kennedy, Gerald, 1982, *Dog-collar Democracy*, London: Macmillan.

Totten, Andrew, 2015, 'Contextual Issues: War and Peace', in Swift, C., Cobb, M. and Todd, A. (eds), *Handbook of Chaplaincy Studies: Understanding Spiritual Care in Public Spaces*, London: Routledge, pp. 215–28.

Tutu, Desmond, 1999, *No Future without Forgiveness*, London: Rider.

Wakefield, G. S., 1995, 'God and Some English Poets: 9. Twentieth-Century Trends', *The Expository Times* 106:5, pp. 138–42.

Wells, H. G., 1916, *Mr. Britling Sees It Through*, London: Cassell.

Wells, H. G., 1917, *God, the Invisible King*, London: Cassell.

'W.T.', 'The Bookshelf', *Challenge* 9:228, 6 Sep. 1918, p. 273.

Works by G. A. Studdert Kennedy

SK, 1917, 'The Religious Difficulties of the Private Soldier', in Macnutt, F. (ed.), *The Church in the Furnace*, London: Macmillan, pp. 373–405.

SK, 1918a, *Rough Talks by a Padre*, London: Hodder & Stoughton.

SK, 1918b, *Rough Rhymes of a Padre*, London: Hodder & Stoughton.

SK, 1918c, *The Hardest Part*, London: Hodder & Stoughton.

SK, 1919, *Lies*, London: Hodder & Stoughton.

SK, 1920a, *More Rough Rhymes of a Padre*, London: Hodder & Stoughton.

SK, 1920b, *Peace Rhymes of a Padre*, London: Hodder & Stoughton.

SK, 1921a, *Food for the Fed-Up: An Exposition of the Christian Creed*, London: Hodder & Stoughton. (Published the same year in the USA as *I Believe: Sermons on the Apostles' Creed*, New York: George H. Doran Company.)

SK, 1921b, *The Sorrows of God and Other Poems*, London: Hodder & Stoughton.

References and Further Reading

SK, 1921c, *Democracy and the Dog Collar*, London: Hodder & Stoughton.

SK, 1921d, *I Believe: Sermons on the Apostles' Creed*, London: Hodder & Stoughton.

SK, 1922, *Songs of Faith and Doubt*, London: Hodder & Stoughton.

SK, 1923, *The Wicket Gate, or Plain Bread*, London: Hodder & Stoughton.

SK, 1925a, *The Hardest Part*, new edition, London: Hodder & Stoughton.

SK, 1925b, *Lighten Our Darkness: Some Less Rough Rhymes of a Padre*, London: Hodder & Stoughton.

SK, 1925c, *The Word and the Work*, London: Longmans, Green & Co.

SK, 1927a, *I Pronounce Them: A story of Man and Wife*, London: Hodder & Stoughton.

SK, 1927b, *The Unutterable Beauty*, London: Hodder & Stoughton.

SK, 1928, *The Warrior, the Woman, and the Christ*, London: Hodder & Stoughton.

SK, 1932, *The New Man in Christ*, edited W. Moore Ede, London: Hodder & Stoughton.

SK, 1940, *The Rhymes of G. A. Studdert Kennedy* (a republication of *The Unutterable Beauty*), London: Hodder & Stoughton.

SK, 1947, *The Best of Studdert Kennedy*, 'edited by a friend', London: Hodder & Stoughton.

Books about Studdert Kennedy

Brierley, M. W. and Byrne, G. A. (eds), 2017, *Life After Tragedy: Essays on Faith and the First World War evoked by Geoffrey Studdert Kennedy*, Eugene, OR: Cascade Books.

This book represents the first concerted effort by modern theologians to examine various themes in SK's writings. Essays on SK are accompanied by others discussing the wider theological and historical context. Recommended for further serious theological engagement with SK.

Grundy, M., 1997, *A Fiery Glow in the Darkness: Woodbine Willie, Padré & Poet*, Worcester: Osborne Books.

A highly accessible and readable biography of SK, profusely illustrated.

Holman, Bob, 2013, *Woodbine Willie: An Unsung Hero of World War One*, Oxford: Lion.

A detailed if at times somewhat hagiographic biography with a particular focus on SK's social concern and work; fully referenced.

Purcell, W., 1962, *Woodbine Willie: An Anglican Incident. Being some account of the life and times of Geoffrey Anketell Studdert Kennedy, poet, prophet, seeker after truth, 1883–1929*, London: Hodder & Stoughton (republished London: Mowbray, 1983).

The first attempt at a biography of SK, well researched but without sources being referenced. Further chapters examine SK's message and the development of his thought expressed in his writing.

Books about Studdert Kennedy

Studdert Kennedy, G. A. (introduction by K. Walters), 2008, *After War, is Faith Possible?*, Eugene, OR: Cascade Books.

This book comprises a 30-page largely biographical introduction and then around 200 pages of extracts from SK's writings, drawn from across his corpus. The motivation for the author was reading Desmond Tutu's reference to SK's theology (Tutu, 1999).

Index of Bible References

Index of Names and Subjects

Index of Names and Subjects

Index of Names and Subjects